Rotter and Bendl, YOUR COMPANION TO ENGLISH LITERARY TEXTS

Wilfried Rotter and Hermann Bendl

YOUR COMPANION TO ENGLISH LITERARY TEXTS

Volume One
Analysis and Interpretation of Narrative Prose

Newspaper Literature
The Essay
Short Narrative Forms
The Short Story
The Novel

Kollegstufe/Abitur/Universität

MANZ VERLAG MÜNCHEN

Herausgegeben von Ute Kretschmann

Unveränderter Nachdruck der zugelassenen Auflage

Manzbuch 531

12 11 10 9 8 1995 94 93 92 91
(Die jeweils letzte Zahl bezeichnet die Auflage bzw. das Erscheinungsjahr)

 Umschlagentwurf: Ingeburg Rothemund, München
Gesamtherstellung: Verlag und Druckerei G.J. Manz AG, München/Dillingen
Printed in Germany

ISBN 3—7863—0531—5

TABLE OF CONTENTS

PREFACE

This book is the first volume of a work in which we try to apply the principles of language learning at an advanced level which we advocated in *Your Companion to English Texts* (München: Manz, 1978) to literary texts – in this first volume to narrative prose, in the second to drama and poetry.
This means that we have started from the assumption that what is needed is first and foremost a strictly monolingual approach in all areas of foreign-language teaching if the general standard of student achievement is to be improved. When applied to the teaching of literature, this means that we are opposed to the use of the students' own language in the explanation and discussion of literary concepts and points of critical study. We also believe that it is not enough merely to offer them a great deal of information about problems of literary analysis and evaluation, even if this is done in the foreign language and done well, because this helps to improve mainly their **receptive** command of English. We are however convinced that it is possible to increase their competence in their **productive** command of the foreign language as well. In fact, we think that this is one of the principal aims in language teaching at all levels — students must be enabled to formulate what they have learnt in clear and correct English.
With this end in view, we have tried to do mainly two things — to provide some basic information on the principal areas of literary study within the spectrum of narrative literature and to offer the most relevant language material in the form of clearly arranged tables. In this way the student can easily memorize the main points in a manner which will be immediately useful to him when he is asked to give his views on this or that problem in the interpretation of a literary work. A most welcome side-effect of this method is that the learner in studying the individual sections of this book will be put in a better position to recognize the general features or the typical characteristics of a certain story type, etc., in the particular text under discussion. If he can be led to see how this text fits into some greater whole, for instance as belonging to the type of short story called 'the classical plot story', or that the individual elements that make up a text have been put together in a way that is typical of the tradition of 'the impressionistic slice-of-life story', then a great step forward in the student's comprehension of the literary process has indeed been taken.
The fact must be stressed again that he is not simply asked to absorb this kind of information by closely studying what is said in a particular chapter, but that he is put in a position which allows him to apply what he has learnt in his own language production. In fact, the tables with the relevant language material usually provide a kind of condensed version of the main information of the particular section of the book in the form of pre-formulated sentences. By memorizing the factual information and the technical terms these tables offer within a sentence context, a

maximum learning effect can be achieved, and at the same time the student can improve his linguistic competence quite considerably.
After an introductory chapter about the nature of literature and literary study, we have attempted to show the relationship and the difference between fact and fiction, to explain the concept of fictionality and to discuss short narrative forms, the short story and the novel and their most important aspects. We have also sought to familiarize the reader with the technical aspects of story-writing and thus to make him understand how stories are put together and how their individual elements are interrelated. A final chapter offering many useful ideas for the interpretation of fiction is meant to round the picture off.
In all this, generalisations and simplifications have been unavoidable, and many paths have been left unexplored, but we do not consider this a disadvantage for learners at this stage. In fact, we believe that there is a great danger of students getting lost among a great mass of technical detail and the constantly increasing number of publications in the field of literary criticism. We have therefore tried to keep things simple, but we trust that the inevitable omissions are not serious and the simplifications sensible, so that the reader who intends to explore further will not have much to unlearn. What we have set out to do is to give a **basic introduction** to a number of problems which are bound to come up in literary study and to indicate the most important answers to them which have been evolved in literary criticism and which have been found useful in practice. (Incidentally, all the material offered in this volume has been tested with various groups of students, to the authors' satisfaction). Anybody who wants to follow up this or that line of study will find valuable suggestions in the lists of 'Suggested Reading' at the back of the book.
One final point. In order to keep the size of this book within manageable proportions, we had to leave out — much to our regret — a number of examples from literature that would have been useful in demonstrating a certain statement or supporting this or that claim. This would however have easily more than doubled the number of pages and it would have seriously changed the character of the book as a whole — after all, it is meant to be a **companion** volume to the study of literary texts.
Some readers may miss a discussion of some important types of fiction, such as detective fiction, science fiction, proletarian fiction, or utopian fiction. We are aware of this omission but plan to tackle the problems involved in introducing students to these fictional types in another book.
We are thankful to Professor Dr Alfred Wollmann (Universität Köln) and Akademischer Oberrat Dr Werner Sedlak (Universität München) for scholarly advice, encouragement and help. Our thanks also go to Mrs Ruth Baumert, B.A., and to Mr Graham Pascoe, M.A., who read and checked the manuscript from the native speaker's point of view.

W. Rotter
Altenerding, June 1981 **H. Bendl**

HOW TO USE THIS BOOK

This book can be used in various ways and for a number of purposes because
- it provides some basic information on important aspects of working with literary texts;
- it offers language material in tables on problems of literary analysis and interpretation;
- it can be used as a reference book.

This means that the book can be read through as a whole or in part, or can be consulted for certain items to be studied separately or simply for reference.
The best course to take is probably to read the book all the way through and then to pick out certain chapters or individual points for detailed study in class or in private; the **Table of Contents** and the **Index** can be consulted for guidance.
A word must be said about the questions and exercises, the points for discussion and further study, etc., which have been included at various points in our presentation of important aspects of literary study and criticism. Here is an example from section 1.2, **What is narrative literature?** which will help to explain what is intended:

Comprehension and revision

1) What is a narrative? Give a definition.
2) What is imaginative literature?
3) What is the precise difference between
   a) fictional and non-fictional narratives?
   b) prose narratives and verse narratives?
4) What is the writer's aim in creating a fictitious reality?

It is quite obvious that these questions are meant to help the student in revising the main information the preceding text offers; they also provide him with an opportunity of practising — and thereby memorizing — the relevant language material, as it is incorporated in the corresponding table, like this:

Narrative literature

Fiction Works of fiction Imaginative literature Works of literary art Fictional narratives	is are	invented. imagined.

p. t. o.

<table>
<tr><th colspan="6">**Narrative literature** (continued)</th></tr>
<tr><td colspan="2">A story
A series of interconnected events</td><td>is</td><td colspan="3">told.
narrated.
recounted.</td></tr>
<tr><td colspan="2" rowspan="2">Non-fiction
Non-fictional narratives
Non-literary narratives</td><td>is
are</td><td colspan="3">factually or historically true.</td></tr>
<tr><td>refer(s)</td><td colspan="3">to the real world.
to the world as we know it.</td></tr>
<tr><td>The narrative
The story</td><td colspan="5">is presented by a narrator.</td></tr>
<tr><td>The writer
The author
The literary artist</td><td colspan="5">orders his material.
imposes a pattern on his material.
establishes connections.</td></tr>
<tr><td>He has</td><td>created
achieved</td><td colspan="4">a world of his own.
a fictitious reality.
an illusion of reality.
a lasting imaginative effect on the reader.</td></tr>
</table>

In some cases, especially in the **Suggestions for further study,** a number of ideas are mentioned which can be used as topics for short talks ('Referate') or for written work ('Facharbeiten', etc.), e.g. in **6.3 Functions and uses of the novel.** Sometimes many more tasks have been listed at the end of individual sections than can probably be dealt with in class. Our intention here has been to offer a wide range of possible points for discussion and further study. The revision and comprehension questions should however not be neglected, because in formulating his answers to them the student is forced to use precisely the language material that he ought to commit to memory and have actively available for the discussion of similar points in different contexts.

The tables normally contain choices of collocations (i.e. words often used together in certain situations). The words and phrases grouped together in one square are **sometimes synonymous:**

e.g.

A story is	told. narrated. recounted.

but not necessarily so. Some may be **rather different in meaning:**

e.g.

A love relationship is	established. strengthened. cemented. challenged. doomed.

At any rate, the language material provided in the tables uses language levels from colloquial to formal style (e.g. told — narrated — recounted). This has to be taken into account in the student's own language production.

Our intention has been to make sure that students at many levels can profit from the book and that it has not exhausted all its usefulness after a first reading. We hope to have included enough stimuli to make it still valuable for a second or third reading. We have made a point of not explaining unusual vocabulary items and have also deliberately refrained from giving annotations of points which may be felt to be difficult without some additional background information. We believe indeed that it is good and salutary for the student to be forced to practise his use of the dictionary and other general works of reference. By not making things too easy for him we hope to provide a stimulus in the right direction — we are firmly convinced that without a proper working technique and some practice in using it, real progress in language learning is just not possible.

This book can of course itself be used as a reference work, especially in its concise explanations of various styles, e.g. 'realism' and 'impressionism' in **6.2.2 The novel can embody many styles,** and in its description of the individual elements that make up fictional narratives and of the most important literary devices, e.g. 'plot', 'viewpoint character', or 'interior monologue' throughout ch. 6. The **Table of Contents** and especially the **Index** can be consulted for help.

1. LITERATURE AND LITERARY STUDY

1.1 What is 'literature'?

The question 'what is literature?' sounds simple, but it cannot always be answered clearly. This is due to the fact that the term 'literature' is somewhat ambiguous and can refer to a number of different things.

It can first of all be understood as **'any printed matter'** — catalogues, holiday prospectuses, text-books, and so forth. Books and articles about a special subject, e.g. surgery or car maintainance, are the 'literature' the medical student or the car mechanic will have to study. In this broad sense a printed account of yesterday's protest march or a few lines advertising a particular brand of cat food are as much literature as Homer's epics, Shakespeare's dramas or E. A. Poe's short stories. But this view would lead to an identification of literature with only the latest epoch in the history of civilization and to a rejection of the literature of many cultures in which literature is transmitted not in printed but in oral form. Literary study as a specific discipline and the development of specific methods for the study of literature would be superfluous and indeed pointless.

A second way of defining literature is to restrict it to **'great books'**, that is to say to books which are notable for literary form and expression, irrespective of their subject. Within the fields of lyric poetry, drama, and fiction, the great books can be selected on the basis of their aesthetic value; great books from other fields can be chosen for their general intellectual eminence together with their distinction in matters of style, composition and general force of presentation. This is a common way of speaking of literature, and most literary histories do in fact mention and discuss distinguished works by philosophers, historians, moralists and others, even some scientists, but these thinkers are usually dealt with in a rather fragmentary fashion, without the context of their subject of discourse. There are other disadvantages in limiting the meaning of 'literature' to the greatest works. For subjects like history and philosophy it means the introduction of an exclusively aesthetic point of view which involves an at least partial disregard of their intrinsic value. In fields of study where knowledge accumulates very quickly and progress has been rapid, as in some sciences, the great books of today can be out of date tomorrow and become historical curiosities practically overnight. As such they can no longer be recommended reading for the beginning student. "Within the history of imaginative literature, limitation to the great books makes incomprehensible the continuity of literary tradition, the development of literary genres, and indeed the very nature of the literary process, besides obscuring the background of social, linguistic, ideological, and other conditioning circumstances."[1]

The best way of defining the term 'literature' seems to be to restrict it to **the art of literature:** that is to say to imaginative compositions, whether printed or oral, whether dramatic, metrical or prose in form. It is, however, not always easy to distinguish between art and non-art, between literature and the non-literary linguistic utterance, and the distinction may be fluid.

One way of solving this difficulty is to distinguish two ways of using language, one artistic, one non-artistic. This is to say that the writer of a science book and the writer of literature use language in a different way. The scientist is concerned mainly with the lexical meaning of words or their 'denotations' (**denotative** use of language). He does not want to appeal to the emotions of the reader, only to his understanding. He intends to make his words mean one thing and one thing only so that confusion is avoided and the intended meaning set forth as unambiguously as possible. The creator of literature, on the other hand, is principally interested in the associations words have acquired through constant use, in the appeal of these words to the feelings, in the ways in which they can move the reader and in which they suggest colour or movement or character. We call these possible suggestions and overtones a word may have its 'connotations'. In this **connotative** use of language it is not mainly dictionary meaning that counts, but the manifold suggestiveness of language (especially in poetry). We can say that the literary artist wants to exploit language to the full — its sounds, its suggestions of other meanings and other words, and its various overtones of multiple associations.

A second way of distinguishing between literature and non-literature is through the study of the intended effect or **the functions of literature.** There are many theories concerning this, but they all agree in one thing — that literature can move the reader or listener, to joy and sorrow, to laughter and tears. The theory of the cathartic effect of literature (Gk katharsis = purgation) can be mentioned here: that the experience of literature causes stability and a harmonization of impulses through the essentially harmless release of emotions. Some would even go so far as to claim that the right kind of literature can cleanse and save society, but if this idea were accepted the distinction between literature and propaganda or sermons would disappear. That literature can in many cases have a didactic purpose and a propaganda value need not be denied. Yet where precisely the borderline is to be drawn is not easy to say. The distinguishing criterion seems to be **aesthetic function.** This is to say that if a piece of literature offers a principally aesthetic experience, such as moving the reader or listener by the sentiments expressed, by the pleasure of finding feelings described which he can share, or by the new insights he has gained, then we are dealing with literature proper. If, however, he is persuaded to some concrete action, such as adopting a different lifestyle, working for certain ideals or fighting for a better world in general, then we are dealing not with literature, but with **propaganda.** In any case, the existence of borderline cases between literature and non-literature and transitional forms, such as the essay, biography, and much rhetorical literature, should be freely admitted. "It seems, however, best to consider as literature only works in which the aesthetic function is dominant, while we can recognize that there are aesthetic elements, such as style and composition, in works which have a completely different, non-aesthetic purpose, such as scientific treatises, philosophical dissertations, political pamphlets, sermons."[2] (That the distinction between literature and non-literature is indeed fluid will be demonstrated in ch. 2; cf. esp. 2.4).

A third way to distinguish literature as a form of art is by the effort that is made to preserve it in script or in oral tradition. Within this context, literature is different from non-literature in that it is regarded as timeless or at least as a valuable instrument in the preservation and transmission of traditional values. The term 'literature' consequently refers to those imaginative compositions which express and communicate thoughts, feelings and attitudes towards life in such a way that an effect of some permanence is achieved. On the basis of this distinction, literature is something that goes beyond the advertisement-writer's or the journalist's concern with what is up to date, of topical interest and the news or fashion of the day. The vast majority of writers want their work to last for generations, for all time; some may even hope for immortality for themselves and those they are writing about. This is not to say that they all achieve this. In fact, most authors, even reasonably good ones, are soon forgotten except by a few scholars and research students and none of us can say with confidence and as a matter of course whether a work of literature is going to last, in the sense of being of interest to future generations. But the very fact that its author intended it to have this **quality of permanence** is certainly something that marks it off from other writings – things like journalism, works of reference and advertising, all of which are not meant to last. Stressing the quality of permanence too exclusively would however result in a very narrow conception of literature, leading back to the idea of literature consisting only of 'great books' and of writings at least intended to be great. We must not forget that a great number of what are quite clearly literary products, in the sense of imaginative compositions, are apparently not intended to last, but are produced for a mass market, to be bought and read today and forgotten and destroyed tomorrow. The fact that this sort of writing, which includes thrillers, westerns and romances, is regarded as something in the nature of **'disposable art'** by authors and readers alike must not blind us to the fact that we are still dealing with literature, with works in other words which are creative fictions which imitate and present people, objects, societies, and ideas, however stereotyped their manner of imitation and presentation. (For a more detailed discussion of the relationship between serious literature and popular literature see 8.4 below).

It is precisely this **quality of fictionality** which is obviously central to the concept of literature and which, even more than aesthetic function, constitutes its distinguishing feature. So it is only natural that the essence of literature and the centre of literary art is to be found in imaginative compositions in which the reference is to a world of fiction, of invention, and not of factual truth, as in the traditional genres of the lyric, the drama and the epic. We think thus of literature in terms of Homer, Dante, Shakespeare, Goethe, and Hemingway rather than of Cicero or Montaigne,

Hegel or Freud. There are of course boundary cases, such as the writings of Friedrich Nietzsche, which seem to lean sometimes more towards the realm of philosophy and at other times more towards pure literature. Most philosophical and literary historians would probably say that Nietzsche belongs primarily in the philosophical tradition, but it is precisely because of this strong element of fictionality that runs through some of his works that he can also be considered a writer of literature.

Comprehension and discussion

1) What possible meanings can the term 'literature' have?
2) Why is 'literature' best limited to the art of literature?
3) What objections can be raised against an identification of literature
   a) with anything printed?
   b) with 'great books'?
4) What is the difference between the denotative and the connotative uses of language?
5) In what ways are recognized forms of writing such as the essay and biography 'transitional forms'?
6) Can highly sensational publications concentrating on violence or melodrama and produced for a mass readership qualify as literature?
7) Can you think of examples of publications with a strongly didactic purpose or in which the propaganda element is very pronounced?
   Can they be regarded as literature? Is the aesthetic element dominant?
8) Can you think of other authors and their works who, like Nietzsche, appear to be somewhere between literature and non-literature?
   Try to decide whether the element of fictionality is central or not.

The character of literature

<table>
<tr><td rowspan="4">Literature</td><td colspan="3">is not easy to define.
is timeless.
is transmitted in printed or in oral form.
expresses and communicates thoughts, feelings and attitudes towards life.
possesses aesthetic worth.
provides an aesthetic experience.
moves the reader or listener.</td></tr>
<tr><td rowspan="3">may have</td><td colspan="2">a cathartic effect.</td></tr>
<tr><td>a didactic
a satirical</td><td>purpose.</td></tr>
<tr><td colspan="2">propaganda value.</td></tr>
</table>

p. t. o.

The character of literature (continued)

Aesthetic function Fictionality	is a	distinguishing dominant essential	feature trait characteristic attribute element	of literature.

Lyric poetry The drama The epic	is a traditional literary genre.

The writer The writer of literature The creator of literature The literary artist	produces creates	works of literary art. imaginative compositions. creative fictions. literary products.
	wants to achieve an effect of permanence. hopes for immortality. intends his work to last.	

Works of literary art Literary products	are	imaginative compositions. creative fictions.

Transitional forms Borderline cases Boundary cases	must be recognized. clearly exist.

The distinction between	art and non-art literature and non-literature	may be fluid.

1.2 What is 'narrative literature'?

A narrative is the telling of a series of events or facts and the establishing of some connection between them. The term is commonly restricted to fiction, that is to say to the recounting of a story that is imagined or invented rather than factually or historically true. But the word can also be used for non-fictional accounts of, say, scientific experiments or for the texts found in do-it-yourself books. Another important example of non-fictional narrative can be found in a historian's presentation of his material — out of what is normally felt to be the chaotic flux of time and experience he creates a lasting imaginative effect on the reader by the way in which he imposes a pattern on the bewildering uncertainties of events. We can say that narrative has two overlapping aspects. One is a question of content, of the

ordering of the material to be used in the narrative and of the nature of the connections that are to be established. The other aspect concerns the problem of how the narrative is presented to the reader, and here the **choice of a narrator** is of crucial importance; this may be the writer himself speaking in his own voice as it were, or a character or several characters may be introduced to tell the story from their individual point of view. For the purposes of this book, the reference in talking of narratives will exclusively be to imaginative literature, in other words to works of literary art in which the author presents actions and events, people, places and situations, all of which he has invented or at least modified to suit his own purposes if they have been taken from real life, as in the case of a historical novel. The main point here is that the writer has created a world of his own, a **fictitious reality**, which may be so convincing that the reader readily accepts this illusion of reality and then follows the events presented to him with a keen interest as if they were really factually or historically true. Another restriction in the use of the word narrative in this book must be mentioned. It concerns the fact that the word is here confined in its meaning to works of fiction **in prose,** such as modern short stories or novels; in other words, ancient epics and romances **in verse** will be ignored although in them certain interconnected events are presented, too, and they therefore, technically speaking, also qualify as narrative literature. What prose is as compared with verse needs hardly any explaining. It is characterised by its apparent formlessness and the use of everyday language whereas verse makes an immediate impact on the reader through such characteristics as metre, rhythm and stanza form. The lack of metre and rhythm does not, however, mean that the composition of good prose is less an art than the writing of distinguished verse.

Comprehension and revision

1) What is a narrative? Give a definition.
2) What is imaginative literature?
3) What is the precise difference between
   a) fictional and non-fictional narratives?
   b) prose narratives and verse narratives?
4) What is the writer's aim in creating a fictitious reality?

Narrative literature

Fiction Works of fiction Imaginative literature Works of literary art Fictional narratives	is are	invented. imagined.
		p. t. o.

Narrative literature (continued)		
A story A series of interconnected events	is	told. narrated. recounted.
Non-fiction Non-fictional narratives Non-literary narratives	is are	factually or historically true.
	refer(s)	to the real world. to the world as we know it.
The narrative The story	is presented by a narrator.	
The writer The author The literary artist	orders his material. imposes a pattern on his material. establishes connections.	
He has	created achieved	a world of his own. a fictitious reality. an illusion of reality. a lasting imaginative effect on the reader.

1.3 What is the relationship between literature and literary study?

Literature and literary study are two distinct activities. Whereas literature is a creative art, literary study refers to the task of the student of translating his experience of literature into intellectual terms and of assimilating it to a coherent rational scheme so that other students can compare their experiences and thereby achieve a deeper understanding of the particular work of literature under discussion.

Not all theorists, however, are convinced that this is the right approach. As they see it, literature cannot be studied at all, but only read, enjoyed and appreciated or otherwise, according to the private taste of the individual student. The only thing possible in this view is an accumulation of all kinds of information 'about' literature, such as biographical details of the author's life, and especially the period when he was engaged in writing the work that is being discussed, or background knowledge of the historical period during which our author wrote.

In our opinion, this is a serious misconception of the study of literature because literary scholarship has developed its own valid methods which ensure that a true study of literature, at once 'literary' and 'systematic', is possible. It is true that attempts to find general laws in literature have always failed and that the case for individuality, that is to say that each work of art has characteristic features and qualities which set it off from other similar works, is well-founded. But it is equally true that each work of literature apart from its individual characteristics also shares common qualities with other works of art and that no such work can be wholly individual and thus unique because in this case it would be totally incomprehensible. It is for this reason that we are sure that the student of literature is justified when he generalizes concerning works of literary art. "Literary criticism and literary history both attempt to characterize the individuality of a work, of an author, or a period, or of a national literature. But this characterization can be accomplished only in universal terms, on the basis of a literary theory."[3] In other words, what literary theory tries to do is to establish methods of characterising and interpreting literature. Without it, literary scholarship could never have become the growing body of knowledge, insights, and judgements that it is.

Comprehension and Discussion

1) Why can literature and literary study be said to be two distinct activities?
2) Why are some people opposed to a study of literature?
3) What is the objective of literary study,
   a) in general?
   b) concerning a particular work?
4) Why is a literary theory necessary?
5) Explain what is meant by the phrase 'the case for individuality'.
6) What makes literature a 'creative art'?

Literature and literary study

<table>
<tr><td colspan="2">Literature</td><td rowspan="2">is to be</td><td rowspan="2">read.
enjoyed.
appreciated.
interpreted.
analysed.
studied.</td></tr>
<tr><td>A (particular) work of</td><td>literature
literary art</td></tr>
<tr><td colspan="4">Literature is a creative art.</td></tr>
<tr><td colspan="2">The individuality
The individual characteristics
The characteristic features and qualities</td><td>of a work</td><td>must be expressed in universal terms.
must be evaluated on the basis of a literary theory.</td></tr>
<tr><td colspan="4">An individual and unique work of art shares common qualities with other works of art.</td></tr>
<tr><td colspan="4">p. t. o.</td></tr>
</table>

Literature and literary study (continued)		
The study of literature		has established methods of characterizing and interpreting literature.
Literary	study scholarship criticism theory	has yielded a growing body of knowledge, insights and judgements. must not be confounded with the accumulation of information about literature.

1.4 What is the purpose of studying literature?

In his novel *Fahrenheit 451*[4] (1954), Ray Bradbury presents a picture of a world in which all books have been banned because they are said to be the cause of all unhappiness and disruption. A four-walled TV screen is in fact the only source of entertainment and information allowed. If any books are discovered anywhere a special task-force of firemen are called in to burn them. There are, however, a few outcasts of society who have formed an underground movement of people who know the contents of one or more of the world's greatest books by heart and pass on this knowledge by word of mouth, hoping that one day a situation will arise in which books and the ideas they contain will be welcome again. The action centres on the experiences of Montag, a book-burning fireman who gradually comes to realize that what he has to do is horribly wrong because without books people's lives are reduced to hardly more than the mere level of subsistence. So in the end he breaks away from his job and everything that binds him to his past life, joins the underground movement and finds his peace of mind with the book-loving outcasts. The message of Bradbury's novel is quite clearly that a world without books is indeed a nightmare world which reduces people to a state of ignorance in which they can all too easily be indoctrinated with any ideology the regime in power happens to favour and thus be manipulated like puppets. To be sure, the reference in *Fahrenheit 451* is to all books and not only to works of imaginative fiction, but works of literary art are obviously counted among the greatest treasures of mankind without which the quality of people's lives would be sharply diminished.

To say that literature is valuable and indeed indispensable to us is in fact the answer to the question of why we study literature. Without the insights it offers into the problems and difficulties people have to face in this world our lives would be quite considerably poorer. It is valuable to us because it is concerned with so many different fields of human knowledge and experience far beyond any individual's reach and his opportunities of personal exploration. In the great works of literature the thoughts and experiences of some of the cleverest people in the world are set down for us. In studying these works, we can share these thoughts and experiences and thus considerably enlarge our knowledge of life. Of course, a study of the problems dealt with in literature cannot replace the actual experience of real life, but we must also realize that the total knowledge of life any one person can acquire through his own personal experience is sadly limited. Through a study of literature, on the other hand, he can make use of the experiences of other people as well. We can learn a great deal about people's behaviour and their motivations from literature. We will be led to **a deeper understanding of ourselves and our fellow human beings** and thus may become more tolerant and perhaps even wise. At any rate, there can be little doubt that we can learn something essential about ourselves and others by grappling with the moral problems involved in the decisions the characters in a work of fiction have to make and by seeing the common faults and weaknesses of mankind exposed in book after book.

Literature is however not only valuable to us because its study may help us in becoming in some sense better people but also because **it provides great pleasure and enjoyment.** Although some experts have forecast that radio, television and film are going to take up more and more of our spare time so that hardly any will be left for reading, all the evidence so far seems to indicate that the mass media encourage rather than discourage the reading of imaginative literature. The sale of books and the use of libraries have in fact been increasing more rapidly than ever before so that there appear to be far more readers now than in the days before TV came along, which is a clear indication that an enormous number of people receive a great deal of pleasure indeed from reading. Most of them simply want to pass the time pleasantly, to imagine strange places and follow exciting stories of adventure and romance. Or they may want to share the emotional experiences of the characters and see how they deal with moral problems. A minority may even be interested in studying the skill of the writer in presenting his materials and in seeing life described in terms of different philosophical approaches. There are probably a number of other reasons, but irrespective of the question of what makes people want to read there can be no doubt that they do enjoy reading and get great pleasure from it.

This pleasure literature provides can be quite considerably enhanced through literary study. It can first of all broaden and refine the interests which a reader brings to literature. It can secondly improve his general taste because it will make him realize that his experience can be extended more fully by reading books which not merely emphasize the elements of violent action and romantic setting but also lead to some understanding of the inner lives of people and to some better understanding of his own life. He will thirdly come to see that suspense in the external action is not everything in a story, but that matters of character, psychological development and moral decision are inextricably bound up with the action and that

> even in the crudest story of violent action, he demands a certain modicum of characterization, a certain concern with the psychological basis of action, a certain interest in moral content and general meaning. And a little further reflection should lead him to the conclusion that his liking for the story may

depend upon the organic relation existing among these elements — that his interest did not depend upon the element of violent plot, or the element of romantic setting, taken in isolation. If he has once faced this question, he may realize that his liking for a story does not depend finally upon his threshold interests, but rather depends, in one sense at least, upon the total structure, upon the logic of the whole, the relationships existing among elements of character and psychology, action, social situation, ideas and attitudes, style, and so on.[5]

We can say that literary study sets in motion a process which leads the reader past his mere threshold interests to the fuller interests implicit in literature and thus causes an enlargement of the area of his potential enjoyment. Literary study is therefore valuable also in this respect.

The most common reason for studying literature is **the desire to pass an examination.** There is of course nothing wrong with this and yet it is in some ways

unfortunate that literature has now become a subject for study and examination in schools and colleges. That young people should be helped and encouraged and guided in their reading is good, but that they should study literature only in order to pass examinations is certainly bad. If anything could make William Shakespeare turn in his much-visited grave at Stratford it would be the thought of millions of English schoolchildren and foreign students painfully reading through his plays, memorising set speeches, and making careful notes on 'characters' — all so that they can pass an Oxford examination, win a Cambridge certificate, or by some other means prove to the world that they are people of education and culture. Yet there is at least one good thing to be said for studying literature in order to pass examinations: it trains students to pay close attention to the printed word, and encourages them to think deeply about the meaning of what is written.[6]

There are many plays, poems and novels which may not seem very attractive at first because they demand careful attention to detail and concentrated reading, perhaps even two or three readings, before they can be fully enjoyed. However, any efforts we are willing to make in this respect will certainly bring rich rewards in the end. There can be no doubt that the enjoyment we may receive from any great work of art — in all fields of art — will largely depend on the time we are prepared to spend in studying it. It is in fact an indication of the permanent character of a great work of art that one can get new pleasures and discover new interesting problems at each successive reading. It is certainly true that most of the greatest works of literature in the world can be fully appreciated only after several readings and much thought and discussion. If the student who for examination purposes is working his way through a list of 'set books' is willing to candidly explore his own feelings and attitudes by comparing them with those of the characters in a work of imaginative literature and to submit his beliefs to the test of imaginative experience, then his time could hardly have been better employed. If the old phrase about **'learning for life'** — *non scholae sed vitae discimus* — has any meaning today at all, it is to be found here, in the enlargement of our awareness of the realities of human experience through the study of some great works of literature.

It goes without saying that **greater benefit can be had from studying a few works of 'good' literature than from reading through one popular story after another.** It is undeniable that popular fiction has a relatively trivial but genuinely useful function — it provides comfort and amusement through a stimulation of the imagination — but it is equally true that a strengthening of our imaginative sympathies and insights can normally only be had in works of serious literature.

> Good fictional pictures of life widen our sympathies, help our sense of proportion, educate our moral judgment; they make human goodness, frailty, sufferings, needs, relationships far more real than abstract definitions or vague exhortations can. They may teach us more of consequences — an important part of learning to make wise decisions — for they show how character traits cause actions, and whither these lead. We may learn more about our selfishness and self-deceiving from Jane Austen, George Eliot, Henry James, Iris Murdoch, than from some tactless older person's rebuke, whose intrusion and ill-temper we resent. The best fiction is a supplementary conscience, a further education, a sometimes disquieting emotional experience.[7]

Summing up we can repeat that we study literature because we regard it as valuable. Its value seems to lie in basically two things — in the pleasure it provides and in the opportunities for education in the widest sense that it offers. Or we could say that Horace's observation *'aut prodesse volunt aut delectare poetae' (Ars poetica,* 1. 333), that writers want either to instruct or to please, **and that all literature is *dulce* and *utile,* sweet and useful,** is still true today. We study literature because it is equally concerned with what we experience as beautiful and as true.

Understanding the text

1) What makes literature so valuable?
2) Why can it be said that literature provides a knowledge of life?
3) In what sense is the study of literature 'learning for life'?
4) What are the reasons for people to read fiction? (Can you add any more?)
5) In what sense can literature offer enjoyment and pleasure?
6) Why can literary study heighten the pleasure one derives from reading?

Talking points

1) What effect would the banning of all books have on society?
2) What are 'threshold interests'? What are the threshold interests which bring you to read fiction?
3) 'Before extensive reading can be profitable, the student must have some practice in intensive reading.' — Discuss.

Reasons for studying literature

<table>
<tr><td colspan="2">People read fiction because they want to</td><td>pass the time pleasantly.
imagine strange places and exciting adventures.
share the emotional experiences of the characters.
see how the characters deal with the moral problems.
escape from a humdrum existence into a world of fantasy.
study the writer's skill.
find out about what the writer has to say.
see life described in terms of different philosophical approaches.</td></tr>
<tr><td rowspan="7">Literature</td><td>is</td><td>valuable.
indispensable.
among the greatest treasures of mankind.</td></tr>
<tr><td>is concerned with
deals with</td><td>the realities of human experience.
many fields of human knowledge and experience.
beauty and truth.</td></tr>
<tr><td colspan="2">enlarges our knowledge of life.
offers insights into the problems and difficulties people have to face in this world.</td></tr>
<tr><td>can teach us</td><td>a great deal about people's behaviour and their motivations.
something essential about ourselves and others.</td></tr>
<tr><td colspan="2">educates our moral judgements.
shows how character traits cause actions and where these lead to.
exposes the common faults and weaknesses of mankind.</td></tr>
<tr><td>provides</td><td>pleasure and enjoyment.
a sometimes disquieting emotional experience.</td></tr>
<tr><td colspan="2">is like a supplementary conscience.</td></tr>
</table>

p. t. o.

<table>
<tr><th colspan="3">Reasons for studying literature (continued)</th></tr>
<tr><td rowspan="3">Literary study
The study of literature</td><td>leads</td><td>to a fuller appreciation of a work of literary art.
to some understanding of the inner lives of people.
to a realization of the organic relation which exists between the various elements that make up the story.
the reader past his threshold interests.</td></tr>
<tr><td>enlarges</td><td>the area of the reader's potential enjoyment.
our awareness of the realities of human experience.</td></tr>
<tr><td colspan="2">broadens and refines the interests which a reader brings to literature.
improves the reader's general taste.
extends the reader's experience.
trains students to pay close attention to the printed word.
encourages students to think deeply about the meaning of what they read.
strengthens our imaginative sympathies and insights.
brings rich rewards.</td></tr>
</table>

2. NEWSPAPER LITERATURE — FACT AND FICTION

2.1 Facts — selected, formulated, and passed on as information in 'straight news'

'Straight news' is expected to be as 'objective' as possible — taking into account that all our experience of reality is necessarily limited and that the gathering of information is always selective. It is directed by the interest of the reader, the work of the journalist, and the selling policy of the paper.
Nevertheless, we can justly call 'straight news' **factual,** i. e. based on facts and not on the interpretation or even imagination of the journalist.
For these reasons, the criteria for the selection, presentation and publication of factual news are:

1) timeliness — Is it a current event?
2) prominence — Is the event or person concerned worth reporting about?
3) proximity — Did the event happen close enough to the reader's sphere of interest?
4) probable consequences — Might it have personal consequences for the reader?

'Straight news' may either be **very short (news bulletin** or **flash)** or take on the form of a **long story (news story,** usually in the form of the 'inverted pyramid story').

2.1.1 A **'news bulletin'** or **'news flash'** (cf L 'bulla' = a short papal edict) is a brief statement of some recent incident or event. Apart from political news, bulletins may cover personal news of births, marriages or deaths. In order to reach the reading public as early as possible, they are often inserted in bold type on the front page of a newspaper at the very last minute. Usually, brief news reports of this type, which are mere summaries of major current events, are later covered in greater detail by a story writer who must first gather more background information to clarify the situation.
The form and style of a bulletin are therefore necessarily very concise. The journalist concentrates on giving the most essential information, guided by the traditional formula of the **four w's — who? what? where? when?**

For study: Determine the **four w's** in the following news bulletin!

> Dallas, Tex., Nov. 22 (1963) — President John Fitzgerald Kennedy was shot and killed by an assassin today. He died of a wound in the brain caused by a rifle bullet that was fired at him as he was riding through downtown Dallas in a motorcade.[1]

As you see, straight news is easily understandable because of its concise and simple language (cf L 'Con-cidere/cis-' = 'cut' to the bone'). Readability is the only criterion of correctness and efficiency. The sentences used are short without any redundancies (L 'redundare' = 'to overflow'; 'redundans' = 'being superfluous'). So, in short, conciseness of language and objectivity are the main characteristics of 'straight news'. In many style books, journalists and reporters have been urged to use simple, clean English so that an **average reader** can read, understand, and remember 'straight news'.
A certain stereotyped monotony, however, can hardly be avoided. It has sometimes been ridiculed by journalists themselves — like James Thurber in the following mock bulletin:

'Dead.
That's what Joe Schmaltz was after he fell down a manhole."

'Straight news' — news bulletin, news flash

This text is 'straight news'. It answers the four w's, namely the who, what, where, when.	
It is stricly	factual. objective.
It does not contain any	subjective element. comment. interpretation. fictional techniques.
Its language is	simple. easily understandable. concise.
It is formulated	in short sentences. without any redundancies. for the average reader.

2.1.2 The **'news story'** — usually in **'inverted pyramid'** form

If an event that has been reported in the form of a news bulletin or flash is of further interest to the reader, he expects his newspaper to provide him with more details and some background information. In other words, on top of the **who, what, where, when,** the reader wants to know about the **how** — and the **why!**
It goes without saying that — in order to provide this additional information — research work is necessary on the part of the journalist or the team of journalists.

Even if this work is carried out without undue haste, with great accuracy and 'objectivity', the subjective element in the news story is likely to be greater than in a bulletin. For this reason, the authors usually sign the article to guarantee that their reporting is authentic — i.e. that they have gathered all the available information from eye-witnesses or publications, and that they have presented all the relevant facts while keeping the subjective element to an absolute minimum.
The factual presentation of news is one of the hallmarks of Anglo-American journalism not often to be found in our own papers. It has a long tradition and has become highly standardized — simply because as a rule a team has to co-operate and finish the story as quickly as possible.
The most important facts are reported first, followed by those of lesser importance. This structure may be diagrammed in the form of an inverted pyramid, like this:

This very graphic comparison has become so widely accepted that the news story of this structure is now often called the 'inverted pyramid story'. For the editor, it has the advantage that he can drop whole paragraphs — particularly towards the end — and, for the reader that he may stop reading as soon as he has got the main information provided in the first paragraphs.

This **'inverted pyramid story'** consists of three parts:
1) the headline,
2) the lead(s),
3) the body.

The function of the **headline** is to catch the reader's interest and to hint at some appealing aspect of the news.
The lead(s) — one or more summarizing paragraphs at the beginning — provide the reader with the most essential information. In fact, they are a sort of summary of the news contained in the following story.
In the **body,** the facts given in the lead(s) are reported in greater detail with each fact being covered in one separate paragraph.

The 'inverted pyramid' news story

This article is	a factual report. an objective report.

p. t. o.

The 'inverted pyramid' news story (continued)	
It consists of three distinct parts,	the headline. the lead(s). the body.
The **headline** has been formulated in this way: — to catch the reader's attention. — to inform him on one appealing aspect of the story.	
The **lead** sums up the news.	
In the lead(s),	the most important information is given. the four w's are answered.
In the **body,**	additional information is given. more details are provided, particularly... the reader is informed **how** the story happened.

For study

Determine and analyse the headlines, the lead(s) and the body of the following news story (abridged).

KENNEDY IS KILLED BY SNIPER
AS HE RIDES IN CAR IN DALLAS;
JOHNSON SWORN IN ON PLANE
Mrs. Kennedy Unharmed

Leftist Suspect Seized in a Theater —
Kennedy Dies in Operating Room —
Body is Flown to Washington

By TOM WICKER
Special to The New York Times.

DALLAS, Tex., Nov. 22 (1963) — President John Fitzgerald Kennedy was shot and killed by an assassin today.

He died of a wound in the brain caused by a rifle bullet that was fired at him as he was riding through downtown Dallas in a motorcade.

Vice President Lyndon Baines Johnson, who was riding in the third car behind Mr. Kennedy's, was sworn in 99 minutes after Mr. Kennedy's death as the 36th President of the United States.

Shortly after the assassination, Lee H. Oswald, described as a onetime defector to the Soviet Union and chairman of a "Fair Play for Cuba Committee," was arrested by the Dallas police.

Oswald, 24 years old, was also held in the slaying of a policeman who had followed him into a theater. Oswald was subdued after a scuffle with a second policeman in the theater...

...The killer apparently fired from a building just off the motorcade route. Mr. Kennedy, Governor Connally and Mr. Johnson had just received an enthusiastic welcome from a large crowd in downtown Dallas.

Mr. Kennedy apparently was hit by the first of what witnesses believed were three shots. He was driven at high speed to Dallas's Parkland Hospital. There, in an emergency operating room, with only physicians and nurses in attendance, he died without regaining consciousness...

Mrs. Kennedy was in the hospital near her husband when he died, but not in the operating room. When the body was taken from the hospital in a bronze coffin about 2 p.m., Mrs. Kennedy walked beside it.

Her face was sorrowful. She looked steadily at the floor. Her hand rested lightly on her husband's coffin as it was taken to a waiting hearse.

Mrs. Kennedy climbed in beside the coffin. Then the ambulance drove to Love Field, and Mr. Kennedy's body was placed aboard the Presidential jet. Mrs. Kennedy then attended the swearing-in ceremony for Mr. Johnson...

The ceremony, delayed about five minutes for Mrs. Kennedy's arrival, took place in the private Presidential cabin in the rear of the plane...

No accurate listing of those present could be obtained. Mrs. Kennedy stood at the left of Mr. Johnson, her eyes and face showing the signs of weeping that had apparently shaken her since she left the hospital not long before.

Mrs. Johnson, wearing a beige dress, stood at her husband's right.

As Judge Hughes read the brief oath of office, her eyes, too, were red from weeping. Mr. Johnson's hands rested on a black, leatherbound Bible as Judge Hughes read and he repeated:

"I do solemnly swear that I will perform the duties of the President of the United States to the best of my ability and defend, protect and preserve the Constitution of the United States."

Those 34 words made Lyndon Baines Johnson, one-time farmboy and school teacher of Johnson City, Tex., the President...

At 2:46 p.m., seven minutes after he became President, 106 minutes after Mr. Kennedy had become the fourth American President to succumb to an assassin's wounds, the blue, white and red jet took off for Washington...[2]

(The second half of the article, which may be regarded as the lower end of the inverted pyramid, has been left out. It contains the report of the doctors who operated on Kennedy, details of Kennedy's activities just before he was shot, and further details of his assassination.)

NOTE that the facts contained in the last two paragraphs of the lead are not mentioned at all in the body. In fact, the identity of the assassin and the circumstances of his arrest provided the subject of a special article in the same edition of *The New York Times.*

2.2 Facts — selectively interpreted in news analysis and interpre(ta)tive story

The ideals of conventional reporting — accurate, 'objective' facts, i.e. 'straight news' — have become increasingly difficult to fulfil, especially in the field of current diplomacy and policy where information is often deliberately distorted before it reaches the mass media.

For these reasons, journalists have felt that they must distinguish between **'official news'** and **'the truth'** which is often hard to guess, even for the most hard-working and competent journalist at the scene of events. It is this background that made the development of a new journalistic technique of research and presentation necessary — the **interpre(ta)tive** or **news analysis story.**

In the following news analysis Reston tries to make his readers aware of the difference between **'what was news'** and **'what was truth'.** In May 1960, the situation was as follows: the U.S.A. were negotiating disarmament with the Russians, when an American sky-spy was shot down and arrested. The Russians, of course, did everything to win a diplomatic victory over the Americans on the mass media. For that reason, their official statements were full of moral indignation. Khrushchev made this attitude clear by taking off his shoe and banging it on the desk to accompany his fierce speech of condemnation. But, at the same time **behind** this official scene, the Russians did everything to prevent a break-down of the disarmament talks.

> ... All this was *news* of boxcar-headline proportions, but was there a difference between *what was 'news'* and *what was 'truth'?* This was the question being asked in Paris Monday night.
>
> The reaction of those experienced and detached diplomats who were not blown over by Khrushchev's storm was that there was an enormous difference.
>
> In the first place *while it was 'news'* that Khrushchev had come in here with what Eisenhower had called an "ultimatum" not to carry out any more flights over the Soviet Union, *the 'truth'* was that Eisenhower had reassured Khrushchev that the Sky-spy flights had been grounded, and Khrushchev knew it.
>
> *Secondly,* while Khrushchev said that his country could not 'be among the participants in negotiations where one of them (the United States) has made treachery the basis of its policy', *the truth was* that his (Khrushchev's) henchmen were running all over the Palais Chaillot Monday night saying that, of course, the Soviet Union did not mean to break off negotiations in Geneva with those "treacherous" American characters who were engaged in the talks on disarmament and the suspension of nuclear testing.
>
> *Third,* the afore-mentioned Soviet officials were also saying that while Eisenhower had really been very irresponsible in the spy-in-the-sky case and was not wanted as a visitor in Moscow, *actually* he was a pleasant man who had merely come close to the end of his term and therefore had no authority to negotiate big issues ..."[3]

So the main purpose of interpretive reporting is

1) to elucidate a complex situation so that an average reader may get some insight into it — by annotations, explanations of interrelations, the function of institutions, etc;

2) to provide additional background information from official bodies or inofficial sources;

3) to indicate some probable consequences as seen by authorities or the author.

Interpretive reporting; news analysis

This is an article of	interpretive/interpretative reporting. news analysis.
The journalist is out	to elucidate the complex situation of . . . to provide the average reader with some insight into . . .
He tries to	explain some of the interrelations between A and B. define the exact function of . . .
Apart from the official statement made by (public institutions), he gives valuable background information.	
He indicates some of the probable consequences of this incident, event.	

Since it is usual for conventional reporting to show a strict division between 'facts' and 'opinion', the views of those in control of the publication on matters of current interest are expressed and given a special place in an article usually written by the chief editor. This **editorial** article (i.e. written by the editor) is also called the **leading article** or the **leader.**

It is printed on the editorial page, along with columns, cartoons, and feature stories — in other words, forms of reporting in which the standpoint of the journalist is prominent and not only the hard facts. In the editorial or leader, the chief editor comments, i.e. expresses his opinion, on current issues of general interest and importance. Its main purpose is to form or influence, sometimes even to manipulate, public opinion. Events are criticized, i.e. praised or denounced. Any leader contains an appeal to the reader to join in, and to support, the arguments propounded.

Although there are no strict general rules, an **editorial** basically consists of three distinct parts:

1) the headline;
2) an introductory paragraph giving the necessary information to enable the reader to understand the column;
3) the body with the highly subjective, and sometimes persuasive, analysis of the issue.

Some newspapers — especially in the U.S.A. — no longer have an editorial of their own. Instead, they buy 'editorials' offered by famous columnists. Some of these columnists have become widely popular (and rich!), since their columns are printed by as many as 500 newspapers. These columns are rightly called **syndicated columns.** Their influence on public opinion is enormous — some critics even think that they endanger the freedom of the press and may be misused as an **uncontrolled** instrument of mass manipulation.

The following **leader** was published in *The New York Times* on November 28, 1963, a week after the assassination of President Kennedy.

THE RIGHT TO BEAR ARMS

The following conversation took place this week in a midtown Manhattan store which sells, among other things, deadly weapons:

CUSTOMER: If I buy a gun, do you check my identification or forward my name to any police agency?

SALESMAN: No, all we do is mark down the weapon number and keep the sales slip for our records.

CUSTOMER: What if I asked for a rifle just like the one Lee Oswald bought by mail?

SALESMAN: Here's the exact model. It's all yours — all you need is to be 18 and have $ 15.95.

A similar conversation could be repeated in many parts of the United States. If any shocked citizen dares to question the whole subject of the easy availability and unregistered nature of weapons, he will be immediately told that the Second Amendment to the Constitution says: "A well regulated Militia being necessary to the security of a free State, the right of the people to keep and bear Arms shall not be infringed."

But the 1960's and not the 1780's is the time at issue. A new examination of this Amendment is needed in the light of the terrible tragedy. State militias play a relatively minor role in our security today. In any event, no city or state law allows people to "keep and bear Arms" for self-protection as such. As a law-abiding people, we are not permitted to take the law into our own hands; we rely on the police instead of turning on each other. The basic constitutional reason given for bearing arms is out of date.

We do not necessarily hold that the Second Amendment should be repealed, but do strongly urge that the Federal and state governments tighten their laws on selling, buying and registering firearms. The principle of regulation of dangerous weapons must apply without exception — for concealed or unconcealed, small arms or large. Legitimate hunters and sportsmen should have no valid objection to registration with an appropriate agency...

What is called for now is a Federal-state conference on regulating arms under the Constitution. The Second Amendment does not prohibit uniformity, or controls. The ownership of firearms should be closely regulated — far more closely than it is today, and surely as closely as that of automobiles.

For study

1) What sort of introduction does the author use?
   Show that it contains the information which is necessary to understand the rest of the column.
2) What is the opinion of the author on 'the right to bear arms'?

2.3 Facts — selected and featured with the focus on 'human interest'

Whereas the **news story** is at its best a fully factual (i. e. objective) report of some recent event, the journalist 'features' (L 'facere' = 'makes') a **'feature story'** in a way so as to arrest human interest: joy or sorrow, admiration or disgust, love or hate, pity or fear — or the humorous side of some otherwise quite deplorable incident. Thus the facts merely serve the journalist as a basis for a rather unusual but appealing treatment. To be sure, the purpose of a feature is also to inform the reader; but it is mainly intended to entertain him, to enlighten him, or give him moral advice by stirring his emotions.

Historically, laying the stress on human interest has had a long tradition in England and America. Some believe that its origin is in the English Gothic ballads and in the American melodrama of the 19th century. This may perhaps help to explain the fact that more often than not feature writers have literary ambitions. In fact, many famous literary men have started their careers by writing features. They are often full of the sometimes quaint (or black) American and English humour. They serve as "the salad or dessert of the journalist diet — a little extra titbit to make the heavier parts of the meal more palatable."[4]

Features may range from the very short report on an incident — they are in that case mere bulletins with the twist on human interest, cf. the first example — to the long report full of appealing and arresting details (second example).

Note how the following fatal incident is reported as a human interest feature. For English and American readers, this means talking about something serious in a funny way — which in this case has got nothing to do with ridicule or sarcasm.

Monk's Fall Fatal To Abbey Worker

Gloucester, England, Nov. 15 (UPI) — Leslie Dally, a gardener at Prinknash Abbey, died yesterday of a broken spine.

He received the fatal injuries when Brother Chirstopher, a monk, fell on him from an apple tree.

On the surface, it is worded according to the principles of 'straight news' — the four w's. But whereas the first lead presents the tragic event in a rather laconic way, the second lead ends in a comic climax.

If details had been added, this human interest incident could have been developed into a human interest story in the form of the inverted pyramid. But, most probably, it would have lost most of its immediate impact and — humour!

Example of a **long feature:** on-the-spot report of President John F. Kennedy's death:

Desperate Hospital Battle to Save the President's Life

By Jimmy Breslin/Special to the Herald Tribune

... John Fitzgerald Kennedy already had been stripped of his jacket, shirt and T-shirt, and a staff doctor was starting to place a tube called an endotracht down his throat. Oxygen would be forced down the endotracht.

Breathing was the first thing to attack. The President was not breathing. Malcolm Perry unbuttoned his dark blue glen-plaid jacket and threw it onto the floor. He held out his hands while the nurse helped him put on gloves.

The President, Dr. Perry thought. He's bigger than I thought he was.

He noticed the tall, dark-haired girl in the plum dress had her husband's blood all over the front of the skirt. She was standing out of the way, over against the gray tile wall. Her face was tearless and it was set, and it was to stay that way because Jacqueline Kennedy, with a terrible discipline, was not going to take her eyes from her husband's face. Then Malcolm Perry stepped up to the aluminium hospital cart and he took charge of the hopeless job of trying to keep the 35th President of the United States from death. And now, the enormousness of his task came over him.

Chest Not Moving

Here is the most important man in the world, Dr. Perry thought.

The chest was not moving. And there was no apparent heartbeat inside it. The wound in the throat was small and neat. Blood was running out of it. It was running out too fast. The occipitoparietal, which is a part of the back of the head, had a huge flap.

The damage a 25-caliber bullet does as it comes out of a person's body is unbelievable. Bleeding from the head wound covered the floor.

There was a mediastinal wound in connection with the bullet hole in the throat. This means air and blood were being packed together in the chest. Dr. Perry called for a scalpel. He was going to start a tracheotomy, which is opening the throat and inserting a tube into the windpipe. The incision had to be made below the bullet wound.

"Get me Drs. Clark, McClelland and Baxter right away", Malcolm Perry said. Then he started the tracheotomy. There was no anesthesia, John Kennedy could feel nothing now. The wound in the back of the head told Dr. Perry that the President never knew a thing about it when he was shot, either.

While Dr. Perry worked on the throat, he said, quietly: "Will somebody put a right chest tube in, please."

Tube Inserted

The tube was to be inserted so it could suction out the blood and air packed in the chest and prevent the lung from collapsing.

These things he was doing took only small minutes, and other doctors and nurses were in the room and talking and moving, but Dr. Perry does not remember them. He saw only the throat and chest, shining under the huge lamp, and when he would look up or move his eyes between motions, he would see this plum dress and the terribly disciplined face standing over against the gray tile wall.

Just as he finished the tracheotomy, Malcolm Perry looked up and Dr. Kemp Clark, chief neurosurgeon in residency at Parkland, came in through the door. Dr. Clark was looking at the President of the United States.

Then he looked at Malcolm Perry and the look told Malcolm Perry something he already knew. There was no way to save the patient.

"Would you like to leave, ma'am?" Kemp Clark said to Jacqueline Kennedy. "We can make you more comfortable outside." Just the lips moved. "No", Jacqueline Kennedy said.

Not a Heartbeat

Now, Malcolm Perry's long fingers ran over the chest under him and he tried to get a heartbeat, and even the suggestion of breathing, and there was nothing...

"Will somebody please get me a stool", he said.

One was placed under him. He sat on it, and for ten minutes he massaged the chest. Over in one corner of the room, Dr. Kemp Clark kept watching an electrocardiogram for some sign that the massaging was creating action in the President's heart. There was none. Dr. Clark turned his head from the electrocardiogram.

'It's too late, Mac'

"It's too late, Mac", he said to Malcolm Perry.

The long fingers stopped massaging and they were lifted from the white chest. Dr. Perry got off the stool and stepped back.

Dr. M. T. Jenkins, who had been working the oxygen flow, reached down from the head of the aluminum cart. He took the edges of a white sheet in his hands. He pulled the sheet up over the face of John Fitzgerald Kennedy.

The clock on the wall said it was 1 p.m. The date was Nov. 22, 1963.

Three policemen were moving down the hall outside emergency room No. 1 now, and they were calling to everyone to get out of the way. But this was not needed, because everybody stepped out of the way automatically when they saw the priest who was behind the police. His name was the Rev. Oscar Huber, a small, 70-year-old man who was walking quickly. Malcolm Perry turned to leave the room as Father Huber came in. Dr. Perry remembers seeing the priest go by him.

And he remembers his eyes seeing that plum dress and that terribly disciplined face for the last time as he walked out of emergency room No. 1 and slumped into a chair in the hall...[5]

For study

1) The scene is described from the standpoint of Dr. Perry. In which way does this standpoint affect the narration and make it more impressive?
2) What is the part played by Jacqueline Kennedy in the description of the scene? Comment on the author's style whenever he mentions her name.

2.4 Facts — selected and featured with the help of fictional techniques — faction

2.4.1 New Journalism

In the early sixties, some newspapers and magazines were in a serious financial plight. With advanced technology, fierce competition had set in between them and the radio, the film and particularly television. Moreover, the costs of production had risen considerably.

To retain their readership, it became necessary for papers and magazines to develop a new sort of reporting that was at once revealing, more colourful and humanly appealing. Neither the reader nor the journalist could be satisfied with the conventional reporting of 'straight news' which did not fully record the complex reality of our time. Even interpretive reporting failed to provide insight into contemporary life and future trends.

For these reasons, the **new journalist tries to reveal the story hidden beneath the surface facts.** He does not only record the official statements of spokesmen of powerful bodies and institutions, but investigates the background that was traditionally considered to be 'off the record', i. e. he inquires about what has been going on before, and what is going on behind the scenes. Besides — well aware of his own limitations — he has given up the standpoint of the omniscient (L 'knowing everything') author, and adopted the role of the eye-witness: he deliberately reveals his own impressions and experiences, and tries to make the reader feel as if he himself had been a witness or gone through the same experience.

This new approach involves more careful research and a more personal kind of interviewing than conventional reporting. It also shows an important change in the relationship of literary art to experience. Some narrative techniques such as inverted chronology or scenic presentation are now used by reporters and journalists, leading to **a fusion of the journalist's passion for detail and the novelist's personal vision.** And more so than before, the once clearly demarcated differences between mere journalism and literature, between elite art and the popular arts, have become increasingly difficult to distinguish.

The use of fictional techniques in factual reporting — characteristic of the New Journalism from the 1960's onwards — is by no means new. Ever since colonial times, writers and literary men in America had written for newspapers and magazines using, of course, some of the literary techniques in their journalistic work.

Mark Twain, O. Henry, Ring Lardner, E. Hemingway were literary journalists. Around 1960, it was Truman Capote, Norman Mailer and Tom Wolfe — all of them literary men of some standing! — who helped to adapt journalism to contemporary needs: choosing documentary form in their new narrative, **they deliberately blended aspects of on-the-spot reporting, the auto-biography and confession with those of the short story, the novel, and the drama.** Their tone is highly personal: happy or sad, matter-of-fact or pensive, humorous or sarcastic.

2.4.2 Criticism of New Journalism

From the very beginning, New Journalism met with hard criticism because it used literary and fictional techniques in a field where facts were expected to be reported in an 'objective' manner. In the view of many of its critics, this 'para-journalism' (Gk 'para' = 'beside' journalism proper) was and is abandoning the real purposes of journalism; in other words, it is distorting the facts by the use of fictional techniques — which means replacing its duty to inform the public objectively by a cult of egotism and profit-making.

In short, it is a mixed form, having it both ways, exploiting the factual authority of journalism and the atmospheric licence of fiction.

2.4.3 Conventional journalism and New Journalism

80 per cent of the news in papers and magazines is still communicated in the form of conventional 'straight news'. The remaining 20 per cent consists of interpretive reporting and background stories published in newspapers, magazines, and television documentaries. This proportion of 'objective' reporting on the one hand and 'interpretive' or 'imaginative' reporting on the other hand should — in the eyes of many of those concerned — be retained.

2.4.4 Fictional techniques used in factual reporting — faction

In order to give the reader the opportunity to form his own impression of a complex situation, the 'New Journalist' tries to give a simplified, but truthful, immediate representation of reality. For this purpose, he uses some techniques originally only found in fictional narrative:

1) instead of giving a summary report of an event in chronological order, he makes use of **'inverted chronology'**, in particular of flashbacks and foreshadowing;
2) instead of giving the mere facts, he **indirectly characterizes people fully by recording 'status details'**, such as their behaviour, their gestures, their home, their car, etc.;
3) instead of giving only occasional quotations, **he records dialogue fully** to provide the reader with an immediate, lively impression of the main personalities;
4) instead of giving the traditional summary report, **he portrays events in dramatic scenes** to make their impact more immediate;
5) instead of using merely direct quotations, **he extensively uses inner monologue and the stream-of-consciousness technique** to provide the reader with some psychological insight;
6) instead of taking the stance of the omniscient narrator, **he extensively uses particular points of view,** i.e. he records how other people see the character he is drawing (portraying);
7) in order to give an immediate, vivid picture of a certain group, **he uses composite characterization.**

Since some of these fictional narrative techniques may be new to you, we have considered it necessary to give a fuller explanation of what they mean, how they work, and why they are used.

1. Inverted chronology (L 'in-vertus' = 'turned round'; Gk 'chronos' = 'time' + 'logia' = 'the science of measuring time')

So, 'inverted' chronology refers to an arrangement in which the 'order of time' has been 'turned around'. This stylistic device, often found in literature, has been adopted by the New Journalists to give the reader the illusion that he is forming his own impressions. So, the story might begin in the middle of a scene, and then — at a moment that lends itself to some deeper reflection — the New Journalist will show what preceded it in a 'flashback' and what might follow by using the device of 'foreshadowing' or 'anticipation'.

1.1 Flashback (G 'Rück-blende')

The 'flashback' or 'backflash' is a narrative or theatrical technique — also used in films or television — that interrupts the current order of time to interject earlier events or scenes. In films, the picture usually becomes blurred when one of the main characters has memories of the past. These are then interjected to provide the viewer with some background information to explain the present state of affairs. After some time, the story continues in the relative present.

1.2 Foreshadowing (G 'Vorauswerfen eines Schattens')
Anticipation (L 'ante' = 'before' + 'capere' = 'to take'; G 'Vorwegnahme')

Foreshadowing or anticipation — as narrative or theatrical techniques — are the reverse of the flashback. The author interrupts the chronological sequence of events to present — or allude to — events that will, or might, happen in the relative future. His aim is to make developments more transparent, quite often with emotional overtones.

2. Depicting 'status details' (L 'status' = 'social standing, rank') is an integral part of the vivid, immediate form of presentation. By recording a person's individual gestures, habits, his peculiar life-style in a particular atmosphere and environment (i.e. his clothing, his home, his friends, etc.), New Journalism manages to achieve an authentic precision of characterization unknown to conventional journalism.

3. Recording dialogue in full (Gk 'dia-logos' = 'Zwie-gespräch', L 'con-versation')

By recording dialogue extensively, the New Journalist intends to reveal a character more fully by the way he speaks, or argues, on a certain topic in a certain situation. It provides the reader with psychological insight, especially if the particular diction (slang, dialect) is captured. Mere quotations fail to characterize a human being's inner life and social behaviour.

4. Dramatic scenes (L 'scena' = 'stage') are episodes so vividly represented that the action seems to unfold immediately before us with its realistic background. These scenes in reporting remind the reader of the scenes in a drama, or the scenic presentation often used in short stories and novels. In longer magazine articles, the action is shown moving from scene to scene. In shorter ones, the most characteristic scene is chosen as a focus to provide a vivid impression.

5. Inner (interior) monologue (Gk 'monos' = 'alone' + 'logos' = talking alone)

In inner monologue, incidents or events are reported, considered, or referred to through the mind of **one** of the characters. Its purpose is to reveal a character's views, his thoughts and his feelings. The interruptions necessary when using direct quotations have thus become superfluous.

6. Point of view, i.e. the standpoint from which someone or something is seen.

By giving up the standpoint of an author who pretends to know everything, i.e. the **omniscient** author, the New Journalist tries to give a portrayal of a person's character or the depiction of an event from the standpoint of several people who were personal witnesses.
So, every new scene is presented through the eyes of a particular character, giving the reader the impression of experiencing the situation himself — along with the accompanying thoughts and feelings which are rendered by inner monologue. Thus, sympathy or antipathy can be generated and the attitude of the reader to the event, the persons or the group influenced, or even manipulated.

7. Composite characterization (L 'com-positus' = 'put together')

Using composite characterization means presenting a typical human character or personality whose peculiarities have been put together by carefully investigating and interviewing many members of a group. If this research has been done carefully, composite characterization can be an efficient literary means to create lively characters representative of a group even in an anonymous mass society. It is this personal atmosphere that makes English or American films or reports on certain problems so lively and so highly impressive. A well-known example was 'Holocaust', where the fate of all the Jews in the Third Reich was crystallized in the fate of a single family.

The good article

<table>
<tr><td>A</td><td>good article
writer knows</td><td>that truth</td><td>may be as strange
can be made as
entertaining</td><td>as fiction.</td></tr>
<tr><td colspan="2">First, he</td><td>studies
investigates</td><td colspan="2">the subject thoroughly.</td></tr>
<tr><td colspan="5">He does not make a difference between the story and the facts.
He tries to write the way he would talk.</td></tr>
<tr><td colspan="5"> </td></tr>
</table>

p. t. o.

The good article (continued)

<table>
<tr><td colspan="3">He uses the tested methods of advertising writing:
— first, he manages to get his readers' attention by . . .
— then, he retains their interest by . . .
— and finally, he secures a positive reaction to his message by . . .</td></tr>
<tr><td colspan="3">He is aware that almost all his readers resist information.
So he deletes most of the laboriously acquired data.</td></tr>
<tr><td colspan="2">He does not weigh down his readers</td><td>with statistics.
with a mass of facts.</td></tr>
<tr><td colspan="2">He does not assume</td><td>a pontifical pose.
the standpoint of an omniscient author.</td></tr>
<tr><td colspan="3">He is never stuffy or dull.
He presents information simply, but animately.</td></tr>
<tr><td colspan="3">He tells those things first which furnish the clearest possible picture of the subject, i.e. the most authentic and appealing ones.</td></tr>
<tr><td rowspan="2">He</td><td colspan="2">'streamlines' facts when he . . .
makes them more palatable by . . .</td></tr>
<tr><td>presents them in such a way that they are</td><td>authentic.
informative.
significant.
palatable.
entertaining.
appealing.
convincing.
persuasive.</td></tr>
<tr><td colspan="2">The good article moves quickly and interestingly</td><td>— because of some 'aids to interest' tested by advertising writing such as . . .
— because of stylistic qualities and techniques developed and perfected by fiction writers such as
— dramatic scenes at the beginning,
— lively dialogue,
— vivid characterization,
— striking anecdotes,
— warm humour.</td></tr>
</table>

p. t. o.

The good article (continued)

<table>
<tr><td rowspan="4">In short, a good article</td><td colspan="3">sounds like an intelligent conversation.
is never boring nor monotonous.
is a short factual narrative based upon careful research.
is full of facts.</td></tr>
<tr><td>is</td><td>more informative
more meaty</td><td>than a fictional story.</td></tr>
<tr><td>is just as</td><td>entertaining
appealing</td><td>as a fictional story.</td></tr>
<tr><td colspan="3">makes use of tricks but is still artistic.</td></tr>
</table>

It is	simple to read, fun to read,	but authoritative and informative.

It is essentially factual, but partly fictional in its approach.

New Journalism

The **New Journalist** first	registers facts. documents reality. interviews all those concerned.
Then he	deliberately blends factual with fictional reality. deepens his work with imaginative conceptions. places composite characters in situations representative of contemporary life. records **and** criticizes reality at the same time. uses a moral vision to serve as a guideline to his readers in human dilemmas.
Sometimes he deliberately	creates a darkly surrealistic atmosphere dominated by absurd and dark humour.

p. t. o.

New Journalism (continued)

In particular, the New Journalist uses **fictional techniques**	such as	— inverted chronology, — flashbacks, — foreshadowing (anticipation); — indirect characterization with the help of 'status details'; — vivid direct characterization by means of — inner monologue and the stream-of-consciousness technique, — extensive dialogues, — full dramatic scenes; — skilful choice of, and change in, the point of view; — criticism contained in — irony, humour, — composite characterization, — the detached implication of future trends.

On September 28th, 1980, *The Washington Post* published the moving story of an eight-year-old Negro drug addict, written by Janet Cooke. Half a year later, this newspaper apologized to its readers after it was found out that the boy had never existed but was a mere product of the journalist's imagination:

Janet's World
The Story of a Child Who Never Existed —
How and Why It Came to Be Published
By Bill Green
Washington Post Ombudsman

"Jimmy" never existed, but his story convulsed the city and humiliated The Washington Post — proud house of Watergate investigations.

The story was a lie and, after all its celebrated achievements, The Post owes its readers an accounting of its spectacular failure...

For Cooke, it was personal tragedy. For The Post, it was inexcusable.

For instance, none of the editors pressed Cooke for confidential details on the identity of "Jimmy" or his family...

Some Post staff members, however, did express suspicions to editors who weren't listening.

While some reporters and editors were talking up their doubts, The Post's top news executives, unaware of newsroom anxieties, were nominating "Jimmy's World" for journalism's highest award, the Pulitzer Prize.

At the center of all this was Janet Cooke. Whether diligence in the newsroom would have prevented her hoax no one can say. Nevertheless, The Post didn't work hard enough.[6]

Now this is Jimmy's story, which may be regarded as a typical example of "faction" (i.e. a fusion of facts and fiction) in the style of New Journalism. (The article has been considerably shortened).

Jimmy's World

8-Year-Old Heroin Addict Lives for a Fix

By Janet Cooke

Jimmy is 8 years old and a third-generation heroin addict, a precocious little boy with sandy hair, velvety brown eyes and needle marks freckling the baby-smooth skin of his brown arms.

He nestles in a large, beige reclining chair in the living room of his comfortably furnished home in Southeast Washington. There is an almost cherubic expression on his small, round face as he talks about life — clothes, money, the Baltimore Orioles and heroin. He has been an addict since the age of 5...

Jimmy's is a world of hard drugs, fast money and the good life he believes both can bring. Every day, junkies casually buy heroin from Ron, his mother's live-in lover, in the dining room of Jimmy's home. They "cook" it in the kitchen and "fire up" in the bedrooms. And every day, Ron or someone else fires up Jimmy, plunging a needle into his bony arm, sending the fourth grader into a hypnotic nod.

Jimmy prefers this atmosphere to school, where only one subject seems relevant to fulfilling his dreams. "I want to have me a bad car and dress good and also have me a good place to live," he says. "So, I pretty much pay attention in math because I know I got to keep up when I finally get me something to sell."...

Jimmy's mother Andrea accepts her son's habit as a fact of life, although she will not inject the child herself and does not like to see others do it.

"I don't really like to see him fire up," she says. "But, you know, I think he would have got into it one day, anyway. Everybody does. When you live in the ghetto, it's all a matter of survival. If he wants to get away when he's older, then that's his thing. But right now, things are better for us than they've ever been... Drugs and black folks been together for a very long time."...

Heroin has become a part of life in many of Washington's neighborhoods, affecting thousands of teen-agers and adults who feel cut off from the world around them, and filtering down to untold numbers of children like Jimmy who are bored with school and battered by life...

Medical experts, such as Dr. Alyce Gulfatte, director of the Howard University Drug Abuse Institute, say that heroin is destroying the city. And D.C.'s medical examiner, James Luke, has recorded a substantial increase in the number of deaths from heroin overdose, from seven in 1978 to 43 so far this year. Death has not yet been a visitor to the house where Jimmy lives....

Jimmy wants most to be a good dope dealer. He says that when he is older, "maybe about 11," he would like to "go over to Condon Terrace (notorious for its open selling of drugs and violent way of life) or somewhere else and sell." With the money he says he would buy a German Shepherd dog and a bicycle....

His mother doesn't view Jimmy's ambitions with alarm, perhaps because drugs are as much part of Andrea's world as they are of her son's.

She never knew her father. Like her son, Andrea spent her childhood with her mother and the man with whom she lived for 15 years....

Addicts who have been feeding their habits for 35 years or more are not uncommon in Jimmy's world, and although medical experts say that there is an extremely high risk of his death from an overdose, it is not inconceivable that he will live to reach adulthood.

"He might already be close to getting a lethal dose," Dr. Dorynne Czechowicz of the National Institute on Drug Abuse says. "Much of this depends on the amount he's getting and the frequency with which he's getting it. But I would hate to say that his early death is inevitable. If he were to get treatment, it probably isn't too late to help him....[7]

For study

1) Which fictional techniques does Janet Cooke use to make her article seem more lively and appealing to the reader?
2) Examine the structure of the article, showing that serious information, which makes this fabricated story more credible, is scattered throughout the text.

3. THE ESSAY

3.1 Characteristics of the essay

3.1.1 General definition

Essay writing is practised at school and university when pupils and students are asked to write about a certain subject and give their own views on it. In fact, anyone who can put pen to paper can compose an essay of a sort. Quite a number of English authors, however, became famous for their essays, and the essay may be regarded as one of the most attractive genres of English literature.
As there is a great variety of essays, a definition applying to all of them must necessarily be very vague. We may say that it is "a piece of prose, usually on the short side, which is not devoted to narrative".[1] The etymology of the word (it comes from the French word 'essayer', which means "to try") suggests that it is a mere attempt on the part of the author — **an attempt to express a few personal thoughts on a certain topic.** This means that the essay does not pretend to completeness and that, moreover, it reflects the personality of its author in a fairly open, direct manner.

3.1.2 Relationship between author and reader

It is perhaps this **directness** which makes the essay different from any other form of literature — except autobiographies... and poetry to a certain extent. When reading an essay, we get the impression that the author is near us and sometimes even that he is talking to us personally; whereas in most other forms of literature, the position of the reader is that of a spectator in front of a stage or a screen... with the author hiding behind. In a drama, a novel or a short story, we meet various characters — they are the author's puppets, mere products of his imagination — and these characters are involved in a plot which has been put together by the author in order to entertain us. There is always something going on — whether it is acted, in a play, or narrated, in a novel or a short story.

3.1.3 Difference between essay and short story

So, according to our general definition, the difference between the essay and the short story — which is also "a piece of prose, usually on the short side"! — is that the essay is "not devoted to narrative". In a short story, the narrative is in the foreground: there may be a particular meaning underlying the story, but even if we fail to grasp it, the story remains and is still enjoyable. Conversely, the essayist may use a few narrative elements to help him to make his point, but these are not essential, and if we fail to understand what he means on the whole, practically nothing remains. Therefore we can say that the essay, being **non-fictional, appeals more to our understanding than to our imagination.**

3.2 Essay and journalism

3.2.1 Influence of the development of the press

Many English essayists reached fame through their contributions to well-known newspapers and periodicals — Charles Lamb and William Hazlitt, for example, at the beginning of the 19th century, or Aldous Huxley in the 20th century. And there is no doubt that it was the development of the press in the 18th century which gave the essay a new scope and caused it to flourish. Papers like *The Tatler* and *The Spectator,* conducted by Steele and Addison, specialized in publishing criticism and comment upon literature and manners rather than in providing news. They denounced the evils of society in those days (like gambling and duelling), discussed all questions of good manners and found the criteria for the ideal gentleman. Their object was to "enliven morality with wit, and to temper wit with morality"[2], and to set up a new standard of good taste — a fair task in the Age of Enlightenment!

3.2.2 Literature and journalism

Still nowadays we find essays of all sorts in newspapers and magazines. Of course, not all of them can be regarded as pieces of literature. The difficulty of defining the border between literature and journalism is at the core of Maurice Hewlett's essay about the essay (!), "The Maypole and the Column" (the maypole standing for the literary essay, and the column for the newspaper article of lesser value). He writes:

> Journalism loves the particular, but literature must hold fast to the general. Journalism accepts the ephemeral, gives you its daily screed for its daily bread; but literature has its eye on posterity, expresses the spirit of fact rather than the body of it . . .
>
> Lamb was essayist first and journalist with what remained over. A column was set up: he made it a maypole. No craftsman has draped his idea or capered about it as Lamb did. He transfigures whatever he touches; more, he transmutes it.[3]

In their book *Elements of the Essay,* R. Scholes and Carl H. Klaus lay the stress on the idea itself, on the message contained in a literary essay:

> Useful writing lasts for a short time. *Artful writing can endure for centuries. What preserves it is its beauty.* And beauty in writing, it should be remembered, is of two kinds: formal perfection and what Plato called "the splendour of truth". All literature involves both kinds of beauty. But the essay is the form most directly concerned with **truth,** most concerned with convincing us of the version of reality that it presents.[4]

3.3 The two main types of essays

3.3.1 An attempt at classification

Being free from any rule, the essay has developed an infinite variety of styles. We cannot possibly classify them according to their subjects — the list would be too long! We might identify them according to the techniques employed: some are chiefly argumentative, some are mainly descriptive, others are based on short narratives, a few will make use of dialogues. But these are only secondary aspects and tell us little about the purpose of the author. When you read a number of essays, you will find that they fall into two main categories — **the serious ones** and **the light-hearted ones.** Nearly all essayists may be regarded as thinkers or **social philosophers,** but it is the **tone** employed which makes all the difference. Aldous Huxley, for example, is not in a joking mood when he warns his readers — in his *Brave New World Revisited* (1946) — of brainwashing and other methods of persuasion. Chesterton, on the other hand, "roars with laughter" when he realizes that he has been sitting on a hill of white chalk, while he was desperately looking for a piece of chalk to draw with.[5] There is, of course, a wide range from the most serious to the most flippant tone, so that each of the two categories itself includes a multitude of styles.

3.3.2 The serious essay, or formal essay

We must bear in mind that the early English essays — Bacon's for example —, with their deliberate **moral purpose,** were necessarily serious. Now some sense of moral purpose runs through most essays in one form or another, but particularly in the formal ones. In his collection of essays entitled *Brave New World Revisited,* Aldous Huxley makes us aware of all the forces that threaten individual freedom and he tries to find ways to resist these forces before it is too late.
The essays, of course, reflect the philosophical views of their authors. T.S. Eliot, for instance, wishes literature to be more closely connected with religion,[6] whereas Bertrand Russell calls all our beliefs in question.[7]

3.3.2.1 Structure

This type of essay is very formal. It is an earnest attempt at **exposing and interpreting facts.** The author, here, speaks as an expert. In his endeavour **to make his point and persuade us to accept his view,** he is concerned with a **logical line of argumentation** and a clear structure: he will state his thesis, justify it by putting forward various arguments, and often imagine counter-arguments which he refutes himself. His conclusion may be a proposal for action, a piece of advice, or an optimistic or pessimistic anticipation of the future.

3.3.2.2 Relationship between author and reader

Formal essays do not always make easy reading. In some cases you need a fair amount of concentration to follow the argumentation of the author or to understand his exposition of facts. (Huxley's approach is rather scientific; in fact, he wanted to become a doctor before he took to writing.) Besides, formal essays are quite **impersonal.** The relationship between author and reader is similar to that of a lecturer to his audience of students. This does not exclude the possibility of a humorous comparison:

> Every man, wherever he goes, is encompassed by a cloud of comfortable convictions, which move with him like flies on a summer day.[8]

But such a stylistic device is an exception and the tone remains serious throughout the text.

The serious, or formal essay

<table>
<tr><td>The tone</td><td>is serious
remains earnest
is rather impersonal</td><td>throughout the essay.</td></tr>
<tr><td rowspan="2">The author</td><td>is out to</td><td>make a point.
establish a view.
warn the reader against...
criticize (certain features of character).
condemn (some trends of society).</td></tr>
<tr><td colspan="2">seeks to convince us of the rightness of what he says.</td></tr>
<tr><td>He is concerned with</td><td colspan="2">the exposition and interpretation of facts.
fundamental questions.
ultimate questions.</td></tr>
<tr><td colspan="3">This essay is mainly argumentative.</td></tr>
<tr><td>The line of argumentation
The structure of the essay</td><td colspan="2">is logical.
is obvious.
follows a clear pattern.</td></tr>
<tr><td rowspan="2">The author</td><td colspan="2">puts forward convincing arguments.</td></tr>
<tr><td>imagines a counter-argument and</td><td>answers it.
refutes it.</td></tr>
<tr><td colspan="3">The essay reflects the philosophical views of the author.</td></tr>
</table>

p. t. o.

<table>
<tr><th colspan="4">**The serious, or formal essay** (continued)</th></tr>
<tr><td>The author</td><td>holds
takes</td><td>a rather pessimistic
a fairly optimistic</td><td>view of the situation.</td></tr>
<tr><td colspan="2">He speaks from the point of view of</td><td colspan="2">a believer.
an atheist.
a humanitarian.
a moralist.</td></tr>
</table>

3.3.2.3 An example of the serious essay

In his essay "Trespass on a Monument", A. MacLeish, an American playwright, comments on his own play, *J.B.*. He fears that some people might criticize him for making use of such a 'monument' as *The Book of Job* as the basis of his drama (hence the title). So, in order to justify his choice, he draws a comparison between his main character and the person of Job in the Bible. This causes him to reflect upon the problem of evil and that of God's relationship to man.
What follows is an abridged version of his essay.

Trespass on a Monument

If the invitation to write this piece means that the drama editor of *The New York Times* regards my play as crying out, like Job's boils, for justification, I can only agree. A man may be forgiven for dramatizing an incident from the Bible and even for modernizing it in the process. But what I have done is not so easy to excuse. I have constructed a modern play inside the ancient majesty of *The Book of Job* much as the Bedouins, thirty years ago, used to build within the towering ruins of Palmyra their shacks of gasoline tins roofed with fallen stones...

...I badly needed an ancient structure on which to build the contemporary play that has haunted me for five years past, and the structure of the poem of Job is the only one I know of which our modern history will fit. Job's search, like ours, was for the meaning of his afflictions — the loss of his children, the loss of everything he possessed, the loss of his wife's kindness, who turned upon him on his agony with those ineradicable words, surely the most dreadful ever spoken by wife to husband: "Curse God and die!" There was no reason for all this: no reason the mind, at least, could grasp. Job was, by witness of God himself and twice repeated, "a perfect and an upright man" and his destruction was, by the same unquestionable authority, "without cause." As for ourselves, there can be very few of us who are perfect, but the enormous, nameless disasters that have befallen whole cities, entire peoples, in two great wars and many small ones, have destroyed the innocent together with the guilty — and with no "cause" our minds can grasp...

...There are those, I know — because I have heard them — who will object that Job's story bears no true relationship to our own because God has changed in the interval. The God of Job is God the Creator of the Universe, and science, they say, now knows that there is no such Creator — that the events of time progress by an automatism of their own — that the watch winds itself and ticks by its own juggling. The modern God of the scientific age, that is to say, does not control events: not, at least, events in the world of here and now.

I have no wish, and certainly no competence, to argue the questions of faith that underlie that attitude. But two things may be said from the merely human position. The first relates to the statement that science knows now there is no Creator. Does it? Einstein has told us that he had sometimes the sense that he was following, in his plumbings and probings of the universe, the track of an Intelligence far beyond the reaches of his own. The second thing to be said is this: that there has been nothing in human history that has brought mankind closer to the immanence of an infinite creativity than the revelation that the minutest particles of inert matter contain an almost immeasurable power. To me, a man committed to no creed, and more uncertain than I should be of certain ultimate beliefs, the God of Job seems closer to this generation than he has to any other in centuries.

My hero, called J. B. after the current fashion in business address, bears little relation, perhaps, to that ancient owner of camels and oxen and sheep. He is not a particularly devout man. But he is, at the beginning of the play, prosperous, powerful, possessed of a lovely wife, fine children — everything the heart of man can desire — and he is aware, as he could hardly help being, that God has made "an hedge about him and about his house and about all that he hath on every side." Not that the name of God is often in his mouth. He is one of those vastly successful American business-men — not as numerous now as they were before the Great Depression — who, having everything, believe as a matter of course that they have a right to have everything. They do not believe this out of vulgarity. They are not Babbitts: on the contrary, they are most often men of exuberance, of high animal spirits, of force and warmth. They believe it because they possess in large measure that characteristically American courage that has so often amused Asian and European visitors, the courage to believe in themselves. Which means to believe in their lives. Which means, if their tongues can shape the words, to believe in God's goodness to them. They are not hypocritical. They do not think that they deserve more at God's hands than others. They merely think that they have more — and that they have a right to have it.

Such a man is no better prepared than Job was for the sudden and inexplicable loss of everything. And such a man must ask, as our time does ask, Job's repeated question. Job wants *justice* of the universe. He needs to know the reason for his wretchedness. And it is in those repeated cries of his that we hear most clearly our own voices. For our age is an age haunted and driven by the need to know. Not only is our science full of it but our arts also. And it is here, or so it seems to me, that our story and the story of Job come closest to each other. Job is not *answered* in the Bible by the voice out of the whirling wind. He is *silenced* by it — silenced by some thirty or forty of the greatest lines in all literature — silenced by the might and majesty and magnificence of the creation. He is brought, not to *know,* but to *see.* As we also have been brought...

(So Job does not get a proper answer to his question. And yet, when God gives him back what he has lost, he accepts the offer to live his life again — without asking for any further explanation. Modern man, in spite of his sufferings, and although his demands for reasons remain unanswered, accepts life just as Job did.)

... Love becomes the ultimate human answer to the ultimate human question. Love, in reason's terms, answers nothing. We say that *Amor vincit omnia* but in truth love conquers nothing — certainly not death — certainly not chance. What love does is to affirm. It affirms the worth of life in spite of life. It affirms the wonder and the beauty of the human creature, mortal and insignificant and ignorant though he be. It answers life with life and so justifies that bravely tolling line of Shakespeare's that declares that love "bears it out even to the edge of doom." Love does: and for us no less than for that ancient man who took back his life again after all that wretchedness. J. B., like Job, covers his mouth with his hand; acquiesces in the vast indifference of the universe as all men must who truly face it; takes back his life again. In love. To live.

I suppose, if I am really to justify my trespass, I must go on to say that, though human beings have taken back their lives over and over, generation after generation since time began, they have, perhaps, never done so with such desperate courage as in these past, strange years. Men, our own contemporaries, have already sat as Job did on an earth reduced to ash-heap, picking in agony at the cinders of a bomb-scorched skin, asking Job's eternal question. We know that they have sat there. We know that we may sit there too. But we know also something more. We know that even men like these can learn, in Yeats' words, to "live it all again."[9]

For study

1) What sort of essay is "Trespass on a Monument"? (What is the tone? What is it concerned with?)
2) Determine the structure of the essay, summing up the ideas of the various paragraphs.
3) What counter-argument does the author anticipate in the third paragraph? How does he refute it in the next one?
4) Would you say that the author speaks from the point of view of an atheist or that of a believer? Give evidence from the text.
5) Which events does the author refer to in the second and in the last paragraph? How did these events make the situation of many people comparable with that of Job?
6) Is the conclusion pessimistic?

3.3.3 The light-hearted essay, or humorous essay

We only need to cast a glance at the table of contents in a selection of essays to realize that a great number of them have been written with a different purpose and to quite a different effect from those mentioned above. "Getting up on Cold Mornings", "A Conversation with a Cat", "On Not Being a Philosopher", "Why We Hate Insects": these are more fanciful subjects — often mere trifles — and their authors usually write in a light and playful vein. Such essayists, unlike the authors of serious essays, do not keep to a systematic structure or rigorous line of argumentation. Even if they do have a point to make, they proceed according to casual associations of ideas, following the swerving path of their fancy. A few unexpected digressions before they return to their main theme provide a somewhat loose and irregular, but not altogether illogical pattern. Their chief purpose is apparently to entertain us — although there is obvious criticism running through their works — and they reach this aim by a very personal approach, a good deal of humour and sometimes even poetry.

3.3.3.1 Personal approach

The tone, here, is more familiar than in the "serious essay" — which does not mean at all that the style lapses into colloquial English or slang, but that the author talks straight at us in a fairly conversational manner, expecting us to meet him on his own level. It is no longer the lecturer standing in front of his students, but a human being sitting near us and telling us about what interests him, his likes and dislikes:

> I hate anything that occupies more space than it is worth, I hate to see a load of bandboxes go along the street, and I hate to see a parcel of big words without anything in them.
> (W. Hazlitt, "On Familiar Style")[10]

> I can look with no indifferent eye upon things or persons. Whatever is, is to me a matter of taste or distaste.
> (Ch. Lamb, "Imperfect Sympathies")[11]

> I am a good lover, but an even better hater. . . . I 'mislike' — to put it no more strongly — a great many women and nearly all men, with a special aversion for the type of man adored by women. . . . I dislike the little ninny who insists that the Moonlight Sonata is by Mendelssohn.
> (J. Agate, "Likes and Dislikes")[12]

The essayist also gets very personal by referring to his own experience. This is where **the narrative element** comes in — an incident is recalled in the middle of the essay to illustrate the topic, or right at the beginning to serve as an introduction:

> The other day, I went into the bar of a railway station and, taking a glass of beer, I sat at a little table by myself to meditate upon the necessary but tragic isolation of the human soul . . . when fate, or some fostering star, sent me a tawny, silky, long-haired cat.
> (Hilaire Belloc, "A Conversation with a Cat")[13]

3.3.3.2 Criticism

We may say that even those light-hearted essays which are chiefly aimed at amusing us are not devoid of moral purpose. Criticism, overtly expressed or concealed with irony, is to be found in many places. The essayist is quick to point out human faults, snobberies, and vanities. In the eighteenth century, for example, Oliver Goldsmith warned his contemporaries against national prejudices (a topic which is still of present interest), after meeting a group of English patriots who spoke badly of other nations in Europe:

> I retired to my own lodgings, reflecting on the absurd and ridiculous nature of national prejudice and prepossession . . . Is it not very possible that I may love my own country without hating the natives of other countries?
> (O. Goldsmith, "National Prejudices")[14]

James Agate, in "Likes and Dislikes", clearly shows his attitude towards religious and racial prejudices: "I have a contempt for the Christian who looks down upon the Jew, the white man who animadverts against the black . . ." and towards ostentatious wealth: "I abhor the belly of the successful man."[15]

W. Hazlitt does not think much of literary critics when he says:

> If we wish to know the force of human genius we should read Shakespeare. If we wish to see the insignificance of human learning we may study his commentators.
> ("On the Ignorance of the Learned")[16]

And J. B. Priestley does not have a high opinion of sociologists either — those people "who understand everything except their fellow creatures . . ." ("Money for Nothing").[17]

Criticism takes on the form of monstrous sarcasm in Swift's *A Modest Proposal.* Swift, who was always indignant at oppression and unfairness, and particularly appalled at the extreme poverty of the Irish people, tried to draw the attention of politicians to this state of affairs by shocking them. His *Modest Proposal For Preventing the Children of Poor People in Ireland From Being a Burden To Their Parents or Country* was . . . to use them as food for the rich (!). The following sentence, full of pungent irony, shows clearly that his satire is directed against the oppression and ruthlessness of the landlords towards their tenants in the eighteenth century:

> I grant this food will be somewhat dear, and therefore very proper for landlords, who, as they have already devoured most of the parents, seem to have the best title to the children.[18]

3.3.3.3 Humour: exaggeration and paradox

Such macabre sarcasm, however, is more typical of Swift himself than it is of the English essay on the whole, the tone of which is usually much lighter: **humorous remarks,** very often in the form of exaggerations, are scattered through its pages to remind us that the author does not take his subject too seriously and that we should not take it too seriously either. In "Walking Tours", for example, Stevenson, talking of Hazlitt's essay "On Going on a Journey", says that it is "so good that there should be a tax levied on all who have not read it",[19] and Chesterton makes the following comment on the content of his pockets: "Once I planned to write a book of poems entirely about the things in my pocket. But I found it would be too long; and the age of the great epics is past." ("A Piece of Chalk")[20]

These are mere jokes — 'logical' nonsense — with no other purpose than to amuse us — while the author himself pretends to remain serious.

Another device often used to a humorous effect is **paradox.** Some titles are paradoxical in themselves: "On the Ignorance of the Learned" (W. Hazlitt), "An Apology for Idlers" (R. L. Stevenson), "A Defence of Nonsense" (G. K. Chesterton), or "The Pleasures of Ignorance" (Robert Lynd). This sort of title is puzzling at first sight, and its startling effect induces us to start reading. The first lines of such an essay usually restate the paradox at more length, and you wonder what the author is actually driving at. Then, as you go along, what seemed to be nonsensical at first develops into a thesis full of common sense, a series of reflexions which strike us as being deeply true.

In "A Defence of Penny Dreadfuls", for example, Chesterton manages to prove that 'cheap' books for youngsters should not be despised as utterly vulgar and harmful. For even if they have no claim to be good literature, they are simply human inasmuch as they are concerned with the kind of adventures that have always kindled juvenile imagination. As to their being immoral, this argument does not stand proof if you consider that such books stick closer to traditional moral principles and are altogether more hopeful and optimistic than many works of modern literature.

> It is the modern literature of the educated, not of the uneducated, which is avowedly and aggressively criminal. Books recommending profligacy and pessimism, at which the high-souled errand-boy would shudder, lie upon all our drawing-room tables . . . These things are our luxuries. And with a hypocrisy so ludicrous as to be almost unparalleled in history, we rate the gutter-boys for their immorality at the very time that we are discussing (with equivocal German

professors) whether morality is valid at all. At the very instant that we curse the Penny Dreadful for encouraging theft upon property, we canvass the proposition that all property is theft... At the very instant that we charge it with encouraging the young to destroy life, we are placidly discussing whether life is worth preserving. But it is we who are the morbid exceptions; it is we who are the criminal class. This should be our great comfort. The vast mass of humanity, with their vast mass of idle books and idle words, have never doubted and will never doubt that courage is splendid, that fidelity is noble, that distressed ladies should be rescued, and vanquished enemies spared. There are a large number of cultivated persons who doubt these maxims of daily life, just as there are a large number of persons who believe they are the Prince of Wales...[21]

3.3.3.4 Poetry

Essayists are not only critics and humorists, they are poets as well when they give short descriptions of landscapes or make use of images to achieve concreteness and vividness. They may speak in favour of familiar style (e.g. Hazlitt's "On Familiar Style"), or warn us against the effects of too much reading and learning (e.g. Hazlitt's "On the Ignorance of the Learned"), but their own style would not reach such a high standard if they did not have a good knowledge of literature, a thorough command of literary devices, and, above all, a poet's imagination.
In "A Few Thoughts on Sleep", for instance, Leigh Hunt uses the following simile to describe the process of falling asleep: "...the spirit of consciousness disengages itself more and more, with slow and hushing degrees like a mother detaching her hand from that of her sleeping child."[22]
There is poetry, too, in the way Robert Lynd compares a bad memory to a hedge, after saying that we often forget the content of the books we have read:

> Little shreds and tags, it is probable, will stick even in the worst memory, just as a succession of sheep cannot leap through a gap in a hedge without leaving a few wisps of wool on the thorns. But the sheep themselves escape, and the great authors leap in the same way out of an idle memory and leave little enough behind.
> ("The Pleasures of Ignorance")[23]

3.3.3.5 A typically English form of literature

Such stylistic devices, as well as the truth of the statements and the personal approach, account for the sure appeal of the light-hearted essay. The author, although he is not a story-teller, succeeds in interesting **us** by writing about what interests **him.** It has been said that it is the essayist's personality that gives infinite variety to the essay — which is true to some extent. And yet there emerges from so many essays a certain **mood** which is common to most essayists. They have a similar attitude towards life, characterized by open-mindedness and a sense of the vanity of human ambition. Now this attitude is closely connected with the sense of humour which pervades their writings even when they reflect upon serious problems and come to conclusions that are not altogether optimistic. In fact it is humour, this characteristic of a nation which "has always regarded reason as a bit of a joke",[24] which makes this kind of essay typically English and gives it its lasting charm.

The light-hearted, or humorous essay

This	essay passage	is not meant seriously.

The tone is	familiar. humorous. playful.

The author	is	in a joking mood. toying with his main idea. capering about his central idea.
	obviously exaggerates when he says...	

His chief purpose is obviously to	entertain us. amuse us.

The subject of this essay	is seems to be	fanciful. paradoxical. a mere trifle.

And yet there is a great deal of	truth common sense	in what he says.

The author	is open-minded. is broad-minded. holds sensible views on the question of...

He seems to be merely joking, but he has something serious in mind.

In fact, he takes the point of view of	a moralist. a philosopher.

There is obviously a moral purpose underlying this essay.

p. t. o.

<table>
<tr><td colspan="4">The light-hearted, or humorous essay (continued)</td></tr>
<tr><td>The author</td><td>overtly
openly
implicitly</td><td>criticizes</td><td>snobberies.
prejudices.
his contemporaries.</td></tr>
<tr><td>His</td><td>irony
satire
sarcasm</td><td colspan="2">is directed against . . .</td></tr>
<tr><td>He feels
He shows</td><td colspan="3">(no) sympathy for . . .
indignation at . . .</td></tr>
<tr><td>There is poetry in</td><td colspan="3">his description of . . .
his imagery.</td></tr>
<tr><td>He achieves</td><td>concreteness
vividness</td><td colspan="2">by making use of images.</td></tr>
</table>

3.3.3.6 An example of the light-hearted essay: "On Doing Nothing"

The subject of Priestley's essay is not new. In "The Superannuated Man", Lamb writes:

> A man can never have too much time to himself nor too little to do. Had I a little son, I would christen him NOTHING-TO-DO; he should do nothing. Man, I verily believe, is out of his element as long as he is operative. I am altogether for the life contemplative.[25]

R. L. Stevenson has written "An Apology for Idlers" mainly to complain that very industrious people often lose their good temper and are a nuisance to others. "There is no duty we so much underrate as the duty of being happy", he says, adding

> There is a sort of dead-alive, hackneyed people about, who are scarcely conscious of living except in the exercise of some conventional occupation. . . . It is no good speaking to such folk: they cannot be idle, their nature is not generous enough.[26]

Priestley's "On Doing Nothing", written almost one century later, is much in the same vein. His essay, which has been shortened here, may be regarded as typical of the light-hearted manner.

On Doing Nothing

I had been staying with a friend of mine, an artist and delightfully lazy fellow, at his cottage among the Yorkshire fells, some ten miles from a railway-station; and as we had been fortunate enough to encounter a sudden spell of really warm weather, day after day we had set off in the morning, taken the nearest moorland track, climbed leisurely until we had reached somewhere about two thousand feet above sea-level, and had then spent long golden afternoons lying flat on our backs — doing nothing. There is no better lounging place than a moor. It is a kind of clean bare antechamber to heaven. Beneath its apparent monotony that offers no immediate excitements, no absorbing drama of sound and colour, there is a subtle variety in its slowly changing patterns of cloud and shadow and tinted horizons, sufficient to keep up a flicker of interest in the mind all day. With its velvety patches, no bigger than a drawing-room carpet, of fine moorland grass, its surfaces invite repose. Its remoteness, its permanence, its old and sprawling indifference to man and his concerns, rest and cleanse the mind. All the noises of the world are drowned in the one monotonous cry of the curlew.

Day after day, then, found us full-stretched upon the moor, looking up at the sky or gazing dreamily at the distant horizon. It is not strictly true, of course, to say that we did absolutely nothing, for we smoked great quantities of tobacco, ate sandwiches and little sticks of chocolate, drank from the cold bubbling streams that spring up from nowhere, gurgle for a few score yards, then disappear again. Occasionally we exchanged a remark or two. But we probably came as close to doing nothing as it is possible for two members of our race. We made nothing, not even any plans; not a single idea entered our heads; we did not even indulge in that genial boasting which is the usual pastime of two friendly males in conference. Somewhere, far away, our friends and relatives were humming and bustling, shaping and contriving, planning, disputing, getting, spending; but we were as gods, solidly occupied in doing nothing, our minds immaculate vacancies. But when our little hour of idling was done and we descended for the last time, as flushed as sunsets, we came down into this world of men and newspaper owners only to discover that we had just been denounced by Mr Gordon Selfridge . . .

. . . All the evil in this world is brought about by persons who are always up and doing, but do not know when they ought to be up nor what they ought to be doing. The devil, I take it, is still the busiest creature in the universe, and I can quite imagine him denouncing laziness and becoming angry at the smallest waste of time. In his kingdom, I will wager, nobody is allowed to do nothing, not even for a single afternoon. The world, we all freely admit, is in a muddle, but I for one do not think that it is laziness that has brought it to such a pass. It is not the active virtues that it lacks but the passive ones; it is capable of anything but kindness and a little steady thought. There is still plenty of energy in the world (there never were more fussy people about), but most of it is simply misdirected. If, for example, in July 1914, when there was some capital idling weather, everybody, emperors, kings, archdukes, statesmen, generals, journalists, had been suddenly smitten with an intense desire to do nothing, just to hang about in the sunshine and consume tobacco, then we should all have been much better off than we are now. But no, the doctrine of the strenuous life still went unchallenged; there must be no time wasted; something must be done. And, as we know, something was done . . . Even at the present time, if half the politicians in Europe would relinquish the notion that laziness is a crime and go away and do nothing for a little space, we should certainly gain by it. Other examples come crowding into the mind. Thus, every now and then, certain religious sects hold conferences; but though there are evils abroad that are mountains high, though the fate of civilization is still doubtful, the members who attend these conferences spend their time condemning the length of ladies' skirts and the noisiness of dance bands. They would all be better employed lying flat on their backs somewhere, staring at the sky and recovering their mental health.

The idea that laziness is the primary sin and the accompanying doctrine of the strenuous life are very prevalent in America, and we cannot escape the fact that America is an amazingly prosperous country. But neither can we escape the fact that society there is in such a condition that all its best contemporary writers are satirists. Curiously enough, most of the great American writers have not hesitated to praise idleness, and it has often been their faculty for doing nothing and praising themselves for doing it, that has been their salvation. Thus, Thoreau, without his capacity for idling and doing nothing more than appreciate the Milky Way, would be a cold prig; and Whitman, robbed of his habit of lounging round with his hands in his pockets and his innocent delight in this pastime, would be merely a large-sized ass. Any fool can be fussy and rid himself of energy all over the place, but a man has to have something in him before he can settle down to do nothing. He must have reserves to draw upon, must be able to plunge into strange slow rivers of dream and reverie, must be at heart a poet. Wordsworth, to whom we go when most other poets fail us, knew the value of doing nothing; nobody, you may say, could do it better; and you may discover in his work the best account of the matter. He lived long enough to retract most of his youthful opinions, but I do not think that he ever went back on his youthful notion that a man could have no healthier and more spiritualizing employment than idling about and staring at Nature. (It is true that he is very angry in one poem with some gipsies because they had apparently done absolutely nothing from the time he passed them at the beginning of his walk to the time when he passed them again, twelve hours later. But this is racial prejudice, tinged, I suspect, with envy, for though he had not done much, they had done even less.) If he were alive to-day I have no doubt he would preach his doctrine more fervently and more frequently than ever, and he would probably attack Mr Selfridge and defend us (beginning 'Last week they loitered on a lone wide moor') in a series of capital sonnets, which would not, by the way, attract the slightest attention. He would tell us that the whole world would be better off if it spent every possible moment it could, these next ten years, lying flat on its back on a moor, doing nothing. And he would be right.[27]

For study

1) Give an abstract of the essay.
2) Comment on the narrative and descriptive elements in the first two paragraphs (style, purpose).
3) What groups of people does the author criticize?
4) What is the tone of the whole essay?
   Find an example of irony and one of paradox.
   Give special attention to the last sentences ("If he were alive to-day...").

4. SHORT NARRATIVE FORMS

4.1 Transitional literary forms

4.1.1 Anecdote

An anecdote (Gk 'sth unpublished') is 'a usually short narrative of an interesting, amusing, or curious incident often biographical and generally characterized by human interest'. *(Webster's Third New International Dictionary of the English Language Unabridged.)* To put it more simply, it is a moment taken from a biography and told in the form of a short, yet complete story. It is a journalistic or literary form in its own right and can be told for its own sake. But it may also be an integral part of longer texts like speeches, newspaper articles, essays, short stories, novels or even dramas. Its main function is then to illustrate a certain idea or a certain trait of the character of a personality.

The first problem an author of an anecdote has to solve is to select such a moment from a biography that can be told in an arresting way. It may be anything like birth, marriage or death; like heredity, environment or education; like duty or escapades; and like failure or triumph. In any case, his skill is to select such a telling moment that throws a light on the character or the life-style of a personality.

His second task is to arrange the material in such a way that it resembles the essay on the one hand and the short story on the other. The anecdote might, in a way, be called a dramatized essay.

In the technique of writing an anecdote, the choice of the point of view — the position from which an incident is seen — is crucial. Moreover, the timing must be good: the teller must come to the point with the right number of words used in the right sequence. Any digression will spoil his effective timing. What is even more important is that the whole of, or part of, the anecdote is given the form of a scene. The reader or listener is then no longer informed about an incident, but **shown a life-like situation.** He has the illusion of participating in the experience himself: of hearing the words spoken in a lively dialogue and seeing the person acting in his characteristic manner.

Particularly important are a lively beginning, the prominence of one controlling idea, and the use of a language that is full of implications to allow for a generalizing interpretation. But most important is how an anecdote comes to the point, i.e. the final objective towards which the whole of the story is directed. The point is usually worded in a surprising, amusing, witty or even paradoxical manner containing the gist of the anecdote and suggesting some generalization.

4.1.2 Sketch

Very similar to the anecdote is the sketch (cf. G 'Skizze'). In fact, a biographical sketch is an anecdote. But whereas an anecdote is normally taken from a biography and based on some personal element, a sketch may be based on any subject. A sketch is originally **'a rough drawing representing the chief features of an object or scene'.** *(Webster's Dictionary.)* Later it also came to mean any 'short literary composition somewhat resembling the short story and the essay but less formal than these and usually intentionally slight in treatment, discursive in style, and familiar in tone'. *Webster's Dictionary.)*
For practical reasons, we may say that a sketch is very similar to an anecdote, except for the following differences:

1) it can be taken from a broader background (i. e. it need not be biographical);
2) it need not be exclusively streamlined towards the point at the end;
3) it is often slighter in treament, more discursive in style, and more familiar in tone.

Both the sketch and the anecdote are some sort of crystallizing point reflecting the most outstanding characteristics of a historical epoch, a place, an institution, or a personality. They suggest many more aspects of the whole truth beyond the mere facts. From the point of view of literature, both the sketch and the anecdote are transitional forms in that they fuse fact and fiction.

Anecdote, sketch

<table>
<tr><td colspan="2">In an anecdote
In a sketch</td><td colspan="2">a telling moment
is selected</td><td>from a biography.
from material that is historically or factually true.</td></tr>
<tr><td colspan="2">In the arrangement of the material</td><td colspan="3">anecdote and sketch resemble a dramatized essay.</td></tr>
<tr><td>A peculiar</td><td>focus
point of view</td><td>is chosen to</td><td>get
retain
arrest</td><td>the reader's attention.</td></tr>
<tr><td colspan="2">An anecdote
A sketch</td><td>is</td><td colspan="2">told.
narrated.</td></tr>
<tr><td colspan="2">An anecdote</td><td colspan="2">deals with
is concerned with</td><td>human behaviour.
individual behaviour in society.
ethical problems.</td></tr>
</table>

p. t. o.

<table>
<tr><th colspan="4">Anecdote, sketch (continued)</th></tr>
<tr><td colspan="2">The author uses language that is full of</td><td colspan="2">connotations.
associations.
implications.</td></tr>
<tr><td rowspan="3">The reader</td><td colspan="3">is not only informed but also entertained.
is shown a common (an exceptional) situation.
has the illusion of witnessing the scene himself.</td></tr>
<tr><td rowspan="2">is shown how</td><td colspan="2">somebody behaved foolishly/brilliantly in a certain situation.</td></tr>
<tr><td>a famous person</td><td>dealt with some crisis.
coped with a difficult situation.
solved a problem.</td></tr>
<tr><td>In the anecdote,</td><td colspan="3">the teller's timing must be effective, i.e. he comes to the point in the right number of words used in the right sequence.</td></tr>
<tr><td colspan="4">The beginning is lively.</td></tr>
<tr><td>The point is</td><td colspan="3">surprising.
amusing.
witty.
paradoxical.
of general human interest.</td></tr>
<tr><td rowspan="2">The narrator</td><td colspan="3">fuses fact and fiction.</td></tr>
<tr><td>creates</td><td colspan="2">a new situation.
a new reality.
a partly fictitious reality.
an illusion of reality.</td></tr>
<tr><td colspan="2">Thus, the transitions from</td><td>fact to fiction
non-art to art</td><td>are fluid.</td></tr>
</table>

The following text may serve as an example of both the anecdote and the sketch:

The Oxford Method

The Oxford School of Litterae humaniores — or "Greats," as it is called — seems to my mature judgment the best scheme of education that I have ever heard of. It is based upon an accurate knowledge of Greek and Latin texts, especially the texts of Plato and Aristotle and Thucydides and Tacitus, and the subjects studied in it are the eternal problems of thought, of conduct, and of social organization. These are discussed, not by means of contemporary catchwords, but by translating them back into another world and another language. Nor could anything be more profitable from the pupil's point of view than the way in which this scheme of education was carried on. The student would prepare a paper on some special subject, and go with it, generally alone, and read it to his tutor, who would then discuss it and criticize it at length; or a group of two or three would meet in the tutor's room for a kind of Socratic discussion of some special point. These discussions were carried on much in the spirit of the Socratic dialogues; and the Socratic irony and assumed ignorance of the instructors, their deferential questions, as if the pupil were the teacher and they the learners, was a method which I found it hard at first to understand.

I remember, for instance, in reading a paper to Nettleship, I mentioned the distinction between form and matter. "Excuse me for interrupting you," Nettleship said, "but this distinction you make, though it is no doubt most important, is one that I find a little difficult to grasp. If it is not troubling you too much, it would be a real kindness if you would try to explain it to me."

"Oh, it's quite simple," I answered patronizingly. "There's the idea, say, in a poem, and there's the way in which it is expressed."

Nettleship still seemed puzzled. "Could you give me an instance?" he pleaded.

"Oh, nothing easier," I answered. "Take the lines, for instance, when Lovelace says,

I could not love thee, Dear, so much,
Loved I not Honour more.

Now he might have said, 'I couldn't be nearly so fond of you, my dear, if I didn't care still more for my reputation.' The form, you see, is very different in both these sentences, but the subject of them — what they mean — is exactly the same."

Nettleship seemed greatly discouraged. "I'm afraid," he said, "I can't see that the meaning of the two sentences is the same. I'm afraid I'm very stupid; but to me they seem to say quite different things."

He was, I thought, curiously stupid; but in my patient attempt to make my meaning clearer to him a dim suspicion began to waken in me that perhaps it was not Nettleship but myself who was playing the part of the fool in this dialogue.

(from Logan Pearsall Smith, *Unforgotten Years)*

For study

1) What does this sketch tell us about the teaching methods practised in the Oxford School of Litterae humaniores? ('School' here is used in a special

Oxford sense — other universities would say 'faculty' or 'department'.) What does the author think of them?

2) How does the author manage to convey an idea of the Socratic method? What does this method consist in?

4.1.3 Utilitarian literature and transitional literary forms

As we have shown in ch.2 **Fact and Fiction in Newspaper Literature,** facts may be passed on as information, they may be analysed, or they may be featured with the focus on human interest. These forms of newspaper articles are obviously part of **'utilitarian'** literature; this is to say that they are useful in the practical affairs of men in that they inform about, or perhaps explain, occurrences of everyday factual experience in much the same way as texts published in scientific journals or books about car maintainance do. The sort of 'truth' and 'reality' which is passed on in the various forms of what we have called 'utilitarian' literature is that of objective, empirically verifiable, experience. The most common form of communication within this field is impersonal, 'objective' information, except for the human-interest story, which is also intended to inform but at the same time tries to make some topical reportage more attractive through the introduction of fictional elements.

In other words, if the author of an article which contains some information that he regards as really useful and important to the reader wants to include also some sort of advice or to provide some general guidance, he will of course try to persuade and urge the reader to accept it. His tone then will be more personally involved and he will usually employ some of the shaping devices of fiction to make his message more appealing and convincing. What is important here is the realization that the fictional devices he uses are exclusively intended for the purpose of strengthening his argumentation and are not employed for any specifically literary aims. So, even though he does occasionally make use of comparisons, symbols, figures of speech, and includes some passages in scenic presentation — all elements which are characteristic of fiction — his overall approach is still that of an author intending to inform, persuade and comment.

In the reportage of New Journalism, which is called 'faction', some shaping devices of fiction are used in such a way that the distinguishing characteristics of what is actual and of what is fictional tend to become blurred — as was drastically demonstrated in the scandal provoked by the story of little Jimmy, an 'invented' eight-year-old heroin addict. (cf. the story on pp. 47 f.). After reading this story and *The Washington Post's* apology for the faked 'information' it used, one can readily understand why New Journalism has often been accused of being only 'para-journalism'.

In the **anecdote** and the **sketch,** the incident from actual life which is selected for presentation may be shown in such a lively manner and with so much entertaining and enlightening comment that it tends to acquire some sort of 'new' reality of its own.

The anecdote and the sketch are **transitional forms** in that they fuse fact and fiction. They make comments on the human situation at large, and in doing so often employ specific devices of creative literature, such as action, scene, character, dialogue, and 'poetic', i. e. figurative, language. The precise relationship between the factual and the fictional elements will of course be different in each individual case, but we can say that if for instance a particular character is portrayed in a form representative of a whole class, generation, or era, actual reality is fused with symbolic reality and the text thus becomes literature proper. In other words, whenever the fictional element gets the upper hand, as it were, and then gives the text a distinctly aesthetic quality, we would no longer speak of utilitarian literature but of imaginative literature. Borderline cases are of course always possible.

Utilitarian literature and transitional forms

<table>
<tr><td rowspan="2">In utilitarian literature
In non-literary texts</td><td rowspan="2">the author's main concern is to</td><td>pass on
transmit
present</td><td>impersonal
empirical
objective</td><td>information.</td></tr>
<tr><td colspan="3">relate incidents that actually happened.
explain complex phenomena.</td></tr>
<tr><td rowspan="2">The so-called transitional forms (anecdote, sketch)</td><td colspan="3">present information with the help of</td><td>fictional techniques.
literary devices.</td></tr>
<tr><td colspan="4">employ some devices of creative literature.
fuse fact and fiction.
may fuse actual reality with symbolic reality.
may acquire a distinctly fictional flavour.
may be infused with a specifically aesthetic quality.
may become literature proper.</td></tr>
</table>

4.2 Creative literature proper

4.2.1 Fable

The fable is usually a tale about animals who are personified and behave as though they were human beings. But the device of personification may be extended to anything inanimate, such as flowers, trees, stones, streams, and winds. Thus it is obvious that the fable is invented, in other words, fictional; it is intended to illustrate some useful truth or some moral lesson that may be learnt. The moral — a rule of behaviour — in which La Fontaine (1621—1695) saw the soul of the fable, may be embodied in the fable itself or explicitly added to its end in some moral tag. Many of these have become so popular that they are now proverbs since they express social attitudes or advice on social or moral conduct in a clear and memorable form. It is particularly this feature of a moral that separates the fable from the ordinary folk-tale — with which it has otherwise much in common. Another characteristic of the fable is that the narrative element is prominent as can well be understood if we consider its etymology (L 'fabula' meaning 'conversation', 'narrative', 'tale'). But what makes the fable a product of creative literature proper is its allegorical nature. In Greek 'allegoria' means 'other-speaking'; in an allegory, then, one thing is substituted for another. So the fable is like a simile or comparison extended into a complete story — a story that is 'fabulous' with the characteristic connotations of 'legendary', 'mythical', 'exaggerated', 'incredible'. But in spite of the incredible tale on the surface, some timeless truth may be told on the allegorical or symbolic level, a universal truth that could never be conveyed by mere information.

The origins of the fable are hidden in the mists of time. Fables appear independently in ancient Indian and Mediterranean cultures. Aesop, a Greek slave (600 B.C.), is generally considered to be the father of the genre because 200 fables were commonly attributed to him, though they had most probably been 'folk-fables'. After a long tradition throughout the Middle Ages, they became an integral part of European literature. Chaucer's delightful version of 'The Fox and the Cock' is just one example in English literature. In 17th-century France the form reached its climax in the works of La Fontaine. Starting with the Aesopian pattern, he later set out to satirize the court, the church, the rising bourgeoisie — indeed the whole scene of human existence at that time. As a skeptic, who was fully aware of human frailty, his great theme was the folly of human vanity.

In modern times, fables have often been trivialized in children's books. But this old genre has also been fully adapted to modern needs. In *Fables for Our Time,* James Thurber revitalized this ancient literary genre. He felt that fables unmask 'the beast in me' — he actually wrote a book with this title. In other words, fables reveal the faults of civilized man. And in *Animal Farm,* George Orwell used the animal story to launch a satirical attack on Stalinist Communism in particular and totalitarianism in general.

Both *Animal Farm* and Thurber's *Fables for Our Time* are examples of creative literature or fiction at its best because of their allegorical structure. They can be understood — and enjoyed — at various levels. The story on the surface can be read for fun, but a careful and systematic literary interpretation is necessary to grasp the deeper — i. e. allegorical or symbolic — meaning hidden behind the story.

The fable

In a fable, animals	are personified. behave as though they were human beings.

p. t. o.

The fable (continued)	
In this fable, the animals	stand for... represent... are substituted for...
Its purpose is	to satirize... to criticize...
Here, the author actually	refers to... alludes to...
The moral	is (not) obvious. is explicitly added to the end in an extra line. is implicit / not directly expressed. (it is for the reader to work it out).
This fable can be interpreted in different ways.	
It is full of	humour. irony.
The author is obviously being ironical when he says...	

The following example of modern fable is taken from *Fables for Our Time* by James Thurber, who was above all a humorist.

The Very Proper Gander

Not so very long ago there was a fine gander. He was strong and smooth and beautiful and he spent most of his time singing to his wife and children. One day somebody who saw him strutting up and down in his yard and singing remarked, 'There is a very proper gander.' An old hen overheard this and told her husband about it that night in the roost. 'They said something about propaganda,' she said. 'I have always suspected that,' said the rooster, and he went around the barnyard next day telling everybody that the very fine gander was a dangerous bird, more than likely a hawk in gander's clothing. A small brown hen remembered a time when at a great distance she had seen the gander talking with some hawks in the forest. 'They were up to no good,' she said. A duck remembered that the gander had once told him he did not believe in anything. 'He said to hell with the flag, too,' said the duck. A guinea hen recalled that she had once seen somebody who looked very much like the gander throw something that looked a great deal like a bomb. Finally everybody snatched up sticks and stones and descended on the gander's house. He was strutting in his front yard, singing to his children and his wife. 'There he is!' everybody cried.

'Hawk-lover! Unbeliever! Flag-hater! Bomb-thrower!' So they set upon him and drove him out of the country.

Moral: Anybody who you or your wife thinks is going to overthrow the government by violence must be driven out of the country.

For study

1) Sum up the fable.
2) Is the moral to be taken seriously?
3) What is funny about the title? Show Thurber's humour in his depiction of how rumours spread.

4.2.2 Parable

A parable (Gk 'parabele' = 'juxtaposition', 'setting side by side', 'comparison') is a short fictitious narrative told to teach a moral or religious lesson. The parable is based on an allegory, i.e. a comparison or simile extended into a complete story. Like the fable, the parable tells a simple story to teach a moral lesson, but whereas the fable mainly uses animals as characters, the typical parable uses human beings as agents. And whereas the storytelling itself is prominent in the fable, the parable shows more interest in the analogy (comparison) it draws between a particular instance of human conduct and human behaviour at large. The simple form of narrative used in parables renders them particularly useful for teaching spiritual values.

In modern times, the purpose of the parable form of presentation is often the analysis and criticism of a particular social system. In former times, the purpose of the parable was rather to remind the listener that such a system exists, that he should not forget it, but act according to it. In any case, the rhetorical appeal of a parable is directed primarily towards an elite that — as an inner circle — has access to a final core of truth. The simple story on the surface is meant to give a clue to those 'hard of hearing'. This structure of a growing concentration of truth towards the core of the parable can clearly be seen in Jesus Christ's parables. He seems to have chosen his disciples as his initiates who 'had ears to hear' the true, i.e. the allegorical or symbolic, meaning of his parables. And he ordered them to pass on their insights and wisdom to the whole world (Matt. 28:20)

The following parable, taken from the *Bible,* is one of the best, in its archaic, classical form:

The Parable of the Sower (Matthew 13:1-17)

[1]The same day went Jesus out of the house, and sat by the sea side. [2]And great
multitudes were gathered together unto him, so that he went into a ship, and sat;
and the whole multitude stood on the shore. [3]And he spoke many things unto them
in parables, saying.

"Behold, a sower went forth to sow. [4]And when he sowed, some seeds fell by the
way side, and the fowls came and devoured them up. [5]Some fell upon stony
places, where they had not much earth: and forthwith they sprung up, because
they had no deepness of earth: [6]and when the sun was up, they were scorched;
and because they had no root, they withered away. [7]And some fell among thorns;
and the thorns sprung up, and choked them. [8]But other fell into good ground, and
brought forth fruit, some a hundredfold, some sixtyfold, some thirtyfold. [9]Who
hath ears to hear, let him hear."
[10]And the disciples came, and said unto him, "Why speakest thou unto them in
parables?"
[11]He answered and said unto them, "Because it is given unto you to know the
mysteries of the kingdom of heaven, but to them it is not given. [12]For whosoever
hath, to him shall be given, and he shall have more abundance: but whosoever
hath not, from him shall be taken away even that he hath. [13]Therefore speak I to
them in parables: because they seeing see not; and hearing they hear not,
neither do they understand. [14]And in them is fulfilled the prophecy of Esaias,
which saith, 'By hearing ye shall hear, and shall not understand; and seeing ye
shall see, and shall not perceive': [15]for this people' s heart is waxed gross, and
their ears are dull of hearing, and their eyes they have closed; lest at any time
they should see with their eyes, and hear with their ears, and should understand
with their heart, and should be converted, and I should heal them. [16]But blessed
are your eyes, for they see: and your ears, for they hear. [17]For verily I say unto
you that many prophets and righteous men have desired to see those things
which ye see, and have not seen them; and to hear those things which ye hear,
and have not heard them.

Now Luke (8:11-15) gives an explanation of this parable by working out the analogy between the sower's seed and God's word:

[11]Now the parable is this: The seed is the word of God. [12]Those by the wayside
are they that hear; then cometh the devil, and taketh away the word out of their
hearts, lest they should believe and be saved. [13]They on the rock are they, which,
when they hear, receive the word with joy; and these have no root, which for a
while believe, and in time of temptation fall away. [14]And that which fell among
thorns are they, which, when they have heard, go forth, and are choked with
cares and riches and pleasures of this life, and bring no fruit to perfection. [15]But
that on the good ground are they, which in an honest and good heart, having
heard the word, keep it, and bring forth fruit with patience.

Throughout the Middle Ages, the parable was used as an effective preaching device. Moreover, pious tales were collected in handbooks such as the *Gesta Romanorum.* These exemplary tales used a simple but lively style, presenting stories of prophets, saints, martyrs, but also of chivalrous knights and ladies. All of them share a strong didactic purpose, namely to show the uninitiated the proper path in earthly, and to heavenly, life. A new, more paradoxical, ambivalent use of the parable led to strange new literary forms. Franz Kafka's parables, for instance, full of doubt and anxiety, concentrate on the loneliness and isolation of modern man. One of his most well-known is 'The Metamorphosis'. His interpretation of modern human existence is one of the most enigmatic in modern literature — allowing some glimpses into the mysteries to those who 'have eyes to see', or, in other words, can interpret the allegorical or symbolic meaning in literature.

4.2.3 The fictional world

There is a widespread intellectual and moral distrust of fiction, because it is felt that it misleads people into believing in things that are not true. The Puritans warned their congregations against reading anything but the Bible, since they regarded imaginative literature as 'fiction', i.e. as something invented and therefore as 'lies'. To be sure, in a work of literary art, the whole atmosphere or a character may become so 'real' that some naive people might even confound the fictional atmosphere with actual life, and experience a character as if he were a living human being and then imitate his moral conduct and behaviour — as may be seen in the fact that many admirers of Sherlock Holmes keep writing letters to him, or that Ian Fleming's James Bond books led to a small revolution in martini-ordering. The kind of 'reality' created by fiction must however not be mixed up with the experience of 'reality' in ordinary life. Reality in fiction must not be confused with actual empirical reality, which is what science, history, or biography deal with. The sort of reality found in literature is obviously of a different nature. It can perhaps best be characterized as 'poetic' or 'fictional' reality. In other words, in a work of literary art, a new form of reality is created with the help of 'poetic language.'

But what does this new sort of aesthetic reality consist of, and how is it created? Evidently, on a certain level, literature 'imitates', 'depicts', 'embodies' people, objects, societies, ideas taken from actual life. It is thus based on imitation (Gk 'mimesis'). This is to say that there is a strong element of factual — i.e. actual, empirical, historical — truth in fiction. To a certain extent, the author records observed facts, but he incorporates these actual or historical facts into his 'creative' or 'imaginative' work of art.

Now, how does he manage to create his fictional world? The essential structural components that help him to build this world are the shaping devices of fiction — character, action, plot, setting, point of view, tone and atmosphere, and world-view and figurative use of language. Marianne Moore rightly speaks of literature as presenting for inspection "imaginary gardens with real toads in them"[1]. Every great novelist creates such a fictional world of his own, which to some extent overlaps the empirical world but is distinct in that it is unique. People therefore refer to something quite definite and unique when they speak of 'the world' of Dickens, or Defoe, or Joyce. The reality of fiction — or rather the illusion of reality it creates — consists in a combination of actual reality and the product of the imaginative process of the author. This can clearly be seen if we compare the world of Dickens with that of Thackeray, which are generally speaking both based on the same actual reality of the nineteenth century. But their fiction is different because their imaginative processes ran in different directions and thus created different fictional worlds — or illusions of reality — from the same material, just as two painters would have produced different paintings. We can say that since the basis of actual reality is the same for both writers, they must have used the shaping devices of fiction in a different way. This difference mainly comes in on a level where the artist interprets reality with the particular scope of his world-view to which he gives expression in his work.

This world-view is different with every author, and it changes with literary-philosophical movements, conventions, and styles. In the course of time, the conceptions of what literature is meant to accomplish with its fusion of reality and illusion have changed again and again. Aristotle thought that the literary artist should not concentrate on presenting the particular, but the universal. For the Neo-Classicists in the seventeenth and eighteenth centuries, art, including literary art, was also something that was expected to present the typical and universal in order to ennoble or idealize life. In the styles of realism and naturalism, on the other hand, the focus was more on actual reality, whereas in expressionism and surrealism the artist's power of interpreting reality in terms of symbols was again felt to be more important than the presentation of particular details. We can say that creative art seems to be infinitely adaptable to different cultural circumstances and the philosophical climate of opinion.

> Meaning, in a work of narrative art, is a function of the relationship between two worlds: the fictional world created by the author and the 'real' world, the apprehendable universe. When we say we 'understand' a narrative we mean that we have found a satisfactory relationship or set of relationships between these two worlds.[2]

In other words, to understand a narrative is to see how the actual world that is imitated is combined with the symbolic world that is the product of the author's creative imagination. This is of course to a large extent a question of credibility. We can say that a writer can do anything with his art so long as he presents and interprets the world of feeling, thought, and sense. The reader must be able to recognize the world that is shown to him as his own, or, if not as his own, at least as a world which might possibly exist or can be dreamed of as existing. Reading thus becomes a process of simultaneous belief and disbelief in the 'truth' or 'reality' of what is presented and interpreted in a work of literary art. And that sort of 'truth' or 'reality' is primarily a product of the imagination — an artistically credible fusion of factual and symbolic reality that does not exist in an actual way in an actual place in actual time.

The reader interprets narrative literature appropriately if he manages to penetrate through the surface action to the symbolic action, i. e. the symbolic truth or reality of a story. And it seems as if the reader's imagination is especially stirred by the comparison he makes between actual reality and symbolic reality on a deeper level of the story; this deeper level is usually called the allegorical level. In this sense, allegory is the level which arouses in the reader or listener a response to imaginative, symbolic, or universal levels of meaning.

Creative literature proper — fiction

<table>
<tr><td>The creative author is not limited by</td><td>facts.
actual experience.
history.</td></tr>
</table>

<table>
<tr><td>He is free to create</td><td>situations
actions
characters</td><td>for his own purpose as long as they are credible.</td></tr>
</table>

<table>
<tr><td rowspan="4">Allegorical
Symbolic
Artistic
Universal</td><td rowspan="4">truth
reality</td><td rowspan="2">emerges from</td><td>the fictitious</td><td>setting.
characters.
actions.</td></tr>
<tr><td>the metaphorical
the figurative</td><td>use of language.</td></tr>
<tr><td colspan="3">is established by means of a network of symbols.</td></tr>
<tr><td>is a product of</td><td colspan="2">the imagination.
fiction.
creative art.</td></tr>
</table>

<table>
<tr><td rowspan="2">He creates</td><td>a setting that is</td><td rowspan="2">life-like.
probable.
credible.
allegorical.
representative of human life at large.
universal.
symbolic.</td></tr>
<tr><td>characters,
actions that are</td></tr>
</table>

<table>
<tr><td>Fiction</td><td>stimulates the intellect.
arouses the emotions.
challenges the conscience.</td></tr>
</table>

<table>
<tr><td>The reader's imagination is stirred by the</td><td>comparison
analogy</td><td>between</td><td>actual reality and fictitious reality.</td></tr>
</table>

5. THE SHORT STORY

5.1 Origins and definition

The telling of tales is probably as old as literature itself, as may be seen in the Egyptian *Tales of the Magicians* (4000 B.C.). Homer's *Odyssey* is virtually a collection of short stories around a loose plot; one of the classical masterpieces it contains is the story of "Ulysses and the Cyclops" — superb in theme, setting, characterization, plot and style. *The Bible,* too, embodies various forms of short fiction, from *The New Testament* parables back to such stories as "Noah and the Great Flood" or "David and Goliath".

In the Middle Ages, too, short fiction flourished. The best known collections of stories from this time are the *Arabian Nights* (1000 A.D.), Boccacio's *Decameron* (1350 A.D.), the *Gesta Romanorum* and Chaucer's *Canterbury Tales* (1400 A.D.). From the 15th to the 18th centuries, the drama and later the novel were predominant as literary genres.

The short story as a literary form in its own right as we know it today is essentially a product of the 19th century. It was in the first half of last century that various writers in a number of countries began to talk about the "short story", which is a fictitious prose narrative longer than an anecdote and shorter than a novel.

5.2 The classical plot story of the 19th century (1820—1900)

Washington Irving, Edgar Allan Poe and **Nathaniel Hawthorne** — generally regarded as the fathers of the (American) short story — at first disagreed about the name to be given to this new literary form, terming it "the tale", "the short prose tale" or "the sketch". Another area of disagreement was the definition of the main purpose and technique of the short story: was it mainly to entertain (W. Irving), to treat serious themes (N. Hawthorne), or to be nothing but a work of art in which artistic unity was an end in itself (E.A. Poe)?

As a consequence of the **rapid spread of newspapers and magazines at that time,** young writers had a great chance of publishing their stories in one single issue of a paper. This led to very lively competition in this field, with positive and negative consequences. It obviously fostered talent, but it also induced some authors to write for a particular readership, and so their products attempted to be 'compact,' 'fast-paced,' and 'forcibly written' — like any other newspaper article, in fact. The practical outcome of all this was what may be called **the classical type of the short story.** It was used by most of the authors of the nineteenth century, with very few individual variations. Its popularity as a major literary form is largely due to the influence of E.A. Poe. He was the first to realize the limited time span of human attention and genuine artistic appreciation and therefore believed that artistic unity could best be achieved in short literary works. It is he who practically invented the most popular form of the short story, namely the **detective story.** In these stories, the revelation of the murder mystery is usually coupled with the revelation of some psychological aberration in the main character. And this basic concept, coupled as it was with a most skilful use of dramatic suspense, was quite readily accepted by a wide readership.

5.2.1 Contemporary comments on the classical plot story

To get a better idea of what those conscious artists who used this new literary form had in mind it is useful to study some of the comments they made on their own works, or the works of their contemporaries.

Washington Irving was the first to realize that he lived in a 'story-telling and a story-reading age.' In a letter written in 1824, he made the following comments on his own short story writing:

> I fancy much of what I value myself upon in writing, escapes the observation of the great mass of my readers, who are intent more upon the story than the way in which it is told. For my part, I consider a story merely as a frame on which to stretch my materials. It is the play of thought, and sentiment, and language; the weaving in of characters, lightly, yet expressively delineated; the familiar and faithful exhibition of scenes in common life; and the half-concealed vein of humor that is often playing through the whole... I have preferred adopting the mode of sketches and short tales rather than long works, because I choose to take a line of writing peculiar to myself, rather than fall into the manner or school of any other writer; and there is a constant activity of thought and a nicety of execution required in writings of the kind, more than the world appears to imagine. It is comparatively easy to swell a story to any size when you have once the scheme and the characters in your mind; ... but in ... shorter writings, every page must have its merit. The author must be continually piquant; woe to him if he makes an awkward sentence or writes a stupid page; the critics are sure to pounce upon it. Yet if he succeed, the very variety and piquancy of his writings — nay, their very brevity, make them frequently recurred to, and when the mere interest of the story is exhausted, he begins to get credit for his touches of pathos or humor; his points of wit or turns of language.'[1]

For study

1) Why does W. Irving consider the story merely as 'a frame'?
2) Name the six elements which, according to Irving, are characteristic of a good short story.

In the following text, **E.A. Poe,** stresses another important aspect of short story writing:

"... in almost all classes of composition, the unity of effect or impression is a point of the greatest importance. It is clear, moreover, that this unity cannot be thoroughly preserved in productions whose perusal cannot be completed at one sitting... The ordinary novel is objectionable, from its length, for reasons already stated in substance. As it cannot be read at one sitting, it deprives itself, of course, of the immense force derivable from *totality.* Worldly interests intervening during the pauses of perusal modify, annul, or counteract, in a greater or less degree, the impressions of the book. But simple cessation in reading would, of itself, be sufficient to destroy the true unity. In the brief tale (i.e. the short story), however, the author is enabled to carry out the fulness of his intention, be it what it may. During the hour of perusal the soul of the reader is at the writer's control. There are no external or extrinsic influences — resulting from weariness or interruption.

A skilful literary artist has constructed a tale (i.e. a short story). If wise, he has not fashioned his thoughts to accommodate his incidents; but having conceived, with deliberate care, a certain *unique or single effect* to be wrought out, he then invents such incidents — he then combines such events as may best aid him in establishing this preconceived effect. If his very initial sentence tend not to the outbringing of this effect, then he has failed in his first step. In the whole composition there should be no word written, of which the tendency, direct or indirect, is not to the one pre-established design.'[2]

For study

1) Why, according to Poe, must a story be **short?**
2) What does he mean by 'incident', and what by 'effect'? Which of the two is — in his opinion — more important for efficient writing?

In an essay (1901), **Henry Seidel Canby** shows that what makes a short story basically different from a novel is in fact the different standpoint of the author:

In a short story... there is a different point of view, and *therefore* a different treatment... While the novel-writer aims at an eminently natural method of transcription, the author of the short story adopts a very artificial one. His endeavor is to give a striking narrative picture of one phase of the situation or the character, as the case may be... We are selecting, far more than in a novel, and this because we are looking only for the chain of related incidents that go to make up one event...; we are looking only for what bears upon our narrow purpose, that the interest may be concentrated and the conception vivified beyond the power of a novel. The process is very artificial but very powerful: it is like turning a telescope upon one nebula in the heavens. Thus it is the standpoint of the author that makes the distinction between a short novel and a long short story. In the one the author digests life histories, or portions of them; in the other he looks only for the episode, which, like the bubble on the stream, is part of and yet distinguished from the main current... He foregoes completeness and gains in force...

The function of the short story is to be interesting, to convey vivid impressions... Such an endeavor has produced its characteristic form, potential for the powerful expression of the daily facts about us.[3]

For study

The author makes his ideas clear by means of two comparisons. Which ones? What does he actually mean?

At the turn of the century, **Brander Matthews,** a university lecturer, gave a synopsis of the theory of 19th century short story writing. Though somewhat generalized, it may help the reader to see the essential traits of the classical short story as it summarizes most of what has been said about the genre so far:

> The difference between a Novel and a Novelet is one of length only; a Novelet is a brief Novel. But the difference between a Novel and a Short-story is a difference of kind. A true Short-story is something other and something more than a mere story which is short. A true Short-story differs from the Novel chiefly in its essential unity of impression. In a far more exact and precise use of the word, a Short-story has unity as a Novel cannot have it. Often, it may be noted by the way, the Short-story fulfils the three false unities of the French classic drama: It shows one action, in one place, on one day. A Short-story deals with a single character, a single event, a single emotion, or the series of emotions called forth by a single situation. Poe's paradox that a poem cannot greatly exceed a hundred lines in length under penalty of ceasing to be one poem and breaking into a string of poems, may serve to suggest the precise difference between the Short-story and the Novel. The Short-story is the single effect, complete and self-contained, while the Novel is of necessity broken into a series of episodes. Thus the Short-story has, what the Novel cannot have, the effect of 'totality,' as Poe called it, the unity of impression....
>
> I have written 'Short-stories' with a capital S and a hyphen because I wished to emphasise the distinction between the Short-story and the story which is merely short. The Short-story is a high and difficult department of fiction.[4]

5.2.2 The main characteristics of the classical plot story (1820—1900)

To be sure, it is literally impossible to list **all** these criteria, or to find all of them in every short story one may care to study; but the following remarks, along with some relevant language material in tables, will be of some help to you when you try to analyse, appreciate and interpret any of the classical short stories of the 19th century. The main characteristics are:

1) a simple, single motive (or theme);
2) a unity of effect or impression, i.e. unique artistic unity;

3) a tightly-knit plot with — an abrupt opening,
— a turning-point,
— a surprise ending.

Individual variations apart, this is the typical scheme underlying practically all of the 19th century short stories.

5.2.2.1 A simple, single motive (as the main idea)

The main idea or theme of a short story is always **simple,** never complex (as in a novel).

> "There is nothing clearer than the difference between the short story motif and the long story motif... Almost in the first germinal impulse the inventive mind foresees the ultimate difference and recognizes the essential *simplicity* or complexity *of the motive.*"[5]

Simplicity of the motif (theme)

<table>
<tr><td>This short story</td><td>is built round
contains</td><td colspan="2">a single theme, namely...
only one or two major scenes/events.</td></tr>
<tr><td rowspan="3">It</td><td>epitomizes</td><td colspan="2">the dangers that threaten man when...
man's dependence on...</td></tr>
<tr><td>illustrates
gives a vivid portrait of
celebrates</td><td colspan="2">the power of human imagination.
man's ingenuity.</td></tr>
<tr><td colspan="3">exposes the darker sides of human nature.</td></tr>
<tr><td colspan="4">It is basically a psychological portrait of...</td></tr>
<tr><td>It presents the</td><td>encounter
clash</td><td colspan="2">of two characters.</td></tr>
<tr><td rowspan="3">The author</td><td rowspan="3">is out to
intends to
tries to
wants to</td><td>reveal X's</td><td>real character.
lack of...
sense of...</td></tr>
<tr><td colspan="2">expose his personal disillusionment.</td></tr>
<tr><td>set forth the hero's search for</td><td>justice.
love.
God.</td></tr>
</table>

5.2.2.2 Unity of effect and impression

In a short story, a single situation and a single character, a single emotion or a series of emotions called forth by a single event are so uniquely interwoven that an artistic unity is achieved which creates an effect of 'totality' or of 'unity of impression.'

Unity of effect and impression

<table>
<tr><td>The story focuses</td><td>attention
interest</td><td colspan="3">on the revelation of one character at some moment of crisis.</td></tr>
<tr><td>Every</td><td>element
detail</td><td colspan="3">is subordinate to a single effect.
helps to create a single effect.</td></tr>
<tr><td colspan="2">Thus, this story is characterized by</td><td colspan="3">unity of action.
unity of impression.</td></tr>
<tr><td>In this story, the</td><td>theme of...
character of...
mood of...</td><td colspan="3">is particularly emphasized, whereas... is never really developed.</td></tr>
<tr><td>In this allegorical tale,</td><td>the events
the characters</td><td colspan="3">are primarily symbols of the central idea, namely...</td></tr>
<tr><td rowspan="2">X's</td><td rowspan="2">nature
character</td><td rowspan="2">is revealed</td><td>through his</td><td>conversation.
gestures.</td></tr>
<tr><td colspan="2">at a moment of moral crisis.</td></tr>
<tr><td>The impact of (this story)</td><td>partly
mainly
entirely</td><td>depends on the</td><td colspan="2">portrayal of X's character.
mood of...
the startling climax when...
the surprising (open) ending.</td></tr>
<tr><td colspan="2">Artistic unity is achieved by the</td><td colspan="3">conciseness of the language.
repetition of keywords.
imagery of... that is used.
recurrence of the theme.
leitmotif of...
tightly-knit plot.
recurring symbol of ...
prevailing mood of ...</td></tr>
</table>

5.2.2.3 A tightly-knit plot

In a short story of the classical type there are no additional, merely ornamental episodes, and there is nothing like a subplot. Quickly, consistently, and forcefully, everything leads up to the climax, i.e. the resolution of action that coincides with a surprising revelation of the main character.

A vivid, abrupt opening

The opening of the story is vivid, and almost always abrupt, e.g. starting in the middle of a dialogue. It provides the reader with an immediate sense of security and sometimes contains a clue that suggests the ending — to those who read closely.

Example: 'I once saw a bloke try to kill himself.' (Alan Sillitoe, "On Saturday Afternoon")

A turning-point

The turning-point comes either when some secret trait of the main character is kept back until towards the end of the story or some dramatic change in the action is brought about. Thus, at a moment of conflict or personal crisis, a completely new aspect of the hero's character can be glimpsed for the first time or the action takes a rather unexpected turn. The term 'turning-point' may therefore be applied both to the moment of a startling revelation of the hero's inner life or of a striking development in the course of the action the story describes.

A surprising ending

Although the turning-point has prepared the reader for some new development, the ending is often abrupt and rather unexpected. Sometimes the story has an 'open' ending, i.e. one that leaves some doubts as to the precise continuation of the story from the point reached when it closes. In any case, this ending is reached step by step, from the opening onwards leading up to the turning-point and from there to the ending, 'with the precision and rigid consequence of a mathematical problem' (E. A. Poe). In a letter to a friend, **R. L. Stevenson** expresses this problem like this:

> Make another end to it? Ah, yes, but that's not the way I write; the whole tale is implied; I never use an effect when I can help it, unless it prepares the effects that are to follow; that's what a story consists in. To make another end, that is to make the beginning all wrong. The *denouement* of a long story is nothing, it is just 'a full close,' which you may approach and accompany as you please — it is a coda, not an essential member in the rhythm; but the body and end of a short-story is bone of the bone and blood of the blood of the beginning.[6]

The classical type: a tightly-knit plot

<table>
<tr><td colspan="4">The author has fused character and action into a simple (not a complex) plot.</td></tr>
<tr><td colspan="4">The story is confined to one setting, i.e. one place and a short period of time.</td></tr>
<tr><td colspan="4">It is focused on one or two significant incidents.</td></tr>
<tr><td>The plot</td><td colspan="3">involves only a few characters.
is developed in only one or two scenes.</td></tr>
<tr><td>It has a(n)</td><td colspan="3">vivid abrupt opening.
single turning-point, i.e. a surprising reversal from which the action develops in a new unforeseen direction.
abrupt ending.
open ending.</td></tr>
<tr><td colspan="2">Towards the end, dramatic suspense</td><td colspan="2">is built up.
leads to an unexpected (a startling) denouement.</td></tr>
<tr><td>The climax is</td><td colspan="3">the resolution of the action, since ...
(= in a simple adventure story)
the solution of the mystery.
(= in a detective story)
the surprising revelation of the main character.</td></tr>
<tr><td colspan="2">The ... constitutes the turning-point in the</td><td colspan="2">revelation of the hero's character.
development of the action.</td></tr>
<tr><td rowspan="2">The</td><td rowspan="2">climax
turning-point</td><td>is reached
comes</td><td>when ...</td></tr>
<tr><td colspan="2">is not explained until the very end of the story and so provides for a surprise ending.</td></tr>
<tr><td colspan="4">The story has an open ending; the reader is left to draw his own conclusions.</td></tr>
</table>

5.3 The short story of the 20th Century

5.3.1 The short story — the most appropriate art form of the 20th century

We can say that the 20th century, so far, has been the century of the short story in England and America. This form of literature is no longer regarded as the "poor relation of the novel". One possible reason for its increasing success may be the hectic rhythm of modern life: the modern reader, always pressed for time, will prefer a story that can be read through at a sitting, to a novel in several volumes.

> More short-story writers are today writing in England and America, and moreover writing better stories, than ever before. That fact is no accident. A particular artistic form does not flourish in a particular age because of a happy accident, but because certain cultural, inventive, revolutionary, or popular forces combine to stimulate its growth: so that finally, perhaps, it becomes the most necessary and natural expression of the age. This was notably true of the drama in Elizabethan times, the heroic couplet in the eighteenth century, the novel in the nineteenth century, and in a lesser but increasing way is true of the short story today.[7]

> For a long time the short story was the poor relation of the novel... We now think differently: the originating genius of Poe in America, of these French and Russian writers and (very late) of Kipling in Britain, has turned out to be decisive and, in this century, writers have had the excitement of a new, intensely individual prose art at their disposal. It is a hybrid. It owes much to the quickness, the objectivity and cutting of the cinema; it owes much to the poet on the one hand and the newspaper reporter on the other; something also to the dramatic compression of the theatre, and everything to the restlessness, the alert nerve, the scientific eye and the short breath of contemporary life. It is the art of the short expectation of life. It fulfills Poe's demand that works of art should be short and immediate in effect.
> The story, on the other hand, wakes the reader up. Not only that; it answers the primitive craving for art, the wit, paradox and beauty of shape, the longing to see a dramatic pattern and significance in our experience, the desire for the electric shock. The modern reader is longing for a revival of the tale.[8]

For study and discussion

1) What other art forms have had an influence on the current short story?
2) Why is it the most appropriate genre to record the reality of contemporary life?

5.3.2 The classical plot story of the 20th century (1900—1920)

Until 1920, when the short story got many new impulses (cf. **5.3.4.1 The psychological, impressionistic, lyric slice-of-life story**), the classical plot story was still very popular.

The classical plot story

<table>
<tr><td colspan="4">The mode of presentation is realism.
The tone is fairly optimistic.
The presentation of events is almost exclusively chronological.</td></tr>
<tr><td>Themes
Thoughts
Events</td><td colspan="3">are fairly explicitly presented
with the emphasis on surface action.</td></tr>
<tr><td colspan="4">The author/narrator is omniscient.</td></tr>
<tr><td colspan="4">This story of traditional plot is based on conflict issuing into action.
This action is progressive, evoking suspense.</td></tr>
<tr><td>The conflict is</td><td colspan="3">sometimes internal but mainly external.
finally resolved by the action.
at the centre of the story.</td></tr>
<tr><td colspan="4">Thus the structure is essentially dramatic.</td></tr>
<tr><td colspan="4">The characters are mostly exceptional, rarely average.</td></tr>
<tr><td rowspan="3">The conflict</td><td>is</td><td>hinted at
stated
alluded to</td><td>at the beginning of the story.</td></tr>
<tr><td colspan="3">follows a line of progression.
is developed by a series of scenes.</td></tr>
<tr><td colspan="3">is resolved at the end.
leads to a crisis and final solution.</td></tr>
<tr><td colspan="4">Thus the story follows a tight plot with
— a vivid opening,
— a turning-point,
— a surprising ending.</td></tr>
<tr><td colspan="4">The message emerges from the surface action.</td></tr>
<tr><td colspan="4">The gist is contained in the end, which is the surprising, but logical, termination of the action.</td></tr>
</table>

5.3.3 The 'formula' or 'magazine' story — degradation and decline of the classical short story
(1900 to the present day)

It is interesting to observe how the abuse of certain of the characteristics of the short story as defined by literary critics led to prolific production and commercialization and in this way to a degradation and decline of the classical short story. By the turn of the century, literary criticism, in particular **Brander Matthews** in his popular essay *The Philosophy of the Short Story (1901),* had succeeded in analysing and describing in simple terms the techniques used by the masters of the classical short story, W. Irving, N. Hawthorne, E. A. Poe, and a few others. At the same time, William Sidney Porter — under the pseudonym of **O. Henry** — made a huge profit by writing around 250 short stories, most of which were sold under contract before they had even been written. It may well be understood that almost all of them bear the mark of haste: they are sketchy, superficial, with his easy-flowing style glossing over the poor substance. While O. Henry's skilful plotting, his economy of means and the effective reversal of the situation are still classical, the endless repetition of the same 'formula' in virtually all his stories made them artificial — action-centred, fast-paced, moving rapidly to a sharp climax that explodes in a surprise ending. Thus the 'magazine story' was 'well-made' in its easy narrative and sophisticated 'punch', yet it was thin and bloodless since it lacked a message worth pondering and remembering.

In a literary review *'Short Story-Writing: An Art or a Trade?',* **N. Bryllion Fagin** heavily criticized O. Henry's most famous short story:

> What is the... story, the famous "Gift of the Magi"? We have discussed it and analyzed it in our texts and lauded it elsewhere. How much of the life of the four million does it hold up to us?...Why is it a masterpiece? Not because it tries to take us into the home of a married couple attempting to exist in our largest city on the husband's income of $ 20 per week. No, that wouldn't make it famous. Much better stories of poverty have been written, much more faithful and poignant, and the great appreciative public does not remember them. It is the wizard's mechanics, his stunning invention — that's the thing! Della sells her hair and buys a fob for hubby's watch; while at the same time hubby sells his watch and buys her a comb. But you don't know all this until they get together for the presentation of the gifts, and then you gasp. We call this working criss-cross, a plot of cross purposes...
>
> Thus an examination of O. Henry's work by any one not blinded up by hero-worship and popular esteem, discloses at best an occasional brave peep at life, hasty, superficial and dazzlingly flippant; an idea, raw, unassimilated, timidly works its way to the surface only to be promptly suppressed by a hand skilled in producing sensational effects. At its worst, his work is no more than a series of cheap jokes renovated and expanded. But over all there is the unmistakable charm of a master trickster, of a facile player with incidents and words . . .[9]

For study and discussion

1) Why is, according to N. B. Fagin, O. Henry's 'The Gift of the Magi' not a genuine literary masterpiece?
2) Name at least three criteria for slick literature.

The more people like O. Henry tried to rise in the world of literature, the more artificial their approach and style became. Their writings were lacking in reality, which was replaced by mere sophistication and prettiness. So these authors failed to interpret the whole range of human experience, both in its contemporary and its timeless forms. Instead, they elaborated mere sensation, sentiment and cheap, insincere romance.
O. Henry's formula, even termed **'O. Henryism',** was further simplified in specific **short story handbooks** written for home correspondence and basic college courses. In no less than 40 of such handbooks published between 1900 to 1930 in the U.S. alone, this 'successful formula' was hammered into the brains of students and housewives whose literary gifts were by no means extraordinary. Equipped with these 'points of information', these scribblers in their turn set out to produce stereotyped products and sell them to magazines — sometimes at a high profit. It may well be imagined that in this way the once classical short story gradually deteriorated and sank to become the **'magazine story',** purely conventional in structure and mechanical in its effect. In the end it became so mercilessly overwrought that even competent and sincere artists could no longer use the once celebrated classical form.

Note how in the following parody **Ring Lardner** exposes the consequences of **ruthless commercialization** for the classical short story. His main intention, of course, is to ridicule the incompetence of mere scribblers, in particular their poor spelling and their poor command of grammar. (The text has been shortened).

How to write short stories

A little group of our deeper drinkers has suggested that maybe boys and gals who want to take up writing as their life work would be benefited if some person like I was to give them a few hints in regards to the technic of the short story, how to go about planning it and writing it, when and where to plant the love interest and climax, and finally how to market the finished product without leaving no bad taste in the mouth.

Well, then, it seems to me like the best method to use in giving out these hints is to try and describe my own personal procedure from the time I get inspired till the time the manuscript is loaded on to the trucks. The first thing I generally always do is try and get hold of a catchy title, like for instance, 'Basil Hargrave's Vermifuge,' or 'Fun at the Incinerating Plant.'...

How to begin — or, as we professionals would say, 'how to commence' — is the next question. It must be admitted that the method of approach ('L'approchement') differs even among first class fictionists. For example, Blasco Ibanez usually starts his stories with a Spanish word, Jack Dempsey with an 'I' and Charley Peterson with a couple of simple declarative sentences about his leading character, such as 'Hazel Goodtree had just gone mah jong. She felt faint.'

Personally it has been my observation that the reading public prefers short dialogue to any other kind of writing and I always aim to open my tale with two or three lines of conversation between characters — or, as I call them, my puppets — who are to play important roles....

To illustrate this, let us pretend that I have laid out a plot as follows: Two girls, Dorothy Abbott and Edith Quaver, are spending the heated term at a famous resort.

The Prince of Wales visits the resort, but leaves on the next train. A day or two later, a Mexican reaches the place and looks for accomodations, but is unable to find a room without a bath. The two girls meet him at the public filling station and ask him for a contribution to their autograph album. To their amazement, he utters a terrible oath, spits in their general direction and hurries out of town. It is not until years later that the two girls learn he is a notorious forger and realize how lucky they were after all.

Let us pretend that the above is the original plot. Then let us begin the writing with haphazard dialogue and see whither it leads:

'Where was you?' asked Edith Quaver.

'To the taxidermist's,' replied Dorothy Abbott.

The two girls were spending the heated term at a famous watering trough....

'I'm getting sick in tired of this place,' went on Miss Quaver.

'It is mutual,' said Miss Abbott.

There was a rap at their door and the maid's voice announced that company was awaiting them downstairs. The two girls went down and entered the music room. Garnett Whaledriver was at the piano and the girls tiptoed to the lounge. The big Nordic, oblivious of their presence, allowed his fingers to form weird, fantastic minors before they strayed unconsciously into the first tones of Chopin's 121st Fugue for the Bass Drum....

That will give young writers an idea of how an apparently trivial thing such as a line of dialogue will upset an entire plot and lead an author far from the path he had pointed for himself. It will also serve as a model for beginners to follow in regards to style and technic. I will not insult my readers by going on with the story to its obvious conclusion. That simple task they can do for themselves, and it will be good practice.[10]

For study and discussion

1) Show that Ring Lardner is making fun of minor writers. What in particular does he satirize and how does he go about it?
2) What is his serious purpose?
3) Try and find some more criteria to define slick literature.

The 'formula' and the 'magazine story' — 'O. Henryism'

In the magazine story, **truth** is often	in the grip of the successful formula. sacrificed to effect.

(reality)	are unrealistic and insincere. artificially narrow the scope of human life and experience.	
O. Henry and his followers Commercial short story writers	accumulate material	that fits into a successful, but sterile stereotype. that is merely romantic and sentimental. that is sensational and has 'punch'. that can be commercialized.

(form)	plays safe, i.e. he: blindly follows the successful formula, concentrates on superficial action, is incapable of creative art.	
A scribbler	uses makes use of employs	the successful **plot** with disregard to truth and reality: — a 'breakneck beginning' (usually in the middle of a dialogue), — a 'fast-paced' narrative moving directly to the 'unknown' climax, — a climax that unexpectedly, but definitely ends the action, — an artificial surprise ending.

The	subject style dialogue setting action character development message	is	subordinated to the service of the formula. squeezed into effective 'high-lights'.

Many **subjects**	are left out, such as stories of quiet homely life, stories of the common man doing his duty, everyday events significant in themselves, stories that end in irony, doubt, . . .

p. t. o.

The 'formula' and the 'magazine story' – 'O. Henryism' (continued)

The **subject** is	limited to restricted to	pseudo-moralistic psychology. social conflicts, such as 'big-business', successful crimes, detective inspectors, cheap sentiment, mere sensation, lascivious romance, blunt sex.	
The **story**	is not based upon real life. is so narrow in subject that it lacks realism. merely supplies what the public wants. follows in the wake of some popular success. is so interestingly featured — with 'love-interest' and a punching climax — that it lies. is full of sentimentality. is full of artificial suspense. shows life as it should be, not as it is.		
It is **peopled by**	dope-fiends. hard businessmen. heroic boys and lovely girls. supermen and heroic maidens.		
Thus,	romance sentimentality sensation	are presented as reality.	
A 'formula story' A'magazine story'	is often	pretty in style. conventional in structure and plot. stereotyped and sterile. mechanical in its effect. a series of cheap jokes continuously repeated and expanded. insincere and superficially flippant.	
		centred on	'love' interest and artificial suspense. cheap sentiment, lascivious romance or blunt sex.
		produced by a master trickster.	

p. t. o.

The 'formula' and the 'magazine story' – 'O. Henryism' (continued)	
Its **message** is	unrealistic. insincere. artificial. thin and bloodless. sentimental and/or sensational. insincerely romantic.
There is often no real message.	

Many **Westerns** of the cheap sort basically follow the pattern of the 'formula short story' then in fashion. The plot may be of the following type:

1) A rather mean chap goes into the redwood forests, prairies or deserts of the West.
2) Quite unexpectedly, the new environment changes him completely (= turning-point or 'O. Henry twist'); he becomes a regular saint fighting continually for justice and a better world (= reversal of the situation).
3) He exhibits some kind of bravery (to keep the reader or TV viewer happy): he catches horse-thieves and rascals; he rescues some down-trodden slut (= love interest) who, in turn, becomes a very rare sample of a good mother and housewife (= definite end of the action and 'happy ending').

It is interesting to note that although the heyday of the 'formula story' is long past, the 'formula story' itself is by no means dead — as anybody who has ever picked up a few **Jerry Cotton stories** and the like cannot have failed to notice. There is obviously still a huge market for this kind of literary product, and so some publishing firms regularly churn out love stories, westerns and detective stories. Once you have read one of them you know them all; names and settings vary, but the 'formula' basically remains the same — as may be seen in any of the cheap TV-series.

That writing short stories according to a certain 'formula' may become very tiresome (though still be very profitable) can be seen in the case of perhaps the most famous of all formula-writers, Arthur Conan Doyle and his immortal **Sherlock Holmes adventures.** The reading public took such a fancy to them that Doyle, who was sick and tired of his hero, and in what he thought would be definitely the last Sherlock Holmes adventure had let him fall down a deep ravine in the Alps, together with his arch-enemy Moriarty, was forced to resurrect him and write a lot more of the immensely popular Sherlock Holmes stories.

5.3.4 The slice-of-life story (1920—1940)

5.3.4.1 The psychological, impressionistic, lyric type

Revolted by the mechanical, rigidly standardized and stereotyped production of 'magazine stories' and frustrated by their lack of genuine artistic message, sincere artists and critics began seeking new directions after World War One. Their criticism of the 'formula' reached its peak in the twenties and thirties of our century and it usually began with denouncing the state of degradation short story writing had reached at that time: It had been spoilt by commercialization, the mere virtuosity of petty, casual, grabbing scribblers. The stereotyped formula limited the subject and the story. Moreover, it was felt that this very technique further titillated the nerves of modern man, whose nerves were already frayed in the whirl of modern life. For that reason, the degraded formula story was compared to the quick-lunch.

The notion of "plot" as a necessary basis for a good short story was strongly criticized by **Sherwood Anderson:**

> There was a notion that ran through all story-telling in America, that stories must be built about a plot and that absurd Anglo-Saxon notion that they must point a moral, uplift the people, make better citizens, etc. The magazines were filled with these plot stories and most of the plays on our stage were plot plays. "The Poison Plot", I called it in conversation with my friends *as the plot notion did seem to me to poison all story-telling*[11]

Even earlier **Henry Seidel Canby** had blamed the stereotyped short stories produced in the wake of O. Henry as mere **'artifices'** and demanded **'greater freedom for fiction'**:

> Better criticism and greater freedom for fiction might vitalize our overabundant, unoriginal, unreal, unversatile, — everything but unformed short story. Its artifice might again become art. And when one thinks of the multitudinous situations, impressions, incidents in this fascinating whirl of modern life, incapable perhaps of presentation in a novel because of their very impermanence, admirably adapted to the short story because of their vividness and their deep if narrow significance, the voice of protest must go up against any artificial, arbitrary limitations upon the art. Freedom to make his appeal to the public with any subject not morbid or indecent, is all the writer can ask. Freedom to publish sometimes what the editor likes and the public may like, instead of what the editor approves because the public has liked it, is all that he needs. There is plenty of blood in the American short story yet, though I have read through whole magazines without finding a drop of it. When we give literature in America the same opportunity to invent, to experiment, that we have already given journalism, there will be more legitimate successors to Irving, to Hawthorne, to Poe and Bret Harte. There will be more writers, like O. Henry, who write stories to please themselves, and thus please the majority. There will be fewer writers,

like O. Henry, who stop short of the final touch of perfection because American taste (and the American editor) puts no premium upon artistic work. There will be fewer stories, I trust, where sentiment is no longer a part, but the whole of life. Most of all, form, the form, the formula, will relax its grip upon the short story, will cease its endless tapping upon the door of interest...[12]

For study and discussion

1) Why are, in Canby's view, formula stories 'artifices'?
2) What are the advantages and the disadvantages of an artifice?

Since reality had become more and more complex it was becoming more difficult to tell what were the causes and what were the effects in the seeming chaos of modern life. Some highly sensitive artists preferred to select some especially telling moments of life and to register the impressions these moments made upon them. And since they concentrated on inner life rather than on outer reality, this new type of story might be called the **impressionistic, psychological slice-of-life story.**

Then it gradually moved inward, and in the hands of many people, almost all of whom had first written poetry — and this includes both Hemingway and Faulkner — it became "a slice of life", as we used to say of Maupassant, but a slice of the mind and the spirit rather than the body.[13]

And it was **Sherwood Anderson** who — in search of new ways — suggested that **short stories ought to be impressionistic tales verging on poetry** rather than constructed on formulas. Notice that he chose the form of a poem to say what he meant in the preface to his *Book of Impressions* — containing 'tales' **and** 'poems':

Tales are people who sit on the doorstep of the house of my mind.
It is cold outside and they sit waiting.
I look out at a window.
The tales have cold hands,
Their hands are freezing.
A short thickly-built tale arises and threshes his arms about.
His nose is red and he has two gold teeth.
There is an old female tale sitting hunched up in a cloak.
Many tales come to sit for a few moments on the doorstep and then go away.
It is too cold for them outside.
The street before the door of the house of my mind is filled with tales.
They murmur and cry out, they are dying of cold and hunger.
I am a helpless man — my hands tremble.
I should be sitting on a bench like a tailor.
I should be weaving warm cloth out of the threads of thought.
The tales should be clothed.
They are freezing on the doorstep of the house of my mind.
I am a helpless man — my hands tremble.
I feel in the darkness but cannot find the doorknob.
I look out at a window.
Many tales are dying in the street before the house of my mind.[14]

This short poem seems to be symbolic of the new approach: since the impressionistic writers developed their approach **in opposition to form,** they attained a highly individualistic, subjective 'lyric' way of writing, concentrating on inward impressions and visions. The term **'lyric story'** was first used by Conrad Aiken in 1921 to characterize the works of Chekhov and Katherine Mansfield.

In their search for a new form, English and American short story writers had to go a long way before they managed to get out of the dead end short story writing had got into at the end of the First World War.
Their progress was lonely at first; quite often they were frustrated because their motives and intentions were ignored, misunderstood or criticized. But gradually they found some helpful suggestions in **painting, philosophy and psychology.** With the development of **impressionism,** a more fluid, flexible and subtle kind of suggestive presentation became predominant, first in French painting, but then in European and world literature.
In the short story, this impressionistic approach shunned consistent plotting, tended towards inaction and formlessness, and merely indicated character. It was primarily concerned with evoking mood and capturing the more elusive qualities of life. The masters of this **impressionistic technique** were **Anton Chekhov** in Russia and **Virginia Woolf** and **Katherine Mansfield** in England.
As a consequence of the impressionistic approach, some new techniques of stylistic presentation were developed, namely **the stream-of-consciousness technique,** i. e. presenting experience through the mind of one of the characters, with the subconscious as derived from **Freudian psychology** often playing an important role. This technique usually involves the use of **inner monologue** and even the introduction of a **fictitious narrator,** i. e. one of the characters who seems to tell the story instead of the author.

In the following text, **Bonaro Overstreet** regards the new **psychological approach** as the basic difference between the short story of the 20th century and the classical plot-story of the 19th century. In her view, the classical plot-story was only possible as long as two faiths were taken for granted by author and reader alike: first, that people "know the difference between right and wrong"; and secondly, "that people are . . . what they seem to be". In the 19th century, outer action could be presented as identical with inner action, whereas in the 20th century, under the influence of psychology, inner action was realized as going far beyond outer action.

> In the twentieth century, because we have lost faiths that must underpin a confident life of action, we are being thrown back upon a study of human nature — human motives, fears, wants, prejudices. The drama of our century is the drama of what goes on in the mind. The outward action — whether it be the slightest gesture of a hand or the ruthless invasion of one nation by another — is significant only as it throws light

upon the obscure mental and emotional states that have bred it. *The characteristic science of our century is psychology.* It has naturalized in our speech such words and phrases as *inferiority complex, stream of consciousness, inhibition, the subconscious, frustration, rationalization.* These are not action-words. They reflect our growing need to understand what goes on in the hidden corners of our human nature. What of the short story in our century? Its future is as unpredictable as that of all our other institutions. But this we can say: during the past several decades it has become a more and more expert medium for the expression of our deep concern about human moods and motives that have shown themselves to be far less transparent than we once thought they were... The twentieth-century story-teller is becoming, in his own way, a master of rigorous form. But to understand this form, we must recognize that it is dictated by psychological materials and processes, not primarily by events in the objective world. Its logic is not, and cannot be, that of dovetailed incidents that total up to a precise plot — a plot that any teacher of English can outline on a blackboard. Its logic is the complex logic of mental and emotional experience. *Associate linkages, personal memories* and *fears* and *faiths, rationalized reasons for behavior, subsurface thinking* that goes on in contradiction to surface talk — all these, and a multitude of other factors, must be recognized by the writer, today, as part of the deeper logic of any given situation. In determining its outcome, *they may be far more important than are objective events.* Some readers complain that nothing happens in modern stories. But we all know from our own experience that a great deal can be happening — that volcanic changes in mind and mood can take place — when there is scarcely a surface ripple for the casual observer to detect.[15]

For study and discussion

1) What criticism is commonly expressed against the twentieth century short story?
2) What — according to Overstreet — dictates its form?

It goes without saying that this style, with its focus on **inner life,** is not always transparent for outsiders; and the reader may be an outsider if he does not happen to be highly sensitive and have had the same impressions or experiences as the writer himself. That seems to be the very reason why this kind of impressionistic narrative prose, in its extreme forms, has not always met with praise but also with criticism. **Frank O'Connor,** for example, does not equally admire all psychological short stories. He has pointed out the danger of blindly imitating Chekhov for a writer who does not have Chekhov's technical devices at his command.

Oh, naturally I admire Chekhov extravagantly, I think every short-story writer does. He's inimitable, a person to read and admire and worship — but never, never, never to imitate. He's got all the most extraordinary technical devices, and the moment you start imitating him without those technical devices, you fall into a sort of rambling narrative, as I think even a good story writer like Katherine Mansfield did. She sees that Chekhov apparently constructs a story without episodic interest, so she decides that if she constructs a story without episodic interest it will be equally good. It isn't. What she forgets is that Chekhov had a long career as a journalist, as a writer for comic magazines, writing squibs, writing vaudevilles, and he had learned the art very, very early of maintaining interest, of creating a bony structure. It's only concealed in the later work. *They think they can do without that bony structure, but they're all wrong...*[16]

For study and discussion
So, according to O'Connor, K. Mansfield and her disciples imitated Chekhov in a one-sided way. In what ways do they fail?

The psychological, impressionistic, lyric slice-of-life story

The author	uses employs	an impressionistic technique.
The story	consists of is based on	a series of impressionistic touches.
It is	obviously greatly	influenced by Freudian psychology.
For the impressionistic writer,	there is	no logical development. no telling what is cause and what is effect.
He does not aim at a clear structure or plot. He hardly ever states things directly or openly. He rather suggests and implies.		
Not much seems to happen in such stories.		
They	lack narrative structure. are rather plotless, static, fragmentary. are often mere sketches of transient moments.	
The author merely captures a mood. To him reality is not definable, but disordered, ambiguous.		
The subject is limited to a "slice-of-life", i.e. a carefully selected moment of time that is fully explored.		
It shows a heavy emphasis on	Freudian psychology. the subconscious. the effect of dreams and nightmares.	

p. t. o.

The psychological, impressionistic, lyric, slice-of-life story (continued)		
The author presents reality through the mind of one of the characters.		
In the presentation, he	uses employs has recourse to resorts to	the stream-of-consciousness technique. inner monologues. a fictitious narrator.
He is	trying to create a certain atmosphere. primarily out to evoke a certain mood.	

5.3.4.2 The expressionistic, symbolic, surrealistic type

As in painting, where impressionism developed into expressionism, writers in the 1920—40s found that such slices of life could be made even more telling if they selected those moments they considered to be typical and left out those which were merely accidental. **Van Gogh,** the famous painter, underwent a similar development in his art. In Arles, he said about his painting that he tended more and more to **exaggerate or emphasize what was typical and telling,** and to leave out what he thought was accidental or casual. In this way, **impressionism developed into expressionism and symbolism.** In literature, this meant that writers had to select typical slices of modern life and work out what was particularly telling in them using a highly suggestive and expressive language. So they chose words that were realistic on the surface but of a deeper symbolic meaning under the surface. In poetry, this metaphorical language had always been used. And so it is a logical development that the short story writing of 1920—1940 verged on poetry.

In *A Critical Survey of the Modern Short Story* (London, 1941), **H.E. Bates** contends that the new suggestive style of the short story may have partly been brought about by the **evolution of the general reader:**

> *The evolution of the short story may . . . have something to do with the evolution of the general reader . . .*
>
> Dickens, often publishing a novel in monthly parts, found it necessary to devote some hundreds of words, and if necessary repeat those words a month later, to a single character. In 1920 Sherwood Anderson remarked simply that "she was a tall silent woman with a long nose and troubled grey eyes"; in 1930 Mr. Ernest Hemingway in a moment, for him, of unusual expansion, said, "He wore a derby hat and a black overcoat buttoned across his chest. His face was small and white and he had tight lips. He wore a silk muffler and gloves." In 1940 Mr. V.S. Pritchett writes, "He had a cape on, soaked with rain, and the rain was in beads in his hair. It was fair hair. It stood up on end." Anderson took up fourteen words, Mr. Hemingway thirty-one, Mr. Pritchett twenty-six. Between Dickens and Mr. Pritchett, then, something has happened. *Is it only the evolution of the short story? May it not also be, perhaps, the parallel evolution*

> *of the reader?* Education, travel, wider social contact, the increased uniformity of life, dress, and manners have made us all familiar with things that were once remote enough to need to be described. Today all of us have seen Sherwood Anderson's woman, the tragic, anonymous representative of a whole inarticulate class; we have seen Mr. Hemingway's tough with the black overcoat and bowler hat; we know Mr. Pritchett's type with its fair hair that stands up on end. The widening of social contact, among other things has relieved these three writers, and their generation of an oppressive obligation. *It is no longer necessary to describe; it is enough to suggest.* The full-length portrait, in full dress, with scenic background, has become superfluous; now it is enough that we should know a woman by the shape of her hands.[17]

In 1934, **L.A.G. Strong** described this method in greater detail.

> The modern short story writer is content if, allowing the reader to glance at his characters as through a window, he shows them making a gesture which is typical: that is to say, a gesture which enables the reader's imagination to fill in all that is left unsaid. Instead of giving us a finished action to admire, or pricking the bubble of some problem, he may give us only the key-piece of a mosaic, around which, if sufficiently perceptive, we can see in shadowy outline the completed pattern.[18]

If we look at this statement more closely, we can see how artists at that time worked:

1) they selected typical segments of reality ("key-pieces" of the mosaic);
2) they presented them in such a way that a creative, sensitive reader could imagine what was missing.

It is precisely this selective realism, suggesting a more complex truth, which is called expressionism — both in painting and in literature.
Richard Kostelanetz, an expert on the modern short story, means exactly the same thing when he defines the short story as a "microcosm":

> The medium (of the short story) is a metaphor in its ability to offer an image of experience which, though not an exact replica, in some way recreates experience; and in contrast to the novel, whose length makes it capable to present a broad picture of reality, the short story devotes its attention to a small area of human existence. If, however, this microcosm is sufficiently resonant, the short story will become a complex symbol for larger worlds. On its surface, it may portray a single situation, but in its depths, it can comment on universal issues. For this reason, as a medium, the short story is more metaphoric than the novel, which in turn is, more metaphoric than reportage.[19]

E. Hemingway, for example, with his spare but powerfully descriptive and suggestive style managed, by depicting "the eigth of the iceberg" above water, to suggest "an entire volume of explanatory matter" (F. Norris).

James Joyce, one of the great short story writers of this period, calls any incident, gesture or bit of conversation that seems to be particularly suggestive and revealing an **'epiphany'**. In *Stephen Hero* (chapter XXV) (1944), he gives an example that illustrates this expressionistic approach clearly.

> He was passing through Eccles' St one evening, one misty evening, with all these thoughts dancing the dance of unrest in his brain when a trivial incident set him composing some ardent verses which he entitled "Vilanelle of the Temptress". A young lady was standing on the steps of one of those brick houses which seem the very incarnation of Irish paralysis. A young gentleman was leaning on the rusty railings of the area. Stephen as he passed on his quest heard the following fragment of colloquy out of which he received an impression keen enough to afflict his sensitiveness very severely.
>
> The Young Lady — (drawling discreetly) . . . O, yes . . . I was . . . at the . . . cha . . . pel . . .
>
> The Young Gentleman (inaudibly) . . . I . . . (again inaudibly) . . . I . . .
>
> The Young Lady — (softly) . . . O . . . but you're . . . ve . . .ry . . . wick . . .ed . . .
>
> The triviality made him think of collecting many such moments together in a book of epiphanies. By an epiphany he meant a sudden spiritual manifestation, whether in the vulgarity of speech or of gesture or in a memorable phase of the mind itself. He believed that it was for the man of letters to record these epiphanies with extreme care, seeing that they themselves are the most delicate and evanescent of moments.[20]

If the author places such an 'epiphany' in an impressionistic slice-of-life story, it will become more suggestive and expressive. The epiphany — a typical, revealing incident, gesture, phrase — will bestow a metaphorical and symbolic meaning on the entire story providing for the reader the key to a deeper understanding and insight. The epiphany will be a "moment of revelation" at which the veil will be lifted from complex reality; some underlying mystery may thus be laid bare and become manifest.

The repeated "pok" of the bottles placed on the fender in James Joyce's short story "Ivy Day in the Committee Room" is such an epiphany: it is symbolic of the vain hopes of some come-down drunkards who try to fool themselves that they are continuing in their heroic fight for Irish independence.

European literature at that time was greatly influenced by **existentialism**, a philosophy giving special emphasis to the absurdity of human life, and by **surrealism**, a mode of presentation that goes beyond the experience of reality as we know it. The best-known of the authors writing in this strain is certainly **Franz Kafka**, who — especially in his story 'The Metamorphosis' — created penetrating and nightmarish symbols of human anxiety and frustration against the background of a modern world geared to the mechanism of bureaucracy and technocracy.

The expressionistic, symbolic slice-of-life story

This slice-of-life story shows great simplicity on the surface but great complexity in depth.

p. t. o.

<table>
<tr><td colspan="5">The expressionistic, symbolic slice-of-life story (continued)</td></tr>
<tr><td colspan="5">On the surface, it portrays a simple situation but in depth it comments on universal issues.</td></tr>
<tr><td>The story is based on a selective realism, i.e. carefully selected moments with</td><td>symbolic value
deeper meaning</td><td>which are particularly</td><td colspan="2">suggestive.
revealing.
telling.</td></tr>
<tr><td>The writer's aim is</td><td colspan="4">to let us see behind things and into man.
to depict the conflict within the character.
to provide a glimpse of what goes on within the mind.</td></tr>
<tr><td>The narrator is often</td><td colspan="4">an eye-witness.
a participant in the action who speaks in the first person.</td></tr>
<tr><td colspan="5">By means of a few simple strokes, the inner truth of things is revealed and suggested.</td></tr>
<tr><td colspan="5">The story offers a succession of subtle indirect suggestions or symbols.</td></tr>
<tr><td>The emphasis is</td><td colspan="4">not upon the sequence of episodes.
not upon progression.
upon their deeper meaning.</td></tr>
<tr><td colspan="5">The action is so much reduced that the story appears rather plotless.</td></tr>
<tr><td colspan="5">There is hardly any conflict revealed through sequential action.</td></tr>
<tr><td rowspan="4">Instead, the author</td><td>resorts to</td><td colspan="3">parallelism.
repetition.
accumulation.
allusions.
implications.</td></tr>
<tr><td rowspan="2">uses</td><td>a(n)</td><td>elliptical
symbolical</td><td>style.</td></tr>
<tr><td colspan="3">figurative language.</td></tr>
<tr><td colspan="4">speaks from various points of view.</td></tr>
</table>

p. t. o.

The expressionistic, symbolic slice-of-life story (continued)			
The aim of the story is to make the reader perceive	a hidden relationship. some aspects of modern life.		
The reader is	expected meant supposed	to	find the key-piece of the mosaic. interpret the symbols. perceive the relationship between various episodes. fill in all that is left unsaid. find out the underlying pattern.
Only at the end does the sensitive reader realize that all the previous seemingly separate scenes fall into a pattern of meaning.			

The surrealistic slice-of-life story

The story is obviously influenced by existentialism.						
The author employs a surrealistic technique.						
He	is out intends	to	express voice	his feelings of	isolation frustration despair alienation apprehension hope love	. . .

. . . by	creating	hallucinatory surrealistic nightmarish	situations. settings.
	using		symbols.

The	exotic surrealistic	mood atmosphere	is	achieved created	by	the masterful rendering of . . .

5.3.5 The fusion of the plot story and the slice-of-life story (1940—1960)

Around 1935, the short story — with its varied historical developments — had obviously ended in dead-ends again:

1) the classical **plot-story of the 19th century** — still favoured by some authors — with its stress on surface action and suspense failed to record the upheavals in the inner lives of 20th century people;
2) the **formula story** in the wake of O'Henry had become so rigidly structured and so ruthlessly commercialized that it failed to grasp any serious substance;
3) the rather subjective, sometimes even egocentric, **impressionistic story** in the tradition of Chekhov and K. Mansfield was often so diffuse in form that many readers — both with or without literary knowledge — simply failed to understand it.

In this situation, it was **William Saroyan** who — in a literary review — rather vaguely claimed that art had to be creative, i. e. it had to be **an organic fusion of "form and substance":**

> What, if anything, is a story? Well, frankly, I do not exactly know, and believe no one exactly *knows*, and if anyone does exactly know, I believe this *knowing* isn't so terrifically important, and if it is important at all, I do not believe it is important enough to stand in the way of the growth of art, which is inevitably the growth of living, and if I myself am interested in anything at all, I am interested in growth, in keeping in motion, in expanding, in not standing still, however artfully. To be petrified, I suppose, is to be perfect after a fashion, but I would rather be wholly alive, in motion, and imperfect. I would certainly prefer to stop writing altogether than to be turned into a pillar of salt. The man who journeys should not turn back to look upon the road he has traveled.
>
> Short, or short story, story or novel, are necessary terms, I suppose, but not necessary to be ignored, if need be, and I think need be. Art is not wholly duration, although duration is part of art. What it is mostly is integration, a making of wholeness. An egg is whole, and is an egg not less because it is small or large, ostrich or robin, white or spotted. The wholeness of a billiard ball is unlike the wholeness of an egg in that it cannot be eaten or hatched into a bird. The wholeness of a billiard ball is form alone: the shape round, the color white, the texture smooth, the density even and sustained: form alone. The egg is form AND substance. That is, living substance, mutability, substance growing.[21]

For study

1) In the first paragraph, the author draws an analogy between a legend from the Bible and short-story writing. What does it suggest about the situation of writers at that time and what their approach should be?
2) In the second paragraph, he compares a billiard ball and an egg. What is the point of this comparison as far as form and substance in art are concerned?

In 1936, **Elizabeth Bowen** in her "Preface" to *The Faber Book of Modern Short Stories* traced two definitely one-sided traditions in short-story writing back to their origins — the "formless", impressionistic type to Chekhov, and the rigidly structured one to Maupassant:

> The influences of two foreign masters on an affectable new form have necessarily run counter to one another. Chekhov stands (or stands with us) for an emancipation of faculties, for a romantic distension of the form of the story to let in what might appear inchoate or nebulous. Maupassant stands for astringency, iron relevance . . .[22]

In the same preface, **E. Bowen** stresses some of the desiderata of a modern short story:

> Poetic tautness and clarity are so essential to it that it may be said to stand at the edge of prose; in its use of action it is nearer to drama than to the novel. The cinema, itself busy with a technique, is of the same generation: in the last thirty years the two arts have been accelerating together.[23]

A compromise between popular art and elite art

In the 1940s there appeared a group of literary scholars in the universities called the **"New Critics".** In their endeavour to analyse the modern forms of fiction appropriately they arrived at the common conviction that a work of art could only be fully appreciated after a careful study of the text itself, and not by the study of the biographical and historical background. Their concern for the internal consistency of every word, phrase, and sentence in regard to theme, structure, atmosphere, character and action has helped to uncover the very making of a work of art. Particularly in the taut forms of fiction, in poetry, and in the short narrative forms, their studies have proved to be penetrating and enlightening.

On the other hand, their dogma of **internal consistency** had a twofold consequence — on the reader and on the artist — that was soon to be criticised:

> Too frequently, it would seem to the lay reader, the New Critics evaluate in terms of complexity of understanding. The value would be in inverse ratio to the number of people who can be expected to understand. The harder one is forced to dig through the symbols, the myths, and the ironies to ferret the meaning the more successful the story. Reading becomes not an experience but an exercise in mental gymnastics for the critics and the initiated few.[24]

What was now in danger of getting lost was the popular appeal, the entertainment of the reader. After a closer study of the most successful short stories — which were also the best in terms of literary quality — **Falcon O. Baker** found out that

> Most short stories that have stood the test of time, the stories that today are accepted as masterpieces, have at the base a great deal of *surface interest.* Regardless of the many cascading levels of meaning, the story can be read entertainingly on a superficial level. All are not reducible to the formula of boy meets girl, pursues girl, marries girl, but they have movement on the surface, an

> interest created by the skill of the author in making the reader want to discover what is going to happen. Certainly Poe and De Maupassant had a sound basis of surface interest. Even the symbolic stories of Hawthorne carry a high quotient of surface activity. Surface plot is the action both by and upon the character which creates a certain suspense for the reader, the abatement of which can be accomplished only by finishing the story. Although it is usually not the real story, it is the vehicle which carries the meaning. It is this surface plot that first catches and holds a great number of readers. *Stories that achieve the highest level of success have both a competent level of meaning and a competent level of* surface action. The author has something to say, and he says it with interest and suspense.[25]

These findings have been deliberately and intelligently used by many writers in the English-speaking world. They have helped to establish **a compromise between popular art and elite art.** The technique applied to that end is **the technique of receding planes:** since most modern short story writers write for a wide readership their stories are often conceived and composed at different levels. The author makes conscious use of connotations, implications, metaphors, symbols, etc. to provide various levels of meaning at which the story may be enjoyed and appreciated.

The technique of receding planes

<table>
<tr><td colspan="6">The author has used the technique of receding planes.
Thus this short story appeals to a wide readership.</td></tr>
<tr><td colspan="3">For children
For people who are no experts in literature</td><td colspan="3">the 'story' itself is fun to read.</td></tr>
<tr><td>For adults
For people with a knowledge of literature</td><td>the full</td><td colspan="3">metaphorical
allegorical
symbolic</td><td>message becomes obvious.</td></tr>
<tr><td colspan="4">For these reasons, this short story has become</td><td colspan="2">so popular.
a best-seller.</td></tr>
</table>

So, a short story, at its best is always **"a miracle of understatement"** (B. Harte). With seemingly spare and simple, but concise means (in terms of language, motive, plot, setting, and characterization) it achieves such a compression of the message that the reader is forced not only to read between the lines, but between the very words.

A miracle of understatement

<table>
<tr><td colspan="3">This story is 'a miracle of understatement'</td><td>because of</td><td colspan="2">its compact brevity.
the economy of means.
the conciseness of its style.
the terse description of the setting.
its bare, but highly suggestive dialogue.
words and phrases charged with connotations and implications.</td></tr>
<tr><td>The</td><td>meaning
message</td><td>is</td><td>intensified
enhanced</td><td>by the use of</td><td>connotations.
implications.
metaphors.
images.
symbols.</td></tr>
<tr><td colspan="5">Thus, it is an artistic masterpiece in terms of</td><td>language.
style.
plot.
characterization.</td></tr>
</table>

The period from 1940 to 1960 is thus a period in which all the existing styles and approaches were fused

The artists wrote in highly individual 'free' forms. Their range included anything from straight narratives following a plot with distinct characters, concentrating on **outer action,** to showing dream visions and symbolic fantasies exploring the mysterious processes of the human mind, with the stress on **inner action.** Of course, all sorts of combinations of these two basic approaches are possible and have been tried. **Angus Wilson** alludes to this **fusion of the classical plot-story and the impressionistic short story,** when he writes:

> The classic short story of Mr. Maugham's era, with its emphasis on narrative and surprise, proved too tight to convey the flow of sensitivity which to Kath. Mansfield was the essence both of art and life. By injecting greater subtlety of mood and deeper levels of consciousness, she almost succeeded in destroying the form and reducing short stories to 'sketches'. **Short story writers for the last fifteen years have been trying to tie the two threads together again.** The history of the novel has not been dissimilar and, on the whole, the short story writers have been more successful than the novelists in restoring shape without losing subtlety. It would not be unfair, I think, to say that the success of

10 short stories is in direct ratio to their *power of maintaining form without losing suggestion and overtone.*[26]

Basically, then, what marks off the scene of short story writing between 1940 and 1960 from all the previous periods is precisely this strong emphasis on the individual writer's freedom of choice between various forms of fusing the old and the new, i. e. of following more or less closely the rules once laid down for the 19th century short story or making use of impressionistic, expressionistic and other elements as they were worked out by the generation of writers during the twenties and thirties.

The fusion of the plot story and the slice-of-life story (1940—60)

<table>
<tr><td colspan="4">This short story blends the classical and the modern.</td></tr>
<tr><td colspan="2">It combines the principles of the plot story:
— clear surface action,
— logical development,
— chronological plot,
— suspense,
— surprise ending,</td><td>with . . .</td><td>elements of the "slice-of-life" story:
— impressionism,
— suggestiveness,
— symbolism,
— psychological insight,
— the use of the subconscious,
— inner monologue,
— the stream-of-consciousness technique.</td></tr>
<tr><td colspan="2">Its major theme is moral failure since</td><td colspan="2">the characters' moral code cannot cope with the realities of existence.
the individual is not able to find a viable morality.</td></tr>
<tr><td rowspan="3">The author</td><td colspan="3">says bluntly what he thinks.
places his own stamp on what he sees.</td></tr>
<tr><td>portrays human</td><td>actions
attitudes
motives</td><td>once thought of as taboo.</td></tr>
<tr><td colspan="3">confronts life honestly and sincerely.</td></tr>
</table>

5.3.6 Some trends in the contemporary short story (1960— . . .)

The period from 1940 to 1960 was an era during which several attempts were made to fuse the highly successful plot story of popular appeal with the expressionistic symbolic slice-of-life story that tended to be favoured by connoisseurs.

Contemporary writers still make use of the long tradition of the short story with its different styles and approaches. But the revolutionary changes in the world brought about by, and in the wake of, World War Two, again urged them to adapt their literary approach to yet a new form of reality. Quite understandably, a systematic historical study based on scholarly research has not yet been provided and can most probably not be given at this stage, since we are too much involved in our own time and lack that critical distance that makes a scholarly study possible.

Some trends, however, have become so dominant that most literary critics have come to acknowledge them.

In the 1960's and 1970's, as a consequence of the cold war in Europe and Asia, of affluence in the highly industrialized nations and poverty in the developing countries, of a sometimes questionable technological progress and environmental pollution, of the space race, and of the growing impersonality in a mass consumer society a need for new modes of perception and presentation in the arts was universally felt.

The following three new approaches to rendering our contemporary world can be made out:

1) **The factual story:** Some authors, who are at the same time journalists, fuse reporting with fictional techniques to record the sometimes fantastic changes in contemporary life — often surpassing the powers of imagination. This fusion of fact and fiction has been called faction.
2) **The 'absurd' anti-story:** A number of authors think that our existence has become absurd. For them, the appropriate means of rendering it is the absurd anti-story. Some committed authors, on the other hand, use an absurd presentation to provoke an insensitive audience to try and find a new sense and meaning in life again.
3) **The meta-story:** Some authors have been influenced by a new technique in art — collages — and by modern linguistics. They offer the reader the linguistic wastes of a consumer society out of which he is expected to produce his own text — in a sort of collage.

5.3.6.1 The factual story — elements of the short story fused with factual reporting

In the 1960's, New Journalists (cf. 2.4.) like Truman Capote, Norman Mailer and Tom Wolfe developed a new form of reporting. To be able to record — like a seismograph — the important changes in contemporary life they gave up the principles of traditional journalism and fused reporting with fictional techniques. They gave up the standpoint of the omniscient author and the news summary. Instead, they tried to put the reader into the position of an eye-witness or participant. Thus their 'stories' became more immediate and vivid. They used inverted chronology, the presentation of characters in dramatic scenes, indirect

characterization, inner monologue, the stream-of-consciousness technique, changes in the point of view, and composite characterization. And they chose whichever of the techniques of short-story writing suited them best **to record the inner life of modern man,** the complex of beliefs, hopes and fears which seem, somehow, to motivate the actions of human beings.
And it was exactly the registering of those hopes, fears and beliefs that was necessary to record the fantastic changes of the 1960's and 1970's: the civil rights movement, women's lib, the identity crisis of the minority groups, of the younger generation, of marginal and isolated groups like flipped-out youngsters or homosexuals.

The factual short story

The writer	deliberately blends factual with fictional reality. places composite characters in situations representative of contemporary life. records and criticizes modern life.
The story lacks a clear-cut structure or plot.	
The theme is diffused throughout the work.	
The story	consists of a succession of almost incoherent moments. consists of a series of brief scenes.
The author resorts to	composite characterization. inverted chronology (flashbacks/anticipation). changes in the point of view. inner monologue. irony. black humour.

5.3.6.2 The absurd anti-story

Some writers find that contemporary life has become so bewilderingly impersonal and complex that they regard it altogether as absurd. And they feel that the only means of rendering an absurd reality is by absurd technique and style.
In the 1960's, the theory of spontaneous prose and the improvisational principle of jazz were integrated into short story writing. Some authors became so preoccupied with the process of composition that their recording of fragmented impressions

became a non-narrative anti-story. A new irrationalism based on the beat scene, the drug scene and an alternative way of life further strengthened these tendencies. What these authors have in common is their endeavour to record reality as absurd, and their irrational opposition to any rules and to society as a whole.
In treating the madness of some individuals, for example, they describe life from the point of view of the madman instead of noting the external symptoms of madness. Among these writers are Samuel Beckett, Dylan Thomas, Ted Hughes, and B.S. Johnson in England and Donald Barthelme, William Burroughs, Kenneth Koch, Jack Ludwig, James Purdy, Hubert Selby, Thomas Pynchon and Curtis Zahn in the USA.

The absurd anti-story

The writer is out to suggest that	the world is ultimately senseless life is absurd there is no meaning in human existence
... by pointing out the contradiction between	values and behaviour. intention and effect. belief and reality.
The world is shown as a non-realistic portrait of thoroughly ridiculous events.	
The central theme is	flight from reality. psychoanalysis as a substitute for religion.
The absurd anti-story is peopled by	outsiders. members of minority groups. flipped-out youngsters. searching adolescents. unhappy criminals. oppressed blacks. frustrated artists and ideologists. marginal or isolated characters. psychopaths. homosexuals.
Realism is completely rejected.	
The omniscient narrator is absent.	

p. t. o.

The absurd anti-story (continued)	
The (first-person) narrator proves unable to understand life.	
The anti-story is based on	spontaneity. creative inspiration.
The chronology is completely distorted.	
The author does not use a plot.	
Without conspicuous notice, he keeps changing	time. scene. point of view.
The story is based on the irrational opposition to any rules and to society.	

Note:

Very similar to the absurd anti-story, yet quite different in its intention, is **the use of the absurd as a means to shock an insensitive or unbelieving readership:** by the presentation of the bewildering, repellent, absurd, grotesque, and mysterious an unbelieving readership may be provoked to try and find a new sense in life. Concerned artists will draw the reader's attention to the distortions in modern life in order to shock him and persuade him to be more critical or even to change his attitude. Even Christian authors like **Flannery O'Connors** are often preoccupied with the negative sides of modern life — and they have been severely criticized for it. It is interesting to see how fully aware they are of their role in an affluent and often superficial society.

> The novelist with Christian concerns will find in modern life distortions which are repugnant to him, and his problem will be to make these appear as distortions to an audience which is used to seeing them as natural; and he may well be forced to take ever more violent means to get his vision across to this hostile audience. When you can assume that your audience holds the same beliefs you do, you can relax a little and use more normal ways of talking to it; when you have to assume that it does not, then you have to make your vision apparent by shock — to the hard of hearing you shout, and for the almost blind you draw large and startling figures.[27]

(What she says of the novel is of course also true of the short story).

For study

What means must the fiction writer adopt to make these distortions "appear as distortions to an audience which is used to seeing them as natural"?

The absurd, grotesque, repellent as means of presentation

<table>
<tr><td rowspan="2">Black humour
Bitter sarcasm
The farce
The caricature
The parody</td><td rowspan="2">is a form of irony used to expose</td><td colspan="2">the absurdity of a certain behaviour.</td></tr>
<tr><td>the hypocrisies
the self-deceit</td><td>of modern man.</td></tr>
</table>

5.3.6.3 The meta-story

In the view of some authors, reality is not only absurd; but they feel that it does not even exist.

> Reality doesn't exist, time doesn't exist, personality doesn't exist. God was the omniscient author, but he died; now no one knows the plot, and since our reality lacks the sanction of a creator, there's no guarantee as to the authenticity of the received version. Time is reduced to presence, the content of a series of discontinuous moments. Time is no longer purposive, and so there is no destiny, only chance. Reality is, simply, our experience, and objectivity is, of course, an illusion.[28]

Since reality is no longer taken for granted, it is considered impossible to represent it by means of imitation. So these writers — like the 'painters' of collages — offer their readers the linguistic wastes of a consumer society and a society that is lacking in communication. It is up to the reader to produce his own text — no longer a story, a meta-story.

Good meta-stories sometimes become vehicles of metaphysical speculations and theoretical discussions on fiction. Other meta-stories, however, are the products of incompetent pseudoartists incapable of communication.

The meta-story

<table>
<tr><td>In the meta-story reality is considered as non-existent.</td></tr>
<tr><td>Chronology loses its meaning.
Personality loses its individuality.</td></tr>
<tr><td>All is considered ambivalent: — point of view,
— action,
— character,
— place,
— time.</td></tr>
<tr><td>p. t. o.</td></tr>
</table>

The meta-story (continued)		
Meta-stories are fragmentary collages of the linguistic wastes of a consumer society. They do not intend to give an illusion of reality.		
For such authors, to write is to produce meaning and not to reproduce pre-existing meaning.		
It is up to the reader to construct his own text out of the linguistic wastes offered.		
The meta-story	approaches approximates to is similar to	poetry in its spontaneity and creative inspiration.

5.3.7 The present situation and possible future development

Although the competition between literature and the mass media has become enormous — straight news, interpretive news, human interest stories, film, TV — there are still many opportunities for capable short story writers. 50 per cent of the world population forms a potential market for short stories written in English.
On the other hand, there are many problems concerned with cultural integration in the English speaking world, and, in the 1960's and early 1970's, the USA was no longer a 'melting pot', but a restless scenery of cultural splintering. The so-called silent majority made up of the average Americans often went unnoticed, whereas minorities and fringe groups got the exclusive attention.

> . . .it is noisy in the literary marketplace. Unless your special noise is that you are a Jew, a Negro, a junkie, a physicist, a homosexual, a prophet of holocaust, a prisoner, a Penrod run away from home and gone on a romp toward Dharma, a bulgy and guilt-laden American, or a spectacular and streamlined coward, it is not so easy to get a hearing.[29]

The consequence was cultural disintegration, especially in the 1960's:

> since World War II, the process of cultural splintering has accelerated enormously, and whatever broad national culture there was has now splintered into a series of distinct subcultures — ethnic, racial, philosophical, artistic.[30]

We must see the formation of the following groups against this background:
- the so-called **Southern Renaissance** — with its emphasis on the country-side, Southern culture and rhetoric,
- the **Jewish Renaissance** — flourishing in the cities and famous for the genuine, tragi-comical humour of the Jewish people,
- the **Black Renaissance** — based on the identity crisis of Negroes, rich in its improvisational rhythmical style.

There is no telling in which direction the genre of the short story will develop, since it has proved up to now to be the most adaptable of all literary forms — alive to any changes in human history and the mind.
Let us hope that good short stories will still be written in the future as in the past, unlike "these little things they publish now, with no beginning and no end and a little incest in the middle."[31]

6. THE NOVEL

6.1 The rise of the novel

The first prose narratives to be called "novels" appeared in Italy from the late thirteenth century onwards. These early *novelle* were not, however, novels in any modern sense, but referred to well-told stories centring around a number of stock characters. Nor did the following three centuries produce real novels. It was in fact not until the beginning of the seventeenth century that a true novel was published by the Spaniard Miguel de Cervantes; his *Don Quixote,* which appeared in two volumes in 1605 and 1615, is a true masterpiece and by many considered not only the first novel in point of time, but perhaps the greatest novel ever published.
Although the Italian stories called *novelle* were being imitated outside Italy by the middle of the fifteenth century in France and towards the end of the sixteenth century in England, it is only much later that one can really speak of an English novel tradition, and we are here mainly concerned with the English tradition of novel writing. It is true that there is a large amount of prose fiction written in the last two decades of the sixteenth century that some literary historians continue to label **"the Elizabethan novel",** but whether we read John Lyly's *Euphues* (1679), Sir Philip Sidney's *Arcadia* (1590), Robert Greene's *Menaphon* (1589), or other works of prose fiction from that time, we are forced to admit that what we find in these books is not the world of the novel as we know it; what they have in common with the novel as we think of it today is hardly anything apart from the obvious fact that they are works of prose fiction. The reader himself finds himself taken into an imaginary world, into **the world of romance** in which ideal love and chivalric adventures among ladies and gentlemen, living as shepherds and shepherdesses with music and madrigals in a lovely and romantic world of constant love and friendship *(Arcadia),* play the all-important role, or in which are recounted the adventures, if we can call them adventures, of a young man of means who commits some of the milder follies of youth and then retires from the world prematurely disillusioned and dejected *(Euphues).* In this last-mentioned Elizabethan prose narrative the narrative element is indeed very limited and to read the book for the sake of the story could be very exasperating. What the author, John Lyly, had in mind when he wrote *Euphues* was less a story than a minutely contrived piece of literary artifice in which the writer's craftsmanship and mental liveliness were devoted to the task of forging a new style, which was later aptly called **'euphuism'** — an elaborate pattern of language and ideas marked by a persistent search for elusive word-patterns and corresponding figures of speech.
With other Elizabethan prose fictions, such as Thomas Nashe's *The Unfortunate Traveller, or the Life of Jack Wilton* (1594) and Thomas Deloney's *Jack of Newbury* (1597) and *Thomas of Reading* (1600), we are a little nearer to what we are used to

in a novel. Their importance in the development of the novel lies in the fact that they provide a context of actuality for the exploits of their respective heroes; they are far removed from such moralistic romances as Lyly's *Euphues* or Greene's *Card of Fancy* (1584), which became a veritable craze among the more cultured reading public, who were willing to turn away from reality and to lose themselves among improbable adventures in Egypt, Greece, or Bohemia. In Nashe's and Deloney's **popular rogue-narratives,** which are heavily indebted to the picaresque tradition that evolved in Spain with the publication of the anonymous *Lazarillo de Tormes* (1554) and the more influential novel by Mateo Alemán, *Guzmán de Alfarache* (1559), we move in a totally different world. It is a world in which the hero is a rogue of some sort (Sp *picaro* = rogue, hence the term **'picaresque'**) who undergoes a number of adventures in foreign parts which involve a lot of fighting but also perilous amours, rollicking merriment combined with practical jokes, episodes of lurid horror and gruesome forms of revenge and torture. Although these novels consist basically only of a collection of tales and events that owe their unity merely to the fact that they occur within the experience of one person, they take us an important step nearer to the novel as we know it today. This is due to the fact that they are written in a plain, unaffected style and breathe everywhere the natural atmosphere of everyday life. They thus unwittingly paved the way for the triumph of realism.
The main reason why we are still a long way from the novel proper in these works of fiction lies in the concern their authors showed for anecdote, almost for its own sake. They were certainly not interested in the light the novel form might throw on man's life and his situation in the world in general, the nature of society, or the interplay of human beings with their fellows, which forms a large part of what we have come to expect from novels. Still, all these Elizabethan fictions are important for the future development of the novel in that they paved the way for the tradition of the **novel of adventure,** which begins with Daniel Defoe's *Robinson Crusoe (1719).* In a way, the pastoral and didactic romances, such as *Arcadia* and *Euphues,* also became important as forerunners of a different development within the field of the novel; these **court novels** — as opposed to the popular rogue novels — were steps towards the **novel of character,** of which the first outstanding example is Samuel Richardson's *Pamela* (1740).
The emergence of the novel as a clearly distinguishable species or as a recognizable type was further helped along by the publication in 1678 of John Bunyan's *The Pilgrim's Progress,* almost a whole century after the first appearance of the Elizabethan fictions mentioned above. The capacity of the novel to show us life as it really is in lifelike sequences, with its full social density and range, can very frequently be felt in this great book, which was intended by its author as an allegory of the Christian in search of salvation. (An 'allegory' represents abstract ideas in the form of characters in a narrative in which the plot serves to communicate a doctrine or thesis, but which also makes sense on the literal level of the narrative). In order to make his point, Bunyan used an ancient, universal image

— the image of life as a journey, as a 'pilgrimage', and so the reader sees the pilgrim ('Christian') going his way on a solid earthy road, through mud, through green fields, and over rocks and hills. Also conveyed behind this external action is the complicated moral life of man, with all its occasions of joy and happiness, feelings of despair, and its challenges to his mortal estate in general. Bunyan's great achievement lies in the **mixture of allegory and realism** his book offers, especially when the allegorical fusion of sense impression and moral concept is complete. The tradition of writing allegories goes back a long time — it was a particularly common form of writing in medieval times — and it is generally remote from reality as we normally experience it. Yet Bunyan managed to bring into his book the very accents of reality, partly through the dialogue which he included, thereby establishing his characters as sharply delineated human beings, and partly through the sheer vividness with which he painted this image of the society of his day. In other words, what makes *The Pilgrim's Progress* so valuable as an important step towards the novel proper is that its allegory is reinforced with a close observation of men and manners, without which novels in a modern sense cannot be written.

In Bunyan's great book we are already very close to the novel, as a very influential critic, William Hazlitt (1778—1830), describes it in his *Lectures on the English Comic Writers* (1819):

> We find here a close imitation of man and manners; we see the very web and texture of society as it really exists, and as we meet it when we come into the world. If poetry has "something more divine" in it, this savours more of humanity. We are brought acquainted with the motives and characters of mankind, imbibe our notions of virtue and vice from practical examples, and are taught a knowledge of the world through the airy medium of romance.[1]

A later critic, however, would scarcely have used the word "romance" in writing on the novel, because historically the novel can be defined as the very opposite of the romance. Indeed, the first great novel, Cervantes' *Don Quixote,* which had an influence on English novelists that can hardly be exaggerated, took as its initial theme precisely the impact of the real world upon an idealist who had been blinded to the world around him as it really was by having read too many medieval romances of chivalry. **This clash between romantic notions about life and the reality of life is a theme that one finds running through the English novel right down to the present day.** We can even say that the great novelists have always been deeply suspicious of mere fiction; what they wrote they wrote in the name of truth — truth to the reality of human nature and society as everybody experiences it.

In a way, Jonathan Swift's *Gulliver's Travels* (1726) continues Bunyan's allegorical approach. The main idea of this book is that of imaginary voyages, in Gulliver's case among the miniature-sized Lilliputians, the giant Brobdingnagians, the moonstruck philosophers of Laputa, and the Houyhnhnms and Yahoos, a race of intelligent and noble horses and their human-like serfs. *Gulliver's Travels* resembles its fellow-allegory *The Pilgrim's Progress* in its human interest and popularity; but in temper and outlook the two books are worlds apart. Bunyan views human weaknesses with a discerning eye, but he can tolerate them through his faith in the presence of divine grace and the possibility of man's redemption and salvation. **Swift's allegorical satire on the illusions and false pretensions of mankind,** on the other hand, is a long elaboration of his contempt and even hatred of the human race. He reduces man to miniature size and then magnifies him into a giant, and he finds him wicked, insolent and mean; he regards man in his so-called wisdom, and he finds him a fool; in despair, in the last book of the *Travels,* he turns from man altogether, and from the non-human Houyhnhnms his hero painfully has to learn that the 'normal' human qualities are actually strange and sometimes revolting peculiarities.

Swift is important in the development of the novel because he contributed to the emerging new form a most important element — the reader is forced to recognize how much of his habitual outlook and valuations rest upon unexamined assumptions. This heightened sense of ordinary experience and of habitual ways of feeling has been a typical feature of the novel form ever since and has made **the novel the most important medium for recording human experience in depth.** *Gulliver's Travels* itself cannot really be called a novel in the customary sense of the word; it is a unique and probably unclassifiable work of great depth and complexity, which needs to be interpreted on many levels, but it has had a lasting influence on the shape of the novel.

A work totally different from *Gulliver's Travels* but published at about the same time is Daniel Defoe's *Robinson Crusoe* (1719), which had an even greater influence on the development of the novel form. The book immediately became famous when it first appeared, especially for its first part, which incorporates the account of shipwrecked Robinson Crusoe's long solitary stay on an island which he gradually transforms into a habitable place that becomes his home. The story is built up with such careful attention to factual detail, and the hero's practical anxieties, his spiritual troubles, and his pride in achievement are presented so convincingly that the account reads like a personal memoir. Defoe's grasp of details and his unerring sense of their supreme literary value, combined with a swift and resolute narrative method and a plain and matter-of-fact style, enabled him to achieve an effect of realism that is rarely approached even by the most ardent of modern realists. His work is thus a landmark in the history of fiction because **it introduced all the elements of formal realism into narratives** and because **it also established character as the very centre of the novel.** Defoe's characterization is however in many ways strangely limited — the relationships of his heroes and heroines with other characters are usually seen only in terms of their value to the protagonists as business-partners. But even though these men and women have little or no sense of beauty and their interest in money and economic affairs occasionally seems excessive, they are portrayed as fully-rounded individuals experiencing life as we all do and confronted with moral choices — in a word, as characters in the modern sense.

Despite its undoubted merits, *Robinson Crusoe* also has grave defects. It simply consists of a number of episodes which are all relatively complete in themselves. The book thus lacks unity of theme, and there is clearly no overall plot design — for Defoe, the novel form apparently was only a handy device for telling a tale. The novel as a new literary form could however be considered fully established only when a narrative embodying realism of presentation and convincing characterization was organized into a plot which was intrinsically coherent; in other words, when it was concerned with character and personal relationships as essential elements in the total structure and all these elements were related to a controlling moral intention.

It was in fact only two decades after Defoe's fictional works were published that all these requirements were fulfilled in the work of **Samuel Richardson** and **Henry Fielding.** For this reason, they may be regarded as **the two founding fathers of the English novel;** in fact, they appear almost as opposed archetypes of later novelists. Unlike their predecessors, Richardson and Fielding were conscious literary innovators. Richardson was writing in the hope that his work "might possibly introduce a new species of writing"[2], and Fielding stated quite definitely that his fictions aimed at being "comic epic poems in prose" and a "kind of writing, which I do not remember to have seen hitherto attempted in our language."[3]

Richardson's first novel, *Pamela or Virtue Rewarded* (1740), is the first European **novel of manners** to deal with the private lives of people of the middle and lower classes. In a series of letters that the heroine writes to her parents, a story is developed which shows how a pretty servant-girl who is at a great social disadvantage resists all temptations to do wrong and eventually succeeds in making a great social position for herself without losing her virtue. Richardson's masterpiece is however *Clarissa Harlowe* (1748), an enormously long novel, which recounts, also in a series of letters, this time written by a number of characters, how the virtuous heroine is persecuted by an aristocratic villain and finally dies of a broken heart.

In these **letter novels,** Richardson was in a position to give the reader the illusion of living in the time-scale of the characters. The epistolary technique enabled him to present a sense of living in a continuous present, always at the cutting edge, as it were, of the character's experiencing, analysing mind; at the same time, he could show that the events are the result, as in drama, of the interaction of the characters and their attitude towards each other. Another advantage of the epistolary technique is the opportunity for character analysis it presents to the novelist. In his letters, a character is shown as he sees himself, minutely analysing motives and emotions, and the picture the reader gets is rounded off through the letters of others, in which this character is discussed from the outside, as it were. Most of Richardson's readers were delighted with his **novels of sentimental analysis,** because they presented life not only as it is, but as it should be. His influence as the initiator of the **psychological novel** throughout Europe has been tremendous, but his competence as a moral teacher was questioned by some even in his own day. These critics were prepared to acknowledge the great merits of his books — insight into character, penetrating analysis of human feelings and emotions, and logical sequence of incident — but they felt that he was altogether too sentimental and that his moral teaching was of doubtful quality. As they saw it, Richardson praised virtue not as something noble in itself, but as a means to an end, as a form of prudence: that virtuous behaviour is commendable because it pays best.

Richardson's most influential critic was his fellow-novelist **Henry Fielding,** whose first novel, *Joseph Andrews* (1742), was written as a parody of Richardson's *Pamela,* but its satirical purpose and parodistic intention was soon forgotten in the process of writing, and the novel developed into a humorous and satirical picture of the society of his day. But it is in his later novel *Tom Jones* (1749) that Fielding made his greatest contribution to the shaping of the English novel. In form, Fielding retreats from the novel of character conflict, challenging what he regarded as Richardson's hypocritical and narrow outlook and his mercenary virtues, and goes back to the model of Defoe and the earlier picaresque tradition. What particularly distinguishes *Tom Jones* is **the handling of a complex plot revolving around the unknown identity of the hero;** Fielding gave his masterpiece greater structural coherence than any previous prose fiction in English. Character is revealed without the help of autobiographical confession or an exchange of letters, but simply through action and speech. The range of characters is also wider than ever before, more lifelike and perhaps even more convincing than in Richardson. The psychological penetration into character is however shallower, but this is more than compensated for by the panoramic vision Fielding achieves and by **the humour with which he views human frailty.** Where Richardson is a didactic sentimentalist, Fielding is a humorist. The tradition of the novel being a vehicle for comments on people's behaviour and social manners and attitudes derives from him.

In summary we can say that with Richardson and Fielding the English novel received its first definite shape and form and its major traditions were firmly established, with the emphasis either on inner conflict or on outward action. A turning away from the idealistic world of romance to the world of ordinary experience, in which clearly individualistic characters are presented in a psychologically convincing manner, combined with formal realism and a clear plot structure, have to a large extent been typical of the novel up to the present day.

For study and discussion

1) In what ways is Elizabethan fiction different from the novel as it emerged in the eighteenth century?
2) What are the characteristic features of this novel-form?
3) Which would you regard as the first English novel — Bunyan's *Pilgrim's Progress,* Defoe's *Robinson Crusoe,* or Richardson's *Pamela?* Try to explain or defend your choice.

The rise of the novel

<table>
<tr><td rowspan="9">The novel</td><td rowspan="2">is different from</td><td colspan="2">the idealistic world of romance.</td></tr>
<tr><td>Elizabethan</td><td>didactic romances.
rogue narratives.
pastoral romances.
court novels.
prose fiction.</td></tr>
<tr><td>is a clearly</td><td colspan="2">distinguishable literary genre.
recognizable type of prose fiction.</td></tr>
<tr><td>is written in a(n)</td><td>plain
unaffected
matter-of-fact</td><td>style.</td></tr>
<tr><td>is concerned with</td><td colspan="2">the nature of society.
social interaction.
character and personal relationships.
character analysis.</td></tr>
<tr><td rowspan="4">typically</td><td colspan="2">shows life as it really is.
pays careful attention to factual detail.</td></tr>
<tr><td>relies on</td><td>realism of presentation.
formal realism.</td></tr>
<tr><td>portrays</td><td>fully-rounded individuals.
sharply delineated characters.</td></tr>
<tr><td colspan="2">is organized into an intrinsically coherent structure.</td></tr>
</table>

p. t. o.

<table>
<tr><th colspan="4">The rise of the novel (continued)</th></tr>
<tr><td rowspan="6">The novel</td><td>may offer</td><td colspan="2">insight into character.
penetrating analyses of human feelings and motives.
a logical sequence of incidents.
a panoramic vision.</td></tr>
<tr><td colspan="3">is based on a close observation of men and manners.</td></tr>
<tr><td colspan="3">conveys a heightened sense of ordinary experience.</td></tr>
<tr><td colspan="3">throws some light on man's life and his situation in the world in general.</td></tr>
<tr><td rowspan="2">has become</td><td colspan="2">the most important medium for recording human experience in depth.</td></tr>
<tr><td>a vehicle for comments on</td><td>people's behaviour.
social manners and attitudes.</td></tr>
</table>

6.2 The triumph of the novel

6.2.1 The novel is adaptable and flexible.

Though story-telling was among the earliest human activities, the novel is the youngest literary form. Its relatively short history has however not hindered it from becoming the most successful literary genre of the last two hundred years. There are two main reasons for this development. One of them is social change and the other lies in the novel form itself.

The novel rose to prominence as a literary form at a time when the traditional religious and hierarchical social frameworks were losing much of their validity. Everything seemed to be changing — a vastly larger middle class and a new urban class were developing as many thousands moved from rural environments to the big cities and suddenly found themselves thrust into new and strange social milieus as the effects of the Industrial Revolution began to be felt. The very conception of history underwent a change from that commonly accepted by previous generations. The reverberations of the revolutions in America and France made people suddenly aware of the fact that they had a part to play in the political process — they were needed as soldiers in a number of wars. The whole idea of wars had not figured very large in people's minds before because wars had appeared as remote events fought by mercenaries for reasons which were not very clear to the ordinary person. All these changes in the sociopolitical setting, which has here been sketched only in its barest outline, plus a number of other factors, such as a higher proportion of literacy than ever before, created perfect circumstances for the triumph of the novel. With its focus on individuals and their behaviour within a certain social order, the novel appeared as the ideal literary form for showing how the sociopolitical setting affected people's attitudes and their actions. It seemed to provide answers to such general concerns as the moral implications of life in an increasingly complex social order by presenting a web of personal relationships. Within this web, a number of realistically portrayed but fictional characters with which the reader could easily identify wrestled with precisely the same problems that he himself was confronted with in his own life — the growth of the city, the change in daily routines and work habits or the new social station he suddenly found himself in. In a situation in which so many things seemed to be changing so quickly and on such a scale that people were often confused, the novel was the ideal literary form for showing how society worked; it alone was capable of encompassing so many people and of showing them in so many situations as they moved through life. **The novel thus functioned as a kind of open forum for a discussion of social and ethical issues.**

But it continued to be an immensely successful form even after people had gradually become used to more or less continuous change. The novel has in fact proved an extremely adaptable and flexible vehicle for the expression of every topical concern it has been employed for — whether it was a preoccupation with the frontier situation, as in some of the first American novels (e.g. J.F. Cooper's 'Leatherstocking' books), or whether it was the discovery of American 'innocence' as compared with the sophisticated decadence of the Old World, as in Mark Twain's *Innocents Abroad* (1869) or in Henry James's novels. It has in fact functioned as a kind of dramatic testing ground for any new idea and topical concern ever since.

We can say that even though it was the massive social changes in the eighteenth and nineteenth centuries which enabled the novel to gain strength in the first place, **the more important reason by far for its continuing success is the adaptability and flexibility of the novel form itself.** It is distinguished by its ability to depict a large social group without losing sight of the nuances of gesture and attitude which characterize individuals within the group. It is also capable of delineating elusive, transient and deeply inward states and experiences, in individuals and also in groups of individuals as they form a society. It can thus portray social and historical affairs of the greatest magnitude and at the same time present the most intimate aspects of private life. In all this, the novel aims at a serious imitation of real life by observing the probabilities of actual occurrence in its use of plot and action and in its portrayal of character. This is what makes the novel so highly convincing and the ideal medium for giving artistic expression to the problems of the age.

No other cognate art form — neither the drama, nor the epic poem, nor, in more recent times, the film — can match the resources of the novel when the artistic task is to bring to immediate, sensuous, passionate life the rather impersonal materials of the sociologist, the historian, and perhaps even the psychiatrist. The novel can accomplish this task because, coming last, it is the heir to all previous techniques, although it has not superseded them. The technique of drama can be used in the novel, as can the devices of the epic and of poetry. It is in fact hardly possible to write a long novel without a mixture of several moods and styles, and length can be a definite advantage for a novelist if he intends to give a presentation not only of character but of a whole society or historical period. There is hardly anything the novel cannot do, there are many experimental paths still to be explored, and there is never any shortage of subject-matter.

Another important element in the success of the novel must also be considered. This is the fact it can command an immensely wide readership among all classes of people and is not limited in its appeal to those who are specifically interested in literature. The reason for this seems to lie in the fact that whereas a literary form such as the ode apparently possesses an inner mechanism which protects it from aesthetic and moral corruption, the novel by its very nature as an unheroic art form carries with it a constant tendency to triviality. What is meant is that since there is no place in it for heroes in the classical or medieval sense and man is shown as unheroic, unredeemed, imperfect, and even absurd, the novel practically invites corruption. Through its characteristic flexibility it leaves room among its practitioners for novelists of the most profound seriousness but also for writers of hard-boiled detective thrillers or of sentimental melodramas. It can even be exploited commercially for pornographic purposes or employed ideologically for propagandistic aims. **It must therefore be seen as an essentially all-purpose medium catering for a great variety of interest and for all the strata of literacy.** It can descend to the lowest commercial and ideological depths but can also attain to the highest reaches of great art. As a literary form embodying all these different tendencies it naturally has an enormously wide appeal among people from all walks of life and, as the steady increase in the number of novels published annually seems to suggest, it will also flourish in the future, despite the competition from other art media.

Understanding the text

1) What made the novel appear as the ideal literary form in a situation of change?
2) What intrinsic qualities of the novel have made it the most successful literary form of the last two hundred years?
3) What makes the novel so attractive to so many classes of people?

The novel's adaptability and flexibility

The novel	is extremely adaptable and flexible.	
	is the ideal literary form for showing how society works.	
	is able to	depict large social groups. portray social and historical affairs.
	is capable of	delineating inwards states and experiences. presenting the most intimate aspects of private life.
	has functioned as a	medium for giving artistic expression to the problems of the age. kind of testing ground for new ideas and topical concerns.
	embodies different tendencies. is essentially an all-purpose medium. caters for a great variety of interest.	
	can be exploited commercially or ideologically.	
	has an	enormously wide appeal among people from all walks of life. immensely wide readership among all classes of people.

6.2.2 The novel can embody many styles.

The novel quite obviously has many intrinsic qualities which make it an ideal instrument for the expression of a great many moods and styles.

The tendency to make use of the novel for the presentation of topical attitudes and interests is already evident in the eighteenth century — in the appearance of two types of novel which clearly reflect some of the preoccupations of the age, the so-called **Gothic novel** and the **sentimental novel.**

In the first type, we find a re-emergence of **the fabulous and marvellous** in new guise. **Scenes of mystery, horror and wonder** and a delight in the mysterious and irrational characterize novels like Horace Walpole's *The Castle of Otranto* (1764) or William Beckford's *Vathek* (1786). Their 'Gothic' style with its pseudo-medieval flavour can psychologically be explained as a reaction to the eighteenth-century belief in 'rationality', in reason and common sense, and as the expression of the apparently inexhaustible human desire for 'romance' (in the sense of the depiction of non-reality), a desire which has manifested itself again and again ever since. In the nineteenth century, for instance, the Gothic style found expression in Mary Shelley's notorious book *Frankenstein* (1818) and reached a climax in some of E.A. Poe's tales, which had an influence that can scarcely be exaggerated. The Gothic atmosphere can also be felt in some early science fiction, such as H.G. Wells' *The Island of Doctor Moreau* (1896), and in some twentieth century novels, where the spirit of the Gothic world with its dark, tempestuous and ghostly setting seems to have been deliberately cultivated, notably in the later novels of Iris Murdoch. It is interesting to note that Gothic fiction has always been approached in a spirit which consciously ignores the ordinary canons of taste — it is meant to be regarded as ingenious entertainment in which sensations such as pity and terror are presented as transient emotions which are, somewhat perversely, to be enjoyed for their own sake.

The **sentimental novel** introduced the concept of sentimentality into fiction. The sentimental style in its eighteenth-century sense is one in which the emphasis is put on an indulgence in refined and elevated feeling. This development was perhaps the natural consequence of the minute analysis of feeling, which was part of Richardson's contribution to literature (cp. 6.1). Henry Mackenzie's *The Man of Feeling* (1771) and Laurence Sterne's *Sentimental Journey* (1768) are outstanding examples of this trend. Most sentimental novels can however command only an academic interest. More important, in fact, than the works themselves is the fact that **they present love as a passionate attachment between the sexes which transcends the merely physical.** The vogue of sentimental love seems to be typical of this age and actually forms part of the Romantic movement which was beginning to make itself felt in the last decades of the eighteenth century. Some of the earlier novels which exhibit the sentimental style possess a certain moving dignity, but the rising commercial demand for bourgeois fiction in the nineteenth century inevitably led to a debasement of the sentimental attitude and to a change in the meaning of the term 'sentimental' itself: it came to denote a self-indulgence in superficial emotions and it implied a deliberate lachrymal appeal. The novel which expressed a sentimental style in this latter sense of emotional excess flourished throughout the nineteenth century both in England and in America, and **even 'serious' writers like Dickens occasionally succumbed to the temptations of sentimentality** and then manipulated tearful responses from their audiences, especially in deathbed scenes. Generally speaking, however, writers of serious fiction have avoided sentimental appeal. That this appeal has certainly not become weaker in the twentieth century and is still vastly attractive to many even in the Atomic Age is demonstrated by the world-wide commercial success of Erich Segal's tear-jerking *Love Story* (1970).

Gothic fiction

<table>
<tr><td rowspan="4">The Gothic novel
Gothic fiction</td><td>shows</td><td>scenes of mystery, horror and wonder.
the fabulous and marvellous.
the mysterious and irrational.</td></tr>
<tr><td colspan="2">uses a dark, tempestuous and ghostly setting.</td></tr>
<tr><td colspan="2">has a pseudo-medieval flavour.
is a reaction to a too exclusive emphasis on rationality.
is the expression of the inexhaustible desire for non-reality.</td></tr>
<tr><td colspan="2">presents pity and terror as emotions to be enjoyed for their own sake.</td></tr>
</table>

Sentimental fiction

<table>
<tr><td rowspan="3">The sentimental novel
Sentimental fiction</td><td colspan="2">is concerned with feeling for its own sake.
puts the emphasis on an indulgence in refined and elevated feeling.</td></tr>
<tr><td colspan="2">exhibits the vogue of sentimental love.</td></tr>
<tr><td>often</td><td>shows emotional excess.
deliberately appeals to the reader's emotions.
tries to elicit a tearful response in the reader.</td></tr>
</table>

Both these tendencies, the Gothic and the sentimental, were satirized in her own novels by Jane Austen at the beginning of the nineteenth century. The recurring theme in her fiction is the contrast between illusion and reality, which is exemplified in all her works by a young girl's painful and chastening progress from illusion about herself and the world around her to the knowledge of reality.

This type of fiction, which produces the **novel of manners,** is based on a close observation of social behaviour and is concerned with the manners of a closed society. In fact, such fiction may be written as readily in the twentieth century as in the centuries before, as is shown, for instance, in Evelyn Waugh's *A Handful of Dust* (1934), in which the hero's personal tragedy appears as a mere temporary disturbance of the collective order, or in Sinclair Lewis' *Main Street* (1920), with its attack on the cultural poverty of the American small town.

The **Romantic spirit** which transformed intellectual life after the French Revolution and which continued to be a powerful force for a great part of the nineteenth century also found expression in the fiction of the time, notably in the novels of Walter Scott. His **historical novels** clearly exhibit the romantic approach to life in their emphasis on idealism, chivalry and strong emotional impulse and their often artificially archaic language full of a remote and magical charm. Scott turns away from 'unheroic' heroes in the tradition of Fielding's Tom Jones and instead offers truly 'heroic' protagonists in his Scottish patriots and idealists. The setting he chooses for his novels is also different from that of the novel tradition — instead of the plain town and countryside he depicts the wild and mysterious landscape of the Scottish Highlands, and in place of the detailed study of middle-class life he constructs a narrative which is at the same time an adventure and a pageant of a bygone age with all its picturesque details.

The romantic style and spirit remained potent until far into the Victorian era and produced novels such as Charlotte Brontë's *Jane Eyre* (1847), which creates an atmosphere of mystery and terror for a love story that is grounded in realism, but carries strong overtones of wish-fulfilment, and her sister Emily Brontë's *Wuthering Heights* (1847), an intense tale of an all-powerful passion set in the wild and disordered world of the Yorkshire moors.

In a sense, James Fenimore Cooper's concern in his 'Leatherstocking' tales (1823–41) with the theme of the American wilderness is also an expression of the romantic interest in wild nature, which is seen as a place of almost mythological significance, and its effect on man. But the romantic style is far less prominent in America than in Britain.

Generally speaking, we can say that the aim of romantic fiction is not so much the presentation of a true picture of reality but the stimulation of the emotions through a depiction of strong and strange passions. Coupled with this is an attempt at firing the reader's imagination through a presentation of wonderful and exciting scenes and events within a more or less exotic setting. For this reason, this type of fiction is not normally classed among the 'novels', but among the 'romances', or it is called **'the novel-as-romance'** (for details cf. 6.4.3.).

The **romantic style** has proved unable to evolve a tradition of novelistic works of high literary merit. It still registered power and truth in the fiction of the Brontë sisters but has since been watered down to the presentation of cheap love stories of an imaginative and emotional appeal but without any real depth of feeling. Even writers like Daphne du Maurier with her novels *Jamaica Inn* (1936) and *Rebecca* (1938) cannot really revive the original romantic élan and works like these are therefore generally classed among **popular escapist fiction.** A kind of decadent romantic spirit can however still be felt in the twentieth century, e.g. in Lawrence Durrell's *Alexandria Quartet* (1957—60). Both the luxuriance of his prose style and the faithful portrayal of the physical feel of the Alexandrian world and the pervasive air of the mysterious and sinister are clearly shaped by something like the original romantic prescription. The whole atmosphere of the tetralogy does however seem somewhat contrived and shows little of the typically romantic transformation of response to life.

The **spirit of Romanticism** in the sense of a search for the identity of the self and the primacy of subjective experience, as it found its most fruitful expression in the work of the great Romantic poets, is still a dominant form in the twentieth century novel on both sides of the Atlantic. The search for reality by means of the quest for self-identity or full self-expression and a discussion of the problem of sustaining in a situation of intellectual isolation the image of the self despite disillusionment, uncertainty, and pain actually figure very large in a great many works of serious fiction. Quite clearly, this form of Romanticism continues to express itself as dynamically and variously today as it did in the first three decades of the nineteenth century. The largely subjective, anti-rational, and emotional elements of the romantic style must however be seen mainly as a historical phenomenon.

Romantic fiction

<table>
<tr><td rowspan="3">The romantic novel
Romantic fiction
The novel in the romantic style
Fiction in the romantic spirit</td><td colspan="2">is subjective, anti-rational, and intensely emotional.
emphasizes idealism, chivalry, and strong emotional impulse.
exhibits the romantic approach to life.</td></tr>
<tr><td colspan="2">is interested in the exceptional soul.
uses a wild, mysterious, or exotic setting.</td></tr>
<tr><td>wants to</td><td>stimulate the reader's emotions through a presentation of strong passion.
fire his imagination through a depiction of wonderful scenes and events within an exotic setting.</td></tr>
</table>

<table>
<tr><td rowspan="3">The spirit of Romanticism</td><td rowspan="2">is concerned with</td><td>a search for</td><td>self-identity.
self-fulfilment.</td></tr>
<tr><td colspan="2">the problem of sustaining the image of the self.</td></tr>
<tr><td colspan="3">is convinced of the primacy of subjective experience.</td></tr>
</table>

In the second half of the nineteenth century, the novel came more and more to embody a widespread dissatisfaction with life, particularly with middle-class life and its materialism, its banal details and its unheroic and dull everyday quality. It thus helped to establish **realism** as the major mood of that time — the exposure of the hopelessness and shallowness of that life and its social forms.

The style of realism found its way into Anglo-American fiction from France. It can be seen as a reaction to the idealism, chivalric passion, and the like, which characterizes the romantic style. The exponents of realism did not want the stark realities of life hidden in the dreamlike haze of romantic fiction, but set out to present the realities of human existence in all their nakedness without any poetic drapery.

Within **the English tradition,** we find the style of realism exhibited in the work of novelists like George Eliot (pen-name of Mary Ann Evans) and Thomas Hardy. Both present a grim view of human life in their novels, remorselessly tracing out the effects of moral choice on people's character and exposing the dreary emptiness of Victorian village life. A fundamental intellectual scepticism, which does not allow her to detect, as the Romantic poets do, a kind of divine benevolence in nature, makes itself felt in all the fiction of George Eliot. She never, however, permits her characters to sink into a deterministic morass of hopelessness. In Thomas Hardy's novels, on the other hand, notably in his final novel *Jude the Obscure* (1896), the determinism which George Eliot manages to avoid is all-pervasive and leads to an unrelenting pessimism. "Behind him one is aware of the new science, initiated by the biologists Charles Darwin and T.H. Huxley, which displaces man as a free being, capable of choice, by a view of him as the product of blind mechanistic forces over which he has little control."[4] In other words, George Eliot lets her characters have free will, or the illusion of it, but Thomas Hardy instils into his fiction a tragic and fatalistic vision and posits man's near-total impotence in a hostile world which appears to be utterly devoid of meaning.

In contrast to British fiction where the style of realism was indeed the dominating force, it was not so generally or so quickly accepted **in America,** where the tradition of romanticism retained a firm grip on many practitioners of fiction. In fact, both realism and romanticism can be felt to be expressions of their time. For one thing, America was changing with staggering rapidity into an industrialized country, a process which entailed all the usual problems of an industrial revolution. For another, there was the realization that the frontier, the open zone of unsettled land, no longer existed and that the almost mythical idea of illimitable territory to the west had to be abandoned. Yet, much was left still of the older, finer America, or at least the illusion of it, as exemplified in the chronic Southern heartache for the time of bygone gracious living *Befo' de War* (a book-title).

In this situation, William Dean Howells, the major champion of realism in the States, at first saw realism as involving no more than writing about people of the kind one meets every day. This harmless version of realism was gradually abandoned when he saw that as a consequence of the rise of capitalism something had seriously gone wrong with the pure, uncomplicated America he had believed in and which had inspired his earlier realism. The industrial brutality of the 188os made him a socialist and led him to describe the moral decay of competitive society in novels such as *A Hazard of New Fortunes* (1890).

The tendency towards realism, which had been growing more and more distinct since the Civil War, found its fulfilment in the work of writers like Hamlin Garland, who called his own variety of realism **'veritism'**. He was among the first who wrote realistically about life in the West and in doing this attacked the almost mystic quality traditionally connected with free land: in the 1880's and 90's, the farmers in the West were going through one of the worst periods in their history, and Garland conveyed with sincerity and dignity the atmosphere of heart-breaking drabness that enveloped their lives.

Another writer of that generation, Stephen Crane, published in 1893 a sombre little novel called *Maggie, A Girl of the Streets,* in which he depicted in the realist style the dreadfully ugly life of the titular heroine in the backstreets of a big city. In his *The Red Badge of Courage* (1894), he introduced the theme of the horror and enormity of war into realist fiction. His description of the brutality which lies beneath the surface of human beings, of the berserk fury which impels them to perform so-called 'heroic acts', and of the helpless confusion which characterizes all the action, highlights in a brilliant manner the view that the world and man's life in it is a chaos where the only consolation is in the tenuous fellowship between man and man.

We can say that the style of realism in the sense of a faithful description of the iniquities of the big city, or of the woes of the farmers out West, and generally of the suffering of the oppressed in whatever context, has been a continuing impulse also **in twentieth century fiction.** The whole atmosphere in more recent novels of this type seems however to be different from that of nineteenth century realism. The reader is still confronted with the baser instincts in man and society which may eventually nullify all human efforts, but realist fiction is now often used as a medium in a reforming design and not any longer as the expression of a hopeless philosophical pessimism or nihilism. As long as realist fiction is put in the service of a protest against the human degradation that some man-made systems entail, we are dealing with a form of qualified optimism. If reform still seems to be a real opportunity, all is not lost: people's lives may be wretched and absurd, but man's power of self-realization through an exercise of his free will is not ruled out. The pain, frustration, and impotent anger which was seen as typical of man's experience of life in the nineteenth century appears to have been modified in the twentieth — the view that people cannot help themselves in their actions and that everybody and nobody is to blame has been largely replaced by the conviction that the origin of all evil is in the human free will and consequently in the wrong moral choices that people make. The mechanistic determinism of a hundred years ago no longer seems a live option.

In a writer like Stephen Crane the realist style in his depiction of the brutality of war and its lack of meaning already shades over into the mood of **naturalism.** This is a style of writing that grew out of realism and also began in France, notably in the work of Émile Zola. Realism and naturalism cannot always be strictly separated, not only in Crane but also in general. The difference between them seems to be essentially one of degree. **Historical naturalism** (as opposed to contemporary naturalism) shares with realism an attitude of pessimistic determinism, but is different from it in its more thoroughgoing concentration on the physical and biological aspects of human existence. **Man is primarily seen as a product of natural forces, of the social milieu around him, but also of genetic influences.** The task of fiction is therefore to show the physical essence of man and his environment. As a consequence, all the exponents of naturalism share an utter frankness about the basic processes of life, and their corresponding outspokenness often brought them into conflict with censorship in many forms — timid publishers, public outcries, confiscation, obscenity indictments, and so on. Theodore Dreiser's first novel *Sister Carrie,* for instance, which has all the usual denominators of a naturalistic book in that it describes how a pretty country girl who comes to Chicago is tempted and seduced by two men, one of whom ruins himself for her, could not be published in America for some time. The book did come out in England in 1901, but Americans had to wait till 1908 to see this first sympathetic study of a 'fallen' woman.

It is typical of the naturalist strain of that period that people are seen as 'chemisms' who suffer for temperaments they did not make and for weaknesses and failings which are not of their own willing or doing, as Dreiser argues in *The Financier* (1912). In his view, conventional fiction mispresents the realities of human existence, whereas realist/naturalist fiction is faithful to its true nature, in the sense that characters are neither 'good' nor 'bad' but are entirely "moulded by circumstance: creatures whose deepest instincts are animal, and who in moments of stress revert to brutishness."[5] The same idea is emphasized in the fiction of Jack London, whose stories of adventure in the Klondike region and elsewhere, especially *The Call of the Wild* (1903), are still widely read today. Instead of good and bad people there are the naturally strong and the naturally weak. Moral judgements are largely replaced by the success of the strong, who rely on deep-seated instincts and on their stature as nature's most highly-developed creation, and the failure of the weaklings, who vainly try to cling to a civilisation which cannot really support them.

After the First World War novelists apparently felt that it was their duty to show the human degradation of the soldier's life and the horrid ugliness of war as such, and so naturalism was infused with a new strength. A real breakthrough was however achieved for naturalism as one of the dominant forms of contemporary fiction with the publication of James Joyce's *Ulysses* in 1922. This truly revolutionary novel seeks to justify total physical candour in terms of its artistic aim, which is **to relate with almost scientific objectivity** every aspect of a single day, June 16, 1904, in Dublin, as mirrored in the consciousness of Leopold Bloom, Marion Bloom, and Stephen Dedalus. The technique of **'the stream-of-consciousness'** or **'interior**

monologue' which Joyce uses attempts to show the unedited flow of a character's unspoken thought and emotion and to catch the very movement of the wandering mind in its reaction to external stimuli and the chain of associations prompted by the outside world and its own drifting course. Such a technique, of course, cannot show a character eating breakfast or having a bath and then refuse to show him defecating or masturbating. Joyce certainly has no prurient or voyeuristic aims but simply strives for the utmost frankness in dealing with natural functions and urges. His intention in *Ulysses* is **to show life as it really is** — and this demands the depiction not only of the traditionally acceptable human functions but also of lust, perversion, and even blasphemy.

The naturalist style in fiction has gradually been taken for granted in the twentieth century. It has in fact become possible for an author like Philip Roth to write in his novel *Portnoy's Complaint* (1969) about a character who is obsessed with sex and is tortured by his erotic fantasies and to focus practically exclusively on the psycho-sexual problems of his protagonist. We can see in this development not only the result of Joyce's pioneering work but also perhaps the reflection of a widespread dissatisfaction with the sordidness of big-city life and a general feeling of frustration in the face of the dismal and dreary quality of so much of modern existence, especially of the dehumanising work process — all this seems strongly to invite the approach of the writer in the naturalist style. The naturalist novel of the last few decades is however different from that before World War I in that it is concerned less with the philosophy of mechanistic determinism which characterizes earlier realist and naturalist fiction than with the technical problems of the fictional presentation of the naturalist's candid look at life.

Realist fiction

<table>
<tr><td rowspan="4">The realist novel
Realist fiction
The novel in the realist style
Fiction in the realist style</td><td colspan="3">reflects a widespread dissatisfaction with life.</td></tr>
<tr><td rowspan="2">exposes</td><td colspan="2">the hopelessness and shallowness of the materialism of middle-class life.</td></tr>
<tr><td>the dreary emptiness of</td><td>stagnant village life.
life in a competitive society.</td></tr>
<tr><td>sets out to present</td><td colspan="2">the realities of human existence in all their nakedness.
the stark realities of life.</td></tr>
</table>

p. t. o.

<table>
<tr><td rowspan="5">The realist novel
Realist fiction
The novel in the realist style
Fiction in the realist style</td><td colspan="3">presents a grim view of life.
conveys with sincerity an atmosphere of heart-breaking drabness.</td></tr>
<tr><td>faithfully</td><td>describes
depicts</td><td>the iniquities of the big city.
the suffering of the oppressed.</td></tr>
<tr><td colspan="3">confronts the reader with the baser instincts in man and society.</td></tr>
<tr><td rowspan="2">is sometimes</td><td colspan="2">used as a medium for the propagation of reforms.</td></tr>
<tr><td>put in the service of</td><td>a protest against human degradation.
a reforming design.</td></tr>
<tr><td rowspan="3">The style of realism
The realist mood</td><td colspan="3">is a reaction against romanticism.
is directed against a romanticist attitude.</td></tr>
<tr><td>is based on</td><td colspan="2">the experience of pain, frustration, and impotent anger in many people's lives.
a loss of faith in the meaningfulness of the universe.
a view of the world and man's life in it as a meaningless chaos.
the belief that the universe is devoid of meaning and that man's life does not make sense.
a fundamental intellectual scepticism.
the doctrine of mechanistic determinism.</td></tr>
<tr><td colspan="2">is the expression of a philosophical</td><td>scepticism.
pessimism.
nihilism.</td></tr>
</table>

Naturalist fiction

<table>
<tr><td rowspan="3">The naturalist novel
Naturalist fiction
The novel in the naturalist style
Fiction in the naturalist style</td><td rowspan="3">wants to
sets out to</td><td colspan="2">take a totally candid look at life.</td></tr>
<tr><td>present</td><td>human life as it really is.
the truth of human nature.</td></tr>
<tr><td>show</td><td>the physical and biological aspect of human existence.
the physical essence of man and his environment.</td></tr>
</table>

<table>
<tr><td rowspan="5">The style of naturalism
The naturalist mood</td><td colspan="3">has many elements in common with the style of realism.
shares with realism an attitude of pessimistic determinism.
concentrates more than realism does on the physical and biological side of human life.</td></tr>
<tr><td colspan="3">wants to be faithful to the true nature of human life.
is concerned with total physical candour.
strives for a total candour in dealing with natural functions and urges.
is utterly frank about the basic processes of life.</td></tr>
<tr><td rowspan="2">sees man</td><td colspan="2">as a product of the evolutionary process.
as a being who is not responsible for the shape of his character.</td></tr>
<tr><td>primarily as a product of</td><td>natural forces.
the social milieu.
genetic influences.</td></tr>
<tr><td>regards people</td><td colspan="2">as being moulded by circumstance.
as ‘chemisms’ whose total make-up is predetermined.</td></tr>
</table>

The realist and naturalist desire to present life with frank objectivity and to be committed to truth and to nothing else led novelists not only to attempt a presentation of aspects of human life which had before been avoided but also to question the validity of the long-established conventions of narrative technique. **If truth was the aim, then some of the long-accepted narrative conventions would have to be reconsidered.** The convention of having the story presented by an omniscient narrator was felt to be particularly offensive — how could one possibly regard as true to life this godlike knowledge of everything that went on? It seemed a much better idea to replace the omniscient narrator by a narrator who is also a character in the story and as such can only recount what he himself sees and hears. In this way one would be much nearer the truth as human beings can know it. By breaking up the narration into what this **observer-narrator** (for details about the narrative process cf. 7.2) actually sees and what he only assumes he is seeing, an effect can be achieved in fiction that is reminiscent of the technique of the French impressionist painters of the late nineteenth century. They tried to show in their pictures that our perception of the visible world is made up of a great number of visual data, of details of light and colour, which together produce a totality of visual perception so that the objects we see seem to be endowed with a firm solidity whereas in reality they are much less definite.

To a certain extent the **impressionist technique** used by painters like Manet or Renoir, which consists in breaking down the visible world into innumerable details of light and colour, can also be employed in fiction. As in those paintings in which a whole scene is suggested through the careful selection of a few dots of colour, the novelist can achieve a similar effect by **a technique of implication** which forces the reader to fill in the details himself. The reader is told what the characters say or do, but there are strictly no authorial comments to guide him in the interpretation of what is presented. He is left to draw his own conclusions. In four or five brief lines of dialogue, masters of this style of meaningful omission like Ernest Hemingway or Evelyn Waugh can convey as much as novelists using a conventional narrative technique manage to say in as many pages. The cooperation of the reader is of course essential when this style is used.

As regards the dialogue, writers in this style sometimes attempt to present speech as it is actually spoken, with all the halting utterances of real-life speech. The idea behind this is that most characters in conventional fiction are impossibly articulate and well-spoken and that the kind of editing process that gives clarity to the often rather meaningless dialogue of real life and produces this artificial articulateness must be stopped if a truthful picture of reality is to be achieved. A development of this technique is the presentation of the stream-of-consciousness, which also eschews editing. It is a typically impressionistic device which enables the writer to show **pre-articulatory thoughts, emotions and sense impressions** which have not been brought into a clearly rational order and thereby to achieve a strong sense of immediacy — the reader is inevitably drawn into the character's consciousness.

Another aspect of the impressionist style is the treatment of time as if it were forever dissolving and reconstituting itself. Temporal progression in strictly chronological order is abandoned for a number of **fragmentary impressions** through which the total picture can be perceived. Ford Madox Ford's *The Good Soldier* (1915), for example, makes extensive use of this technique. The narrator, who is not omniscient but limited in his knowledge to what a fallible human being can know, recounts his story in the form of stringing together his reminiscences. These are

however not arranged in a chronological order, but the narrator ranges freely through time, thereby fragmenting whole sequences of events.
The impressionist style of writers of the early twentieth century has had an immense influence throughout the century, and techniques such as the interior monologue, **an impressionist dialogue,** which gives only the words as they are actually spoken, and **the broken-down time continuum** have become generally accepted.

Impressionist fiction

<table>
<tr><td rowspan="7">The impressionist style
Impressionist writing
Impressionist fiction</td><td>gives only
merely presents</td><td>a number of fragmentary impressions.</td></tr>
<tr><td colspan="2">stimulates the reader's imagination.
is intensely implicational.
constantly asks the reader to cooperate.</td></tr>
<tr><td colspan="2">does not describe, explain, or moralize, but simply presents impressions.
omits every word which does not help to create a certain atmosphere.
conveys a maximum of meaning in a few lines.
makes use of a spare brilliance of observation.</td></tr>
<tr><td>presents</td><td>real-life speech.
speech as it is actually spoken.
action and speech without comment.</td></tr>
<tr><td colspan="2">makes use of an observer-narrator.</td></tr>
<tr><td colspan="2">shows pre-articulatory thought, feeling, and sensuous perception.
employs the technique of the interior monologue.
makes use of the stream-of-consciousness.
achieves a strong sense of immediacy.</td></tr>
<tr><td colspan="2">breaks down the time continuum.
ignores the chronological order of events.</td></tr>
</table>

Twentieth-century novelists drew inspiration also from the **expressionist style,** which derives from the movement of Expressionism which arose in Germany at the beginning of this century. It found its most congenial artistic media in painting and drama, and its most persistent influence has in fact been in the theatre and the film, but it sometimes also found expression in poetry and in prose fiction.

We can say that the decisive feature of expressionism is **a radical revolt against realism.** Instead of imitating reality, the writer wants to express inner experience by depicting the world as it appears to his state of mind, or to that of one or more of his characters, and it is generally a troubled or even an abnormal mental condition. Or he may undertake to convey the essence of a particular theme or an important idea. In any case, fidelity to life as it really is or probability of action in the old realist sense play a very minor role or are sacrificed altogether.

The greatest of the expressionist novelists was **Franz Kafka,** who created a hallucinatory atmosphere which is appropriate to nightmare in his novels *The Trial (Der Prozeß,* 1925) and *The Castle (Das Schloß,* 1926). His intention was apparently to express **the theme of man's alienation from the world around him** and to imply that the state of mind of his characters is representative of anxiety-ridden man in an industrial and technological age which is moving in the direction of disintegration and chaos.

The central conviction of expressionism, that **the presentation of a particular theme is more important than the imitation of reality,** has exerted a considerable influence among novelists, and especially among those who try **to follow propagandistic or didactic aims** in their fiction. In his trilogy of novels *U.S.A.* (1930—36), for example, **John Dos Passos** attempted to present a massive indictment of America and to show up the defeat of the individual on all fronts. It is typical of the expressionist style of these novels that the narrative focus is on many characters, swinging from one to another and often leaving them again rather abruptly; some of them never re-appear even though the reader's interest in them has been aroused — the attack on the values of the dehumanising society of the United States clearly takes precedence over the depiction of character or the arrangement of plot. Typically expressionist is also the use of a number of literary devices which have been taken over from expressionist theatre, such as Brecht's plays with their symbols, music, dance, choral speech, etc. This is to say that Dos Passos employs **devices such as headlines, newsreels,** biographies of important men and women published in **tabloid newspapers, popular songs, esoteric verse,** and the like, presumably in order to emphasize the documentary nature of the trilogy.

Generally speaking, one can say that although the expressionist style is still occasionally used by novelists — such as William Burroughs, who in his *Nova Express* (1964) employs obscene fantasy for the presentation of a kind of metaphysical struggle between enslaved flesh and free spirit — it has never become a dominant force in fiction comparable with that of the impressionist style. All in all, it seems as if expressionism in fiction belongs more among the experimental techniques than among generally accepted historical or contemporary styles. Expressionist elements can indeed be found in many works of twentieth century fiction, but they hardly ever determine the character of the work as a whole.

Expressionist fiction

<table>
<tr><td rowspan="7">The expressionist style
Expressionist writing
Expressionist fiction</td><td colspan="4">revolts radically against realism.
is not interested in imitating reality in the usual sense.</td></tr>
<tr><td rowspan="2">wants to express
undertakes to convey</td><td colspan="3">inner experience.</td></tr>
<tr><td>the essence of</td><td colspan="2">a particular theme
an important idea.</td></tr>
<tr><td colspan="4">shows the world not as it really is but as it appears to the state of mind of the writer or of a character.</td></tr>
<tr><td>sacrifices</td><td colspan="3">fidelity to real life.
probability of action.</td></tr>
<tr><td>typically</td><td>uses
makes use of
employs</td><td colspan="2">a number of devices taken over from non-literary media.</td></tr>
<tr><td>sometimes uses</td><td colspan="3">a dislocated time-sequence.
a stylized dialogue.</td></tr>
</table>

One could claim with some justification that change has been the dominant mood of the twentieth century. More important, however, than the *fact* of change as such, with its vast social and economic upheavals, seems to be the accelerated *pace* of change, which leaves scarcely any time for the assimilation of new situations.
Unassimilated change is certainly one of the most important reasons for the quickened succession of **experimental movements**, such as the production of throw-away art, the staging of "happenings", the concern with anti-literate theatre, and experimenting with innumerable avant-garde techniques.
It lies in the nature of experimental works that they break with the conventions of a dominant literary tradition. In the twentieth century, this break has been directed mainly against nineteenth-century realism, that is to say against the conventions of mimesis and against conventional ways of looking at man and society and of defining the nature of reality. Much experimentalism has also been – at least in part — a reaction to new intellectual tendencies, such as the growth of Freudian psychology, of theories of economic determinism and of sociology and anthropology, all of which made the art of realism, in the sense of mimetic presentation, seem somehow inadequate because it can capture only the illusion of surface reality. **The protest against the conventions of realism in fiction has taken many**

forms, but they can perhaps all be subsumed under the styles of impressionism and expressionism. In fact, even a work like James Joyce's *Finnegan's Wake* (1939), which employs for its attempt to realize a comprehensive vision of human experience a language that is largely made up of a great number of invented words and cryptic puns from many languages, remains within the impressionist style, even though it clearly pushes it to the limit. Novels of Samuel Beckett like *Molloy* (1951) and *The Unnameable* (1953), on the other hand, stay firmly within the expressionist tradition. They are often felt to be entirely revolutionary in that they reject realistic settings, logical reasoning and a consistently evolving plot and tend to destroy the logical and syntactical coherence of language itself, their own medium. But although Beckett's fiction is no doubt truly remarkable in its technical presentation, this aspect of his novels is not his main concern. In fact, he is typically expressionist in subordinating everything to his central theme — the showing up of the senseless irrationalism and absurdity of life and of the character of man as a totally deprived creature resentful of a God he cannot believe in. (cf. also his *Waiting for Godot,* 1954). So it is not surprising that Beckett presents man's language as inadequate for the expression of the human condition.

We can say that **this concern with man in his loneliness is indeed the dominant theme in twentieth century fiction,** but it is of course expressed in a great variety of ways and with vastly different emphases. What many writers seem to have in common is a conviction that the social circumstances that press so closely on the individual are, in the last analysis, irrelevant to the meaning of experience; in other words, if one is looking for meaning in life, the social context cannot any longer provide it. It is thus not surprising that after a period of probing analysis and diagnosis, which all tended to underline man's essential loneliness, there should be a revival of interest in a novelistic presentation of truth, and therefore of meaning, as it is seen by writers of various shades of religious conviction. Writers in the Catholic tradition (e.g. Graham Greene's *The Heart of the Matter,* 1948), or in the Protestant tradition (e.g. Joyce Cary's *A Prisoner of Grace,* 1952), or the authors of new allegorical novels in which a denominational background is irrelevant (e.g. William Golding's *The Lord of the Flies,* 1954), have apparently all taken to heart a saying by Eugene Ionesco, one of the leading writers of the drama of the absurd, who wrote: "Cut off from his religious, metaphysical, and transcendental roots, man is lost; all his actions become senseless, absurd, useless."[6] In fact, the writers of **'the religious revival',** if one can call them so, **set out to hint at the possibility of finding meaning in life in some form of religious commitment.**

Writers under the influence of **existentialist philosophy,** on the other hand, have found themselves unable to provide positive answers in any form. The world they present is **a fantastic and nightmarish world in which comic, brutal, horrifying, and absurd events take place simultaneously.** In this they demonstrate their "rebellion against the essential beliefs and values both of traditional culture

and traditional literature. Central to this earlier tradition had been the assumptions that man is a rational creature who lives in an at least partially intelligible universe, that he is part of an orderly social structure, and that he is capable of heroism and dignity even in defeat."[7] In opposition to these beliefs, each man is now seen as an isolated being who is mercilessly thrown into an alien universe which possesses no inherent human truth, value, or meaning. Man's life is consequently presented as a form of existence which is both anguished and absurd. Man's tragedy consists in the fact that in his search for identity and meaning he cannot find either, as he has no means of seeing through the opaque spatio-temporal world to its meaning, purpose, and central nature. He cannot rely on other people or on any moral system because he can never be certain of anything outside himself. In effect, he is totally free, left alone with his moral decisions, but totally responsible for them, and above all totally isolated.
When this existentialist attitude finds expression in fiction, as it frequently does in the works of post-war writers, it is often coupled with **black humour** (e.g. Joseph Heller's *Catch-22,* 1961), apparently in an attempt to make the basically absurd situation a bit more tolerable. Its main feature is however always the presentation of the isolation of the individual and his inability to establish satisfactory and lasting relationships with others, but his search for identity, which never comes to an end, and the absurdity of the world in general, in which **the "tragic farce"** (Ionesco) **of man's life** takes place, can also be emphasized.

Experimental fiction

<table>
<tr><td rowspan="6">Experimental fiction</td><td>is a reaction to</td><td colspan="2">shifts in society.
social and economic upheavals.
the accelerated pace of change.
unassimilated change.
new intellectual tendencies.</td></tr>
<tr><td>regards</td><td rowspan="2">the conventions of realism</td><td>as inadequate.</td></tr>
<tr><td>protests against</td><td>in many forms.</td></tr>
<tr><td rowspan="2">breaks with</td><td>the conventions of</td><td>a dominant literary tradition.
nineteenth-century realism.
mimetic presentation.</td></tr>
<tr><td>conventional ways of</td><td>looking at man and society.
defining the nature of reality</td></tr>
<tr><td colspan="3">is concerned with experiments in technical presentation.</td></tr>
</table>

p. t. o.

Experimental fiction (continued)

Experimental fiction	uses avant-garde techniques.
	wants to be revolutionary.

Fiction of 'the religious revival'

Fiction of 'the religious revival' Fiction influenced by a religious attitude towards life	is concerned with the presentation of man's search for meaning in life. hints at the possibility of finding meaning. sometimes makes use of an allegorical presentation of truth.

Fiction influenced by existentialism

Fiction influenced by existentialism Fiction influenced by theories of the absurd Existentialist fiction	rebels against the essential beliefs and values both of traditional culture and traditional literature.	
	sometimes rejects	realistic setting. logical reasoning. a consistently evolving plot.
	is concerned with man's essential loneliness.	
	sets out to show the	senseless irrationality and absurdity of life. character of man as a totally free being.
	presents	man as being totally free. man as being totally isolated. man's life as meaningless and absurd. a fantastic and nightmarish world.

p. t. o.

<table>
<tr><th colspan="4">Fiction influenced by existentialism (continued)</th></tr>
<tr><td rowspan="5">Fiction influenced by existentialism
Fiction influenced by theories of the absurd
Existentialist fiction</td><td rowspan="3">tends to stress</td><td colspan="2">the isolation of the individual.</td></tr>
<tr><td>the individual's</td><td>lack of identity.
inability to establish satisfactory and lasting relationships with others.</td></tr>
<tr><td colspan="2">the opacity and absurdity of the world.</td></tr>
<tr><td colspan="3">emphasizes the 'tragic farce' of man's life.</td></tr>
<tr><td colspan="3">cannot provide positive answers to questions about the meaning of existence.</td></tr>
</table>

Comprehension and revision

1) Name the typical features of the styles of writing discussed above.
2) What is typical of fiction in the nineteenth century?
3) What distinguishes twentieth century fiction?
4) Explain the reasons for the lack of a dominant style of writing in the present century.

6.3 Functions and uses of the novel

There seem to be few limits on what a good novelist can do with the novel. It can fulfil a number of functions and has in fact been put to many uses.

Very commonly, novels are **an expression of an interpretation of life.** These novels are not usually meant to be didactic, but, in varying degrees of implicitness, they express a philosophy of life, a world-view. In bourgeois fiction (e.g. in Jane Austen), life is seen as essentially good and just, with a well-ordered universe behind it. Or it may be regarded very pessimistically by writers in the tradition of realism (e.g. Thomas Hardy) as showing no sense of justice at all so that evil and stupidity must prevail; nothing of what happens is for the best, and the universe is seen as malevolent. Writers in the 'Catholic' tradition (e.g. Graham Greene), who view this attitude as morbid, tend to express in their novels a philosophy of life which accepts life for what it is in their view — mysterious, full of evil and injustice, but also full of hope, in any case inexplicable in merely human terms — because of their belief in an inscrutable, but somehow benevolent God. Novels can also be based on a philosophy of optimistic liberalism (as in the case of H.G. Wells), on the doctrine of the strength of 'natural man' (as in Hemingway), or they can express the assumption that man is imperfect and life possibly or definitely absurd (as with writers in the existentialist tradition). We can say that the novel as an expression of a certain view of existence generally reflects certain historical developments; realistic pessimism, for instance, obviously has much to do with the agnosticism and determinism which dominated nineteenth century science.

Novels are also very often used for the purposes of **entertainment or escape.** A well-known and highly-valued writer like Graham Greene has in fact no scruples about calling his books not novels but 'entertainments', but novelists who primarily seek to take the reader away from a humdrum existence and from his often dull and oppressive daily life are not generally highly esteemed. It is apparently taken for granted by many 'serious' critics that a novel ought to be committed to the exposure of social injustices or the propagation of progressive ideas and not function as a mere form of diversion. Nevertheless, the provision of laughter and dreams has always been regarded as one of the legitimate occupations of literature. This point of view is well put in this extract from an article on the novel in an encyclopedia: The use of the novel as a form of diversion

> can be condemned by serious devotees of literature only if it falsifies life through oversimplification and tends to corrupt its readers into belief that reality is as the author presents it. The novelettes once beloved of mill girls and domestic servants, in which the beggar maid was elevated to queendom by a king of high finance, were a mere narcotic, a sort of enervating opium of the oppressed; the encouragement of such subliterature might well be one of the devices of social oppression. Adventure stories and spy novels may have a healthy enough astringency, and the very preposterousness of some adventures can be a safeguard against any impressionable young reader's neglecting the claims of real life to dream of becoming a secret agent....
>
> Any reader of fiction has a right to an occasional escape from the dullness or misery of his existence, but he has critical duty of finding the best modes of escape — in the most efficiently engineered detective or adventure stories, in humor that is more than sentimental buffoonery, in dreams of love that are not mere pornography. The fiction of entertainment and escape frequently sets itself higher literary standards than novels with a profound social or philosophical purpose. Books like James Buchanan's *Thirty-nine Steps* (1915), Graham Greene's *Travels with My Aunt* (1969), Dashiell Hammett's *Maltese Falcon* (1930), and Raymond Chandler's *Big Sleep* (1939) are distinguished pieces of writing that, while diverting and enthralling, keep a hold on the realities of human character. Ultimately, all good fiction is entertainment, and if it instructs or enlightens it does so best through enchanting the reader.[8]

Novels have occasionally been used for **propaganda** purposes. We must, however, distinguish here between purely propagandist novels, which quickly become dated as soon as the injustices they attack are put right or are superseded by some new ones, and novels which primarily have an aesthetic purpose but which are also concerned with social, religious, or political issues in such a way that the reader is somehow put under a moral obligation to do something about them, or at least to feel indignant at the situation described. Pure propaganda novels, such as a large portion of Communist fiction, are often dull and unreal because they too frequently neglect man as a totality and view him almost exclusively in terms of social phenomena or politics. A writer like Charles Dickens, on the other hand, who drew his reader's attention to some of the grave social wrongs of his time, such as the horrors of poor-houses in his *Oliver Twist* (1838), was able to go beyond these topical issues by giving his attacks on social injustices a timeless human validity, mainly through the vitality with which he presented his material in the form of an intense drama of character conflict. If the reader's reaction does not lead to an immediate desire for action, possibly of a violent kind, but to a modification of his own sensibility, then this fusion of propagandist purpose with aesthetic intention can be considered one of the legitimate functions of serious fiction.

As books like Truman Capote's *In Cold Blood* (1965) and Norman Mailer's *The Armies of the Night* (1968) have shown, the documentary report can gain strength through its presentation in fictional form. The tendency to present fiction as **reportage** goes back to the example of Defoe, who presented his *Journal of the Plague Year* (1722), a fictional re-creation of the London plague of 1665, in the form of plain journalistic reportage. The example he had set was however not followed until the middle of the present century when factual material and actual events were again presented in a basically novelistic approach, but disguised as reportage. Mailer's *Armies of the Night,* for example, seems to merge the art of fiction with the craft of reportage and records, in highly personal detail but narrated in the third person, his part in a protest march on Washington, D.C.

It is rare, but not totally unheard-of, for a novelist to influence attitudes to life and supply the vocabulary of such attitudes, as opposed to effecting actual changes in the social and political order, which was achieved by books such as Karl Marx's *Das Kapital* or Adolf Hitler's *Mein Kampf*. The novel can in fact sometimes function as **an agent of change in the language and thought of a culture.** In support of this claim we need only point to George Orwell's *1984* (1949), which expressed in a brilliant manner the political choices which are open to mankind in the second half of the twentieth century. By coining terms such as "Big Brother", in the sense of 'leader of an authoritarian state', and "doublethink", meaning 'a paradoxical belief in contradictory ideas', Orwell also considerably influenced and modified the political vocabulary of English.

The novel has, in varying degrees, always been used as **an expression of the spirit of its age.** This use of the novel is neatly summed up in the following text:

> The novelist, like the poet, can make the inchoate thoughts and feelings of a society come to articulation through the exact and imaginative use of language and symbol. In this sense, his work seems to precede the diffusion of new ideas and attitudes and to be the agent of change. But it is hard to draw a line between this function and that of expressing an existing climate of sensibility. Usually the

nature of a historical period — that spirit known in German as the *Zeitgeist* — can be understood only in long retrospect, and it is then that the novelist can provide its best summation . . .

The novel can certainly be used as a tool for the better understanding of a departed age. The period following World War I has been caught forever in Hemingway's *The Sun Also Rises* (1926), F. Scott Fitzgerald's novels and short stories about the so-called Jazz Age, the *Antic Hay* (1923) and *Point Counter Point* (1928) of Aldous Huxley, and others.

Similarly, the unrest and bewilderment of the young in the period after World War II still speak in novels like J.D. Salinger's *Catcher in the Rye* (1951) and Kingsley Amis' *Lucky Jim* (1954). It is notable that with novels like these — and the beat-generation books of Jack Kerouac; the American-Jewish novels of Saul Bellow, Bernard Malamud, and Philip Roth; and the Negro novels of Ralph Ellison and James Baldwin — it is a segmented spirit that is expressed, the spirit of an age group, social group, or racial group, and not the spirit of an entire society in a particular phase of history. But probably a *Zeitgeist* has always been the emanation of a minority, the majority being generally silent. The 20th century seems, from this point of view, to be richer in vocal minorities than any other period in history.[9]

The novel can last of all also be used as **an expression of mythic and symbolic truth.** It happens again and again that the aesthetic value of a novel is determined by subliminal forces which invest the elements of the story that is set forth with a deeper mythical or symbolic significance. These forces apparently operate independently of the writer's conscious preoccupation with the presentation of incident, the portrayal of character, and the handling of exposition, conflict and resolution. Sometimes, however, writers deliberately set out to give a work of fiction a significance beyond that of a mere story. This is for example the case in James Joyce's *Ulysses* (1922) or John Updike's *Centaur* (1963), which are based on classical myths. These myths are obviously meant first of all to ennoble a lowly subject matter and then also to hold down a complex and, as it were, centrifugal picture of existence. As regards Joyce's *Ulysses,* there can be no doubt that with the help of the classical parallel the account of an ordinary summer day in Dublin, which makes up the 'story' of this book, is infused with a richness, irony and universality which could not have been accomplished by any other method. The mythical or symbolic intention of a novel may also manifest itself in little, seemingly factual, details or even in the choice of a character's name. For instance, the name of Sammy Mountjoy in William Golding's *Free Fall* (1959) symbolizes a person who has by an act of his own free will fallen from the grace of heaven, the mount of joy, as the title also implies. There are also some novels which are an expression of some hidden mythical or symbolic truth, even though it cannot easily be stated what that truth is as it seems to subsist on an unconscious level. Melville's *Moby Dick* (1851), the story of the hunting of a white whale, is a case in point.

Thus, to recapitulate, we encounter in the novel a literary form which has proved itself capable of being a vehicle for the expression of many concepts, intentions and meanings. It frequently transcends the mere telling of a story and the setting forth of character and interprets life in that it embodies a world-view and comments on the meaning of existence. It may provide entertainment and escape; sometimes it is also used for the purposes of propaganda and of heightening the effectiveness of factual reports; it can in rare cases even function as an agent of change in the language and thought of a culture and as the expression of mythical and symbolic truth; more commonly, however, the novel is simply an expression of the spirit of its age.

Revision and discussion

1) What functions can the novel fulfil and what can it be used for?
2) What interpretations of life can be expressed?
3) Why is entertainment a legitimate use of the novel?
   What can make this use illegitimate or dangerous?
4) Should the novel be used for propaganda purposes? Discuss.
5) When is fiction nobler — when it is purely fictional or when it is more or less a record of real life? Discuss.
6) In what ways can the novel function as an agent of change? Try to list a few such influential novels and to say what their influence has mainly consisted in.
7) Explain what is meant when it is said that the novel is an expression of
   — the spirit of its age;
   — mythical and symbolic truth.
8) What could be the reasons for the fact that there are so many different expressions of 'the spirit of the age' after World War II? Discuss.

Suggestions for further study

1) Try to find out more about
   — bourgeois fiction;
   — the fiction of realism;
   — the 'Catholic' tradition in fiction;
   — fiction about 'natural man';
   — existentialist fiction;
   and about the most important and influential exponents of each of these traditions.
2) Prepare a short talk or write a paper on
   — any of the writers who produced distinguished fiction mainly for the purpose of entertainment;
   — Charles Dickens as a social critic;
   — Truman Capote or Norman Mailer and their fiction;
   — George Orwell and the ideas he put forward in his *1984;*
   — Hermann Melville's use of symbols in his *Moby Dick.*

Functions and uses of the novel

<table>
<tr><td rowspan="8">The novel</td><td rowspan="6">can function as
can be used as</td><td colspan="2">a vehicle for the expression of many concepts, intentions and meanings.</td></tr>
<tr><td>an expression of</td><td>an interpretation of life.
a world-view.
a philosophical conviction.
a religious belief.
a philosophy of life.
a comment on the meaning of existence.
the spirit of its age.
the existing climate of sensibility.
mythical and symbolic truth.</td></tr>
<tr><td colspan="2">entertainment and escape.
a form of diversion.
a mere narcotic.
a sort of enervating opium.</td></tr>
<tr><td colspan="2">propaganda.</td></tr>
<tr><td colspan="2">a fictional strengthening of reportage.</td></tr>
<tr><td colspan="2">an agent of change in the language and thought of a culture.
a tool for the better understanding of a departed age.
the articulation of the inchoate thoughts and feelings of a society.
a summation of a historical period.</td></tr>
<tr><td rowspan="2">may</td><td colspan="2">instruct and enlighten the reader.
draw the reader's attention to some of the grave social wrongs of the reader's time.
lead to a modification of the reader's sensibility.
take the reader away from a humdrum existence.
enchant the reader.</td></tr>
<tr><td colspan="2">interpret life.
embody a world-view.</td></tr>
</table>

p. t. o.

Functions and uses of the novel (continued)

The novel	may	influence modify	attitudes to life.	
		provide	laughter and dreams. entertainment and escape.	
		falsify life through oversimplification.		
		deal with	topical controversial	issues.
		be concerned with	social political religious philosophical	issues.
		be committed to the	exposure of social wrongs. propagation of ideas.	

6.4 The theory of the novel

6.4.1 Literary theory and the novel

It is rather a strange phenomenon that the novel, which undoubtedly has been the chief form of printed fiction and perhaps the most influential literary genre for at least two centuries, should seem to be "an entity without a definition, an art without an aesthetic, and a tradition without a theory for perceiving its continuity."[10]

There are several reasons for this, and a first reason is suggested by the word "novel" itself — something new in the field of literature. At whatsoever point one dates the beginnings of the novel, a true sense of its generic identity is little more than two hundred years old. This is a comparatively short time, as artistic forms go, for the establishment of a substantial body of theory.

A further reason seems to lie in the fact that the novel has suffered from the widespread idea that it is an inferior art form. This is to say that its artistic integrity has not been taken with the same seriousness as that of other art forms. In part this appears to be due to the old prejudice against imaginative literature which, in the last analysis, goes back to Plato who rejected poets from his ideal republic as he saw evil in all fiction. This prejudice against fiction centres on the notion that anything invented and imagined is 'fiction', in the sense of 'not true', and therefore constitutes something in the nature of a lie. This ancient charge against fiction was vigorously taken up during the puritan regime in Britain which, among other things, led to the closing of all the theatres. This distrust of fiction lingered on and as recently as 1862 a Quaker, Arthur J. Naish, could still write: "Indiscriminate novel-reading, or even frequent novel-reading, is about the most dangerous employment that can occupy a young person."[11] The low estimation of the novel as an art form also has to do with extra-artistic pressures brought to bear on it — by publishers, serializing editors, the tastes of the reading public and also, to a large extent, with the willingness of the novelists themselves to treat their artistic seriousness rather lightheartedly. Thus in the history of the novel we find Defoe, in the 18th century, stating quite explicitly that he is nothing but the editor of true memoirs, Dickens, in the 19th century, claiming to be simply a public entertainer, and Faulkner, in the present century, enjoying immensely the sport of pretending not to be a great writer. The very fact that a good many of the chief practitioners of the novel conspired to produce the impression that they and their art are anti-intellectual and even anti-artistic has certainly discouraged rather than encouraged the critics' interest in the theory of an art form which has refused to take itself seriously as art.

The main reason, however, for the fact that "literary theory and criticism concerned with the novel are much inferior in both quantity and quality to theory and criticism of poetry"[12] and that "criticism in the past has given to the novel little sense of its generic uniqueness, no very clear sense of its formal conventions, comparatively little sense of its aesthetic possibilities, and little sense of its origins"[13], lies in the very nature of the novel itself. It is first of all a mixed genre touching on reportage and history at one extreme and on high literary formalism at the other. Historically, it derives from a number of different forms, from epic and romance, from diary and letter, from biography and comic and sentimental drama, and so on. Through its use of the most familiar and open form of language and its apparent lack of strict formal conventions, the novel is, moreover, open to a wide variety of registers, structures and typologies and thus appears to be a highly eclectic and variable genre. All of this has made the task of the critic trying to work out a satisfactory theory of the novel a difficult one because a really adequate critical definition of the novel will have to cover all this traditional range of the flexibility and indeterminateness of the novel form. Finally, the novel has by its apparent link with realism given critics cause to doubt the possibility of establishing a general theory. What is meant is that these critics have seen the novel basically as a mimetic species (Gk mimesis = imitation), as a form of writing which imitates real life, life as we know it, so closely that it can hardly be distinguished from unfictionalized versions of reality, from non-fictional prose forms, particularly from those used in journalism, history and sociology. In other words, the difference between fiction and non-fiction seems to disappear, or to be too thin for the novel to be recognized as a respectable literary genre.

Another problem is that the novel forms a genre which can give form to certain attitudes concerning the social and historical situation and the general culture of which the novel is a part.

"Almost anything that one can say about Western culture from the beginning of the eighteenth century to the present can serve to characterize the novel since it is almost inevitable that the novel will express, criticize, or minister to that aspect of culture. Of society, one may speak of the decline of the organic community and the growth of individualism, the steadily increasing possibilities of class mobility, and the growth of urbanization — and all of these the novel as a genre concerns itself with. Of the transformations of consciousness, one may speak of the decline of belief, the growth of a secular ethic, and the increasing fragmentation of personality into professional and social segments — and the novel reflects, shapes, and enlarges upon these also. Of the great events of intellectual history, one may speak of the growth of psychology, sociology, and scientific method, the thought of Hume and Burke, Marx and Freud — and inevitably the emphases of intellectual history are the emphases of the novel. There is something slightly circular in defining the novel by defining the dominant traits of the culture in which the novel occurs; yet it is a way of looking at the identity of the novel which can hardly be ignored, since the novel tends to insist upon its own cultural relevance."[14]

Yet the criticism which the situation of the novel as understood in this text is apt to lead to stands in danger of treating the novel as a cultural and ideological document, a case history or a history of a life and its times rather than as art, and the novel's standing as a form of literary art is again neglected or at least underrated.

A last difficulty for theorists of the novel lies in the inextricable relation between any given element of a novel, such as character constellation, plot, point of view, etc., and the fictional structure as a whole in which it appears. This is to say that any theory which does not treat novels as organic wholes and tries to isolate certain parts is pointless because it ignores the fact that all the elements of the novel exist within a total form which is ultimately indivisible.

To sum up, all these factors have made the serious study of the novel in the sense of the establishment of a substantial body of theory rather difficult, and thus basic definitions and a clear critical terminology are still among the *desiderata* of literary scholarship.

Comprehension and discussion

1) What are the reasons for the phenomenon that literary criticism concerned with the novel has not been very successful in establishing a substantial body of theory?
2) Why has the novel been so often underrated as an art form?

3) Explain the prejudice against fiction.
   What forms of fiction are not valued at all highly even today and what could be the reasons for this?
4) Describe the situation of the novel as understood in the quoted text (ll. 65–81) in your own words.

Understanding the terminology

Try to paraphrase the underlined words and phrases:

a) The novel seems to be an entity without a definition, an art without an aesthetic, and a tradition without a theory for perceiving its continuity. (ll. 3–5)
b) A true sense of its generic identity is little more than two hundred years old. (ll. 8 f.)
c) The novel's 'artistic integrity' has been doubted. (ll. 12 f.)
d) This ancient charge against fiction ... (l. 19)
e) The novel is a mixed genre touching on reportage ... (l. 43)
f) It is open to a wide variety of registers, structures and typologies and thus appears to be a highly eclectic and variable genre. (ll. 48 f.)
g) The novel has been regarded as 'a mimetic species'. (ll. 55 f.)
h) ... unfictionalized versions of reality ... (l. 58)

For further study

1) Find out about Plato and his *Republic* in a good encyclopedia.
2) Try to find out about the closing of the theatres during the puritan regime in Britain and about their re-opening during the Restoration.
   You could use the information you have collected for a short talk in class.

Literary theory and the novel

<table>
<tr><td colspan="1">The novel has been</td><td colspan="3">the chief form of fiction
the most influential
literary genre</td><td colspan="2">for at least two
centuries.</td></tr>
<tr><td rowspan="3">A true sense
of its</td><td>generic</td><td>identity
uniqueness</td><td rowspan="3">was not</td><td rowspan="3">accomp-
lished
achieved
reached</td><td rowspan="3">for a long
time.</td></tr>
<tr><td>identity
uniqueness</td><td>as a genre</td></tr>
<tr><td colspan="2">formal conventions
aesthetic possibilities
origins</td></tr>
</table>

p. t. o.

Literary theory and the novel (continued)

The novel has been treated as a(n)	form of art. cultural and ideological document. case history. history of a life and its period. inferior form of art (artform).

<table>
<tr><td>A(n)</td><td>comprehensive
adequate
satisfactory</td><td>general theory of the novel</td><td rowspan="2">has not been established.
is still missing.</td></tr>
<tr><td colspan="3">A substantial body of theory concerning the novel</td></tr>
</table>

A critical definition of the novel Basic definitions A clear critical terminology	is/are still missing.

The serious study of the novel has hardly begun.

The novel as a fictional prose form differs greatly from	unfictionalized version of reality. non-fictional prose forms.

<table>
<tr><td rowspan="5">The nature of the novel is not easy to determine because</td><td>it is</td><td>a mixed genre.
a highly eclectic and variable genre.</td></tr>
<tr><td colspan="2">it touches on reportage and history at one extreme and on high literary formalism at the other.</td></tr>
<tr><td colspan="2">of the wide range of the flexibility and indeterminateness of the novel form.</td></tr>
<tr><td colspan="2">of the great variety of registers, structures and typologies.</td></tr>
<tr><td colspan="2">its apparent lack of strict formal conventions.</td></tr>
</table>

p. t. o.

<table>
<tr><th colspan="5">Literary theory and the novel (continued)</th></tr>
<tr><td rowspan="2">The novel</td><td>is a</td><td colspan="3">mimetic species.
form of writing which imitates real life, life as we know it.
respectable literary genre.
valid form of literary art.</td></tr>
<tr><td colspan="4">has cultural relevance.</td></tr>
<tr><td colspan="4">The old prejudice against imaginative literature
The ancient charge against fiction
The distrust of fiction
The low estimation of the novel as an art form</td><td>lingered on.</td></tr>
<tr><td colspan="5">The novel was regarded as an inferior art form.</td></tr>
<tr><td>Its artistic</td><td colspan="2">seriousness
integrity</td><td colspan="2">was doubted.</td></tr>
<tr><td colspan="3">All the elements of the novel</td><td colspan="2">contribute to the fictional structure as a whole.
form an organic whole.
exist within a total form which is ultimately indivisible.
stand in an inextricable relation to each other.</td></tr>
</table>

6.4.2 Problems of definition

Poetry, drama and novel constitute the three main kinds of literature, but whereas the first two are fairly easy to define the novel has always posed great problems of definition. A clear and unambiguous definition of what the novel is simply does not exist. Consider the following attempts at defining the novel and then try to say what the elements are that all these definitions have in common:

a) "A fictitious prose narrative of considerable length, in which characters and actions representative of real life are portrayed in a plot of more or less complexity." *(Shorter Oxford English Dictionary)*
b) "An invented prose narrative that is usually long and complex and deals with human experience through a connected sequence of events." *(Webster's New Collegiate Dictionary)*
c) "A fictitious narrative in prose, usually of sufficient length to fill a volume, portraying characters and situations from real life." *(Cassell's English Dictionary)*

d) "A fictitious prose narrative or tale presenting a picture of real life, especially of the emotional crises in the life-history of the men and women portrayed." *(Chambers Twentieth Century Dictionary)*

e) "A fictitious prose tale dealing with the adventures or feelings of imaginary persons so as to portray, by the description of action and thought, the varieties of human life and character." *(Collins's Dictionary)*

It is not difficult to see that all of these definitions, vague as they are, stress three defining constituents of novels. They are

— fictitious prose narratives
— involving characters and actions
— which must be true to real life or to human life and experience.

If, however, one takes a closer look at these three attributes one finds that only one element is totally unambiguous — that novels are **prose** narratives, as distinguished from **verse** narratives such as Chaucer's famous *Canterbury Tales* (14th century) or Spenser's *Faerie Queene* (16th century). All the other elements, which for brevity's sake can be subsumed under the heads 'fictionality', 'story' (including 'plot', 'action', and 'character'), and 'realism', are themselves complicated concepts which are not too easy to define.

If we consider the **concept of fictionality** and argue that a novel is essentially a work of fiction, something based on the author's imagination and his invention of events, situations and characters, then we run into difficulties with the so-called 'historical novels'. The events they describe have not been invented, but are firmly rooted in history. This is the case in many of Scott's novels, the so-called 'Waverley novels' which are grouped around various events in 18th century Scottish history, among them the Jacobite rising of 1745, which is the theme of *Waverley* (1814), the first of these novels. Another well-known example is Bulwer-Lytton's *The Last Days of Pompeii* (1834), a book which is concerned with what its title proclaims — the last days of a flourishing Roman town before the eruption of Vesuvius in 79 AD which practically buried the place and killed every living thing. Or novels may be largely biographical or autobiographical with the author telling the reader about certain formative events in the life of a historical figure or in his own life. In *The Moon and Sixpence* (1919), for example, the author, Somerset Maugham, tells about a stockbroker who forsakes his wife because of an urge to paint. Eventually he goes to Tahiti where he lives with a native woman. The book is clearly based on the life of Gauguin, the French painter, and the author makes little attempt to disguise this fact. Autobiographical material is included in Maugham's most famous novel *Of Human Bondage* (1915) in which Philip Carey, an orphan with a club foot tries in vain to become an artist. Of course, there is still a strong fictional element in the make-up of all these novels, but just what it is or how far it goes within the total conception of such a work is not easy to say. Still, the concept of fictionality is undoubtedly there; it is, however, hard to define. The situation is totally different in the case of books normally classed as novels in which the fictional element seems to have disappeared altogether. A case in point is Truman Capote's *In Cold Blood* (1965). In this 'non-fiction novel' the author does no more than lay before the reader the accumulated evidence he unearthed in several years of research about the brutal murder of a farmer's family by two psychotics — how they got to know about the family, their plans and expectations, how they carried out the murder, went away, and were finally caught and sentenced to death; yet for all this factual documentation *In Cold Blood* is still considered a novel, and not a mean one.

If the concept of fictionality is of somewhat doubtful standing as a defining characteristic of the novel, so is **the story element.** There are quite a number of first-rate novels where the story is of little or no importance. This is especially so in what has been called 'the didactic or propaganda novel' in which the author tries to influence the readers in a certain direction. Erico Jong's *Fear of Flying* (1973) is such a book: The author is mainly interested in putting across her femininist convictions and in showing the problems of a woman who wants to live freely and independently in what she sees is principally a man's world. Much of what 'happens' in this novel is a description of people's reactions when a woman demands the same freedom in sexual relations as a man. The story-line is also very thin in novels in which the so-called 'stream-of-consciousness technique' is used and in which consequently the internal action takes clear precedence over the external action. In Virginia Woolfe's *Mrs Dalloway* (1925), for instance, the incidents, if one can call them that, take place on a single summer day in the life of Clarissa Dalloway, but the substance of the book is contained in mental reflections and flashbacks that reconstruct Mrs Dalloway's past. Another group of novels where the concept of story presents some difficulty is made up of books in which we can find not only one but several stories. Sometimes this takes the form of a main story with a number of 'sub-plots' subordinate to it; sometimes the various stories are of equal status, as in Dickens' *Bleak House* (1852) which skilfully intermingles several stories to form "a vigorous satire on the abuses of the old court of Chancery, the delays and costs of which brought misery and ruin on its suitors."[15] That a novel can get along quite well without a proper story was brilliantly demonstrated as early as the 18th century by Laurence Sterne in his novel *The Life and Opinions of Tristram Shandy, Gent.* which appeared in several instalments between 1760 to 1767. The book presents very few incidents and is chiefly occupied with exposing the author's own personality and whimsical ideas. It offers the reader practically nothing of the life and opinions of the nominal hero, who is not even born until vol. iv and simply disappears from the book in vol. vi. Apparently Sterne was more interested in flouting the emergent conventions of novel-writing than in presenting a story, and yet the book succeeds brilliantly. Especially since the end of the nineteenth century a constant experimentation with new fictional techniques and procedures has been going on in which the traditional story element has been considered less and less important.

> In recent decades such experimentation has reached a radical extreme. Vladimir Nabokov is a supreme technician who writes "involuted fiction" (a work whose subject involves its own author, genesis, and development — for example, his *Pale Fire),* employs multilingual puns and jokes, incorporates strategies from chess, crossword puzzles, and other games, parodies other novels (and his own as well), and sets elaborate traps for the unwary reader. This is also the era of what is sometimes called the *anti-novel* — that is, a work which is deliberately constructed in a negative fashion, relying for its effects on emitting or annihilating traditional elements of the novel, and on playing against the expectations established in the reader by the novelistic methods and conventions of the past.[16]

This clearly goes to show that practically all the standard novelistic elements — characterization, descriptions of states of mind, normal relations of time and space, some frame of reference for the guidance of the reader, and above all a clear story line — can be thrown overboard and we may still be dealing with a novel (in the *Tristram Shandy* tradition), with a novel, that is, that functions precisely because it turns the standard conventions upside down.

A further weakness of the claim that a novel is essentially a long story lies in the fact that story-telling is a major element also in other narrative forms, notably the short story. And even there the plot story concept, as we have seen above (cf. ch. 5), is typical mainly of the tradition of the nineteenth century.

If 'fictionality' and 'story-telling' as defining attributes of the novel are problematic to a certain degree, perhaps the essence of the novel lies in its so-called **'realism of presentation'**, in its life-like portrayal of life-like characters and their actions in life-like situations. In fact, the case for realism as a defining characteristic of the novel is the strongest, but it poses some problems, too. There is first of all the basic fact that the concept of 'reality' is many-faceted and that consequently there is a certain element of uncertainty about the precise quality of what is regarded as 'real'. This is basically a philosophical problem, but it does have its repercussions on the evaluation of the degree to which any given novel gives a 'realistic' portrayal of people and their actions, or feelings and so on, in certain situations. Then there is an additional complication. Quite a number of widely-known and highly-valued books are undoubtedly 'unrealistic' in that they centre on situations that do not as such exist, have never existed and are not even likely ever to exist. The reference is here to some science fiction novels, such as Arthur C. Clarke's *2001, A Space Odyssey* (1968), and to utopian novels like George Orwell's *1984* (1949). In these and similar books a future situation is presented that is meant to throw some light on the present. But it is certainly odd to read about a computer falling in love, as in Clarke's book, and it is also very hard to imagine a situation in which the control exercised by the state over its population is total. In other words, books of that type are not 'realistic' in the sense of giving a true picture of the world as we know it. What is involved here is the presentation of an alternative world which must be accepted by the reader as 'real', during the time he reads the story, and only then can the action proceed as if the novel were dealing with a present or past, in any case a known, socio-cultural situation. These books, then, are 'realistic' only in as far as they show people who move in a world that is in a large measure or even totally foreign to us, but who — once the illusion the author has created is accepted — act, feel and think in accordance with the demands made on them by their situation.

The conclusion to be drawn from all the foregoing discussion is clearly this: Novels are notoriously difficult to define unambiguously, borderline cases are not infrequent, and it is always possible to point to certain books which are normally classed as novels but in which this or that element of those definitions of the novel that have been attempted is either missing or this element must be understood in a new sense. **All one can really say with any confidence is that the attributes of fictionality, story and realism are to be found in the vast majority of novels, but not necessarily in every novel.**

Leaving the theoretical aspect behind now and turning to **more practical problems,** we can diagnose a remarkable interpretative skill in most readers of novels. Practically everybody possesses what at first sight seems an astonishing ability which we never even think about — we can tell at once whether we are dealing with a novel or not. In other words, we know a novel as soon as we see one even if we are not able to give a precise and comprehensive definition of what a novel is. In fact, most readers can tell after the opening sentence whether the book they are reading is a novel or not. You can test yourself with the sentences in the following list. They have all been taken from famous books, and each is **the opening sentence.**[17]

1) When he was nearly thirteen, my brother Jem got his arm badly broken at the elbow.
2) No household in the English-speaking world is properly furnished unless it contains copies of the *Holy Bible* and of *The Works of William Shakespeare.*
3) I am always drawn back to places where I have lived, the houses and their neighbourhoods.
4) My father's family name being Pirrip, and my christian name Philip, my infant tongue could make of both names nothing longer or more explicit than Pip.
5) It is a commonplace to say that the British are a people of mixed blood.
6) I was set down from the carrier's cart at the age of three; and there with a sense of bewilderment and terror my life in the village began.
7) There is an old Anglican hymn of which I am very fond called "The Day Thou Gavest, Lord, Has Ended."
8) To many people conscience is almost all they have by way of knowledge of God.
9) He lay flat on the brown, pine-needle floor of the forest, his chin on his folded arms, and high overhead the wind blew in the tops of the pine trees.
10) Emma Woodhouse, handsome, clever, and rich, with a comfortable home and happy disposition, seemed to unite some of the best blessings of

existence; and had lived nearly twenty-one years in the world with very little to distress or vex her.

This was not a very serious test. You will certainly have noticed that sentences nos. 1,3,4,6,9, and 10 have been taken from novels, nos. 2,5, and 8 from non-novels, and that one cannot be quite sure about no. 7. The point is not whether you got the answers right but what enabled you to find the correct answers. **How** could you tell the sentences from novels from those from other prose writings?

The essential distinction seems to be between **concreteness** and **abstraction.** When a sentence conjures up a vivid picture in the mind of the reader he almost automatically assumes that a narrative is under way. When no such concrete pictorial or auditory image is created but a rather abstract idea or concept is offered instead, the reader does not think of a narrative. In other words, we have come to associate concrete imagery with novels and to connect specific information, hard facts and abstract ideas with non-novels.

This is the reason why no. 7 is a little difficult to classify. The sentence contains a highly personal statement by an I-narrator, but since a discussion of favourite church hymns does not figure very large in the novels he knows, the reader would be a little hesitant about attributing such a sentence to a novel. It is in fact the opening sentence of a rather controversial book which ran into many impressions offering a personal account of what the Church looks like to the outsider.[18]

This is to say that there is another criterion for distinguishing novels from prose forms which are not novels: One commonly associates **certain themes** with novels rather than non-novels, above all with the passage from a state of ignorance, innocence or moral blindness to a state of maturity and experience, from a situation of blissful ignorance through a process of gradual disillusionment to a mature recognition of the actual way of the world.[19] This is the reason why so many novels begin with the hero's birth or with some situation during his childhood (cp. nos. 1,4,6, perhaps even 10 above) and then pass on to describe his gradual initiation into the adult world and his recognition that the reality of the world is not identical with his dreams, wishes and desires. In other words, he is likely to discover that he has to let go of his pride and his wishful thinking, that there is no future for heroism, and that an adjustment to the realities of the material world and of human life in society necessarily involves the overcoming of his illusions. Thus, the protagonists of novels often move from the restricted awareness of childhood and adolescence to the wider experience of maturity; or, in the case of an older hero, he may come to realize that much of his previous life has been wasted, that he has lived in a state of illusion about himself or others, or both. In any case, at the end of the novel he has learned to see things differently and thus has gained new insights. He is no longer the person he was at the beginning and has changed in the direction of disillusionment and recognition. Appearances no longer deceive him, but it may be too late for him to do anything about that, if the novel ends tragically, or he may be able to start a new life, as in the case of a 'happy ending.' A great many variations are of course possible. Summing up, we can say that the novel characteristically deals with the difference between appearance and reality and that its themes centre around the notions of change and of education in the widest sense.

Another way of distinguishing the novel is through **structure**. Novels differ from other forms of prose writing in that they introduce conflicts and tensions concerning the main characters which are carried right through the whole length of the books and which are brought to a solution only at their ends. In other words, the novel presents an action, with all the materials that make up this action arranged and interrelated in such a way that an image of coherence, continuity and wholeness is created. We can say that the idea of the novel includes action and that a novel is a novel only inasfar as it is **a unified action,** that novels cohere as actions and that if the total architecture of a piece of prose does not support some sort of action, then it is not a novel but something else.

A very important distinguishing feature of novels and one that is not always admitted or seen is their close relationship of what they present with the reader's experience. The characters' behaviour must be **true to the reality of human experience.** As soon as one of the characters assumes super-human dimensions and becomes 'larger than life', in the sense of being stronger, wiser, more capable and resourceful than any of us, the work which contains such a character cannot legitimately be called a novel. In such a case we are dealing with a **romance.** (see 6.4.3 Novel and romance).

A last decisive criterion for distinguishing the novel not only from other prose forms in general, but from other narrative prose forms, such as the short story, is **the criterion of length.** But it is not an accident that of the five definitions of the novel given above only a, b and c mention 'length' as a distinguishing feature of the novel whereas d and e do not. The novel differs from shorter narrative forms by being an extended work of prose fiction, but what a phrase like 'of considerable length' really means is of course impossible to determine. We generally accept that **a novel fills a book,** yet how many pages it ought to have cannot be said with any precision. Compared with the short story, the novel is normally expected to contain a greater variety of characters, greater complication of plot, possibly involving a number of subplots, an ampler development of milieu, and a more sustained and subtle exploration of character[20]. Borderline cases are, of course, always possible; these are sometimes called 'long short stories', 'short novels', or 'novelettes' and 'novellas'. The last term, however, is ill-chosen because 'novella' is already used to designate the stories by Boccaccio and his imitators. Perhaps the most unambiguous term for a prose narrative which falls between the novel and the short story is **'novelette'.** A comprehensive definition is again difficult to give, but one can say that a novelette is longer than a short story and shorter than a novel; it tends to be less concentrated than the short story but does not have the diffuseness of the novel, which is to say that it is more limited as regards theme, plot, characters, descriptive narrative and background, so that there is a unity of mood comparable to the mood of the short story; on the other hand, character is usually developed as in the novel and not revealed as in the short story. A case in point is Steinbeck's *Of Mice and Men* (1937), which is a short narrative (95 pages in the Pan edition), has no subplots, the action is concentrated on events covering a short time and there are only about ten characters in the story, most of them relatively important. Another well-known example is Hemingway's *The Old Man and the Sea* (1952).

Comprehension and discussion

1) What are the main kinds of literature?
2) Name the defining constituents of the novel.
   Why is it so difficult to provide a comprehensive definition of the novel?
3) What is meant by the phrase 'the novel's realism of presentation'?
4) Name some of the conventions of the novel.
   What is a 'convention'? Try to give a definition
5) Are experimental novels useful? Are they necessary? Can they make an important contribution to literary developments?

For further study

1) Can you find some more examples of historical novels, biographical and autobiographical novels, propaganda novels, stream-of-consciousness novels, non-fiction novels, and novels without a proper story, in English, in your own language or in any other language?
2) Try to find out who Nabokov is and what he wrote.
3) What is meant by 'picaresque novel', 'novel of incident', 'novel of character', 'epistolary novel', 'Gothic novel', 'Bildungsroman', 'sociological novel', 'regional novel', 'roman à clef', and 'nouveau roman'? Can you find examples for each type.
   You will find relevant information in general works of reference and especially in a good dictionary of literary terms (consult the bibliography at the end of this book).
   Look first of all under 'novel'.

The novel — problems of definition

Poetry Drama Novel	are kinds of literature.

A(n)	clear unambiguous precise comprehensive adequate	definition of	the novel what the novel is	is impossible.

p. t. o.

The novel – problems of definition (continued)

<table>
<tr><td rowspan="3">A novel</td><td rowspan="2">is</td><td colspan="2">a unified action
a fictitious prose narrative
a fictitious narrative in prose
an invented prose narrative</td><td colspan="2">of considerable length.</td></tr>
<tr><td colspan="4">an extended work of prose fiction.</td></tr>
<tr><td colspan="5">fills a book.</td></tr>
<tr><td colspan="2">Defining
Distinguishing
Essential</td><td>features
characteristics
elements
attributes
constituents
traits</td><td colspan="2">of the novel include the criterion of</td><td>length.
fictionality.
action.
realism.
concreteness.</td></tr>
<tr><td colspan="2">The novel</td><td colspan="4">tends to present a slice of life itself.
gives a true picture of the world as we know it.
presents a picture of real life.
presents life as it really is.
represents ‘real’ men and women in ‘real’ situations.
portrays the varieties of human life and character.
gives a realistic portrayal of people and their behaviour.
tends towards giving the imaginary the formal guarantee of the real.
presents a fictional world which the reader must accept.
creates an illusion of reality.
introduces conflicts and tensions concerning the main characters.
presents an action.
coheres as action.</td></tr>
<tr><td colspan="3">The novel is concerned with
deals with</td><td colspan="3" rowspan="2">the difference between appearance and reality.
human experience.
change and education in the widest sense.</td></tr>
<tr><td colspan="3">The novel’s theme is</td></tr>
<tr><td colspan="2">Novels may be</td><td>concerned with
dealing with</td><td colspan="3">the author’s convictions.</td></tr>
</table>

p. t. o.

The novel – problems of definition (continued)

<table>
<tr><td>Novels may be</td><td>largely autobiographical.
written around historical events.
written for propaganda and didactic purposes.
made up of several stories.
made up of a main story with several subplots.
experimenting with new fictional techniques and procedures.</td></tr>
</table>

<table>
<tr><td colspan="2">The conventions of novel-writing</td><td rowspan="2">can be</td><td rowspan="2">turned upside down.
flouted.
experimented with.</td></tr>
<tr><td>The standard
The traditional</td><td>novelistic elements
conventions</td></tr>
</table>

<table>
<tr><td rowspan="5">The novelistic hero
The protagonist
The main character</td><td>passes from a state of</td><td>innocence
ignorance
moral blindness
illusion</td><td>to a state of</td><td>maturity.
experience.
recognition.
disillusionment.</td></tr>
<tr><td colspan="4">becomes disillusioned (gradually or abruptly).
reaches a mature recognition of the actual way of the world.
finds himself in a new situation.
realizes that the reality of the world is not identical with his dreams, wishes, fancies and desires.
adjusts to the realities of the material world and of human society.</td></tr>
<tr><td>overcomes his</td><td colspan="3">illusions.
fancies.
wishful thinking.</td></tr>
<tr><td>learns to see</td><td colspan="3">things differently.
through appearances.</td></tr>
<tr><td colspan="4">gains new insights.</td></tr>
</table>

<table>
<tr><td>A character</td><td>is true to life.
is larger than life.
assumes super-human dimensions.</td></tr>
</table>

<table>
<tr><td>A novelette is a prose narrative which falls between the novel and the short story.</td></tr>
</table>

6.4.3 Novel and romance

Many classifications of fiction have been tried, ranging from the all-too-easy identification of fiction with the novel to rather elaborate systems of classification. We do not, however, have to follow all the critical discussion about the generic identity of this or that line of tradition in fiction; for our purposes it is quite sufficient to look at the two by far most common forms of extended prose fiction, the **novel proper** and the **romance.** The two are not always clearly distinguished, but there is an important difference between them which must not be obscured.

Before we go on any further, however, it seems essential to point out the ambiguity of the term 'romance'. It can refer to ancient narrative poems which are concerned with idealized characters and situations, such as the old Greek love idyll *Daphnis and Chloe* (probably second century A.D.) or to the medieval narratives of ideal love and chivalric adventure, e.g. *Sir Gawain and the Green Knight* (fourteenth century). It can also refer to some works of Elizabethan fiction, such as Spenser's *The Faerie Queene* (1589 and 1596) or to the Gothic novel of the later eighteenth century, such as Ann Radcliffe's *The Mysteries of Udolpho* (1794). Today, the term 'romance' seems most commonly to mean 'a love story', usually the sentimental pap produced for the mass market.

When, however, we speak of the **romance** as being different from the **novel proper,** we refer to **a basic distinction between two conceptions of fiction.** In the novel proper we find a realistic portrayal of the world as it actually is rather than as it should be or possibly might be. In the romance, on the other hand, we encounter an idealized world which relies on the powers of the imagination rather than on a strong facticity which is absolutely true to life. We can perhaps say that whereas the novel tends to expand into a fictional approach to history, the romance is concerned with an avowedly fictive world. This is to say that the writer of romance frequently makes little attempt to disguise the fact that what he is presenting is not a fictional picture of an aspect of empirical reality (for details see below), but a world which can in some respects be different from ours. The reader of such a text will therefore not be prepared to believe in what is being presented, in the sense of accepting it as a factually true rendering of reality as we know it, but will for the purpose of losing himself in the story "suspend disbelief", in T.S. Eliot's phrase.

The difference between the novel and the romance appears to be **the result of certain historical developments** — the two forms typify the double descent of extended prose fiction. The novel goes back to the lineage of largely non-fictitious narrative forms, such as the journal, the letter, the memoir or the chronicle. It has developed, so to speak, out of documents, whereas the romance seems to continue the tradition of the epic and the medieval romance — two openly fictitious narrative forms which neglect verisimilitude of detail. The fictional attempt to give the effect of realism, which is typical of the novel, is thus largely ignored in the romance.

Romance probably reflects an eternal tendency of the human mind which is essentially unaffected by change. That it has persisted after the birth and eventual triumph of the novel, simply by adapting its methods and matter to the tastes of a different social background, is quite clearly an indication of its continuing strength. We can say that its function, which is to provide **escape,** and its action, which centres on **adventure,** have not changed; only the externals of the setting have undergone an alteration. The tales of chivalrous adventure, with their battles with dragons and their quests for the grail, have largely been replaced by settings which reflect more recent cultural situations, such as crime and its detection and pursuit, international espionage, the American West, etc. In any case, there is a clear analogy between the heroic cowboy of a western romance and the chivalrous knight of Arthurian legend. Both the western and the Arthurian romance are forms of escape — the world of everyday reality is replaced by the picture of an idealized world which appeals to the emotions and imagination of the reader, inviting him to marvel at what is essentially **an enchanted world.** The **novel,** on the other hand, constantly calls the reader back to **reality** by questioning the very basis of romance; and the more sophisticated or the more devastating the process becomes, the less 'popular' the novel is likely to be. It is not an accident that the history of the novel proper begins with Cervantes's *Don Quixote* — the great Spaniard clearly saw the essential difference between **the realistic world of the novel** and **the idealistic world of the romance** and in conceiving his *Don Quixote* as an anti-romance produced the first genuine novel of world literature.

If we take a systematic look at **the distinguishing characteristics of the romance,** we will find that a first identifying feature is the special world it presents; it may be the enchanted world of triumphant adventure in the more trivial forms of romance; or it may be a setting away from the ordinary social nexus, with the events occurring in isolation and much of the patterns of life as we know it blocked out, as in romances which are clearly intended as 'serious' literature. A famous example of a romance of that type in the English tradition is Emily Brontë's *Wuthering Heights* (1847); within the American tradition we can point to Herman Melville's *Moby Dick* (1851); a contemporary writer of romances is Saul Bellow (cp. his *Henderson the Rain King,* 1959, and others of his books). In all these examples we encounter an isolated setting where people seem to be governed by primitive emotions, without the pressures of ordinary social environments to restrain them.

Another characteristic feature of the romance is the curiously suspended sense of time it shows. In much the same way as the chivalrous heroes of medieval romances move through a timeless world, the people in modern romances appear to live outside the referential frame of chronological time. Time is apparently not measured by the normal standards of social activities and human development and may seem to stagnate entirely.

A third identifying trait of the romance seems to be the questionable reliability of the narration itself. The events are often related only indirectly, perhaps to enhance our sense of wonder at the strangeness of what is being recounted. The action itself frequently remains unexplained.

We can say that the focus in **a romance is generally different from that in a novel,** where the emphasis may lie on social interaction, psychological development, or on ideas and philosophical concerns (for details cp. 8.3 Modes of fiction). In a romance, we are given an abstracted vision of the state of human society in its larger forms; we are offered insights into the tensions existing within the contemporary social order, but the focus is never only on one problem or one kind of human experience within that society. The romance is thus relatively free from the necessity of presenting historical truth in any particular factual sense, though it may well deal with history as myth, or as metaphor. Whereas the material of the novel is confined to the narration of common and daily occurring events and the grouping and delineation of characters in the ordinary conditions of society, the romance does not confine itself to what is known, or even what is probable; it can even include elements which go beyond the humanly possible and thus arrive at a projection in symbolic form of the primal desires, hopes, and subconscious anxieties and terrors in the depths of the human mind. Indeed, from the romancer's point of view, the novelist constantly runs the risk of becoming so bogged down with meaningless detail as to obscure the truth which all art must in some way reveal.

The most important characteristic of the romance and the one which perhaps most clearly distinguishes it from the novel is its conception of characterization. We can say that the romance deals with heroes, whereas the novel deals with real people. The romance thus seems to stand somewhere between the novel and the myth, which deals with gods. The novelist presents "complex characters with mixed motives who are rooted in a social class, operate in a highly developed social structure, interact with many other characters, and undergo plausible and everyday modes of experience."[21] The writer of romance, on the other hand, does not attempt to portray 'real people' so much as simplified and stylized figures which are larger than life and more intense than any 'real person' could possibly be. In trivial escapist romances, the characters are sharply distinguished as heroes and villains, whereas in 'serious' romances characters are presented which expand into psychological archetypes. "It is almost as if they came out of another dimension — out of legend, or myth, or recesses in our psyche long suppressed by civilisation."[22] The heroes of a romance can usually fulfil their heroic potential, whereas the novelistic hero finds that the real world does not allow him to elaborate his dreams of glory and success; he is constantly led back to the world as it really is and has to undergo a process of disillusionment with his conception of himself and of his surroundings. The novel is thus 'deflationary' in a way, and the romance seems to rely on the art of inflation — on showing characters and situations which loom larger than life.

This ‘inflation’ of real-life situations is in fact also the point the romance is mainly criticized for. The reader, it is argued, is seduced into applying the values presented in a romance, especially if it is on the trivial type, to the real world where he will find that pain has a genuine sharpness which cannot be explained away and that life is not simply a big adventure which comes out right for those who follow a decent course of conduct. What may be appropriate enough in the artificial world the writer of romance has created may be painfully unrealistic in the real world. Happy endings do not follow as a matter of course in the world as we know it. It is thus wrong to lead people into a never-never land of fancy when it is more useful to prepare them for the process of disillusionment real life always brings with it. Criticism of the romance is therefore essentially a moral one, not a literary or artistic one. Whether literature must of necessity be moral and didactic, or whether the writer is not free to choose what method he thinks best for the presentation of truth as he sees it, is however a debatable point. There are many who will insist that the romance addresses itself to a higher reality and a deeper psychology than the novel and that it is therefore analogous to the materials of dream, **myth, ritual** and **folklore,** all of which present ‘truth’ in a non-factual and non-realistic way. The fact that romance is older than the novel has perhaps led to the historical illusion that it is something outgrown, a juvenile and undeveloped form. But if this were really so, we could no longer find any truth in such a hopelessly non-realistic writer as Homer. It is simply not enough to describe the romance as escapist and non-realistic and imagine one has explained everything. There is an important sense in which all art is an escape. In fact, the capacity to escape from his present experience is man’s greatest and distinguishing ability. We must not forget the force of Aristotle’s argument that literature is valuable because it shows men not simply as they are, but as they ought to be or as they are capable of becoming. This **fantastic quality of art,** that it takes us out of the real world so that the mind is awakened and enlarged, this quality is not a trivial or accidental by-product but the very essence of the value of art. If art did in fact merely paint a picture of what is, in the sense of a photographic reproduction, it would be a much less valuable form of human activity, for it would not alter people’s consciousness but merely confirm it. To criticize the romance on the ground that it is not realistic but idealistic is thus largely beside the point. **What is important is only that the romance tends to oversimplify ethical questions.** Life then becomes a battle between Good and Evil; and characters, instead of being truly human — neither wholly good nor wholly bad — tend to become entirely black or white. If such a static, idealist moral code is imposed on the actual movement and complexity of human behaviour, then this is bound to lead to inadequate results.[23] The best of the romances, of course, avoid these crudities and are then artistically as convincing as the best of the novels. **Literary merit must clearly be seen as independent from an ultra-naturalistic form of presenting reality.** (For criteria for distinguishing between ‘good’ and ‘bad’ literature cf. 8.4 below).

We said at the beginning that novel and romance are not always clearly distinguished. In fact, many people, instead of referring to 'novel' and 'romance', prefer to speak of **novel-as-history** and of **novel-as-romance.** The reason for this lies in the fact that the romance often contains much concrete, realistic detail which is meant to give a certain credibility to a story which is basically not realistic. As a result, the romance often, though not invariably, has about it a certain spurious realism which is however not to be seen as its heart but rather as an incidental attribute. Conversely, the novel frequently incorporates romantic elements, especially in its portrayal of the main characters, so that we can say that 'pure' examples of either form are hard to find or may not exist at all. The popular demand in fiction, of course, always goes for a mixed form — something in the nature of a **'romantic novel'.** It must be sufficiently romantic for the reader to project his wishful thinking and his fantasies on hero and heroine; and it must be sufficiently realistic to ensure that these projections are kept in a familiar world.

Comprehension and revision

1) Explain the possible meanings of the term 'romance'.
2) Explain the different conceptions of fiction in novel and romance.
3) How true is it to say that
   a) novel and romance typify the double descent of extended prose fiction?
   b) romance reflects an eternal tendency of the human mind?
   c) the novel questions the very basis of romance?
4) What are the distinguishing characteristics
   a) of the romance?
   b) of the novel proper?

   Name these characteristics first and then explain them.
5) What is the main criticism of romance? Explain.
6) Can the romance be criticized for its idealistic orientation? Give reasons.
7) Why are the terms 'novel-as-history' and 'novel-as-romance' sometimes preferred?

Novel and romance

The novel proper and the romance are	the two most common forms of extended prose fiction. based on different conceptions of fiction.	
	not always clearly	separated. distinguished.

p. t. o.

Novel and romance (continued)

The romance The **novel-as-romance**	presents shows portrays depicts is concerned with	the world	idealistically. as it should, could or might possibly be.
		an idealized world. an enchanted world. an avowedly fictive world. a world which is in some respects different from ours.	
	provides escape. centres on adventure and love. is idealistic. is non-realistic. appeals to the powers of the imagination. invites the reader to suspend disbelief. may neglect verisimilitude of detail. addresses itself to a higher reality and a deeper psychology. reflects an eternal tendency of the human mind. tends to over-simplify ethical questions. often has a certain spurious realism about it.		

The	distinguishing characteristics identifying features typical elements characteristic traits	of the romance of the **novel-as-romance**	are include	the special world that is presented. an isolated setting. a (curiously) suspended sense of time. the questionable reliability of the narration itself. an action that remains largely unexplained. a concern with a higher reality. an inflation of real-life situations. the presentation of truth in a non-factual and non-realistic way.

p. t. o.

Novel and romance (continued)

The	distinguishing characteristics identifying features typical elements characteristic traits	of the romance of the **novel-as-romance**	are include	the characterisation of the protagonists as	heroes. stylized figures. people who loom larger than life.
The	distinguishing characteristics identifying features typical elements characteristic traits	of the novel of the **novel-as-history**	are include	a narration of common or daily occurring events. a portrayal of real people. a delineation of characters in the ordinary conditions of society.	
				a stress on an emphasis on	ordinary social environments. real-life situations. the pattern of life as we know it. social interaction. psychological development. an idea or philosophical concern. one problem or one kind of human experience. the process of disillusionment real life always brings along withit.

p. t. o.

<table>
<tr><th colspan="4">Novel and romance (continued)</th></tr>
<tr><td rowspan="4">The novel
The novel proper
The novel-as-history</td><td rowspan="2">shows
presents
portrays
depicts</td><td>the world</td><td>as it really is.
realistically.</td></tr>
<tr><td colspan="2">a realistic world.
the pattern of life as we know it.</td></tr>
<tr><td>stresses
emphasises
focuses on</td><td colspan="2">facticity.
empirical reality.
what is factually true.
verisimilitude of detail.</td></tr>
<tr><td colspan="3">gives the effect of realism.
tends to expand into a fictional approach to history.
constantly calls the reader back to reality.
goes back to the lineage of non-fictitious narrative forms.
frequently incorporates romantic elements.</td></tr>
</table>

7. THE CRAFT OF FICTION

This section is intended to help you understand **the shaping devices of fiction.** We have set out to show how fictional works are put together and to provide the technical vocabulary which is essential for a discussion of the writer's craft — how he manages to transform the outline of a story into a work of imaginative art with meaning.

7.1 Problems of composition

7.1.1 The theme, i.e. the central idea or purpose of the author

Unless he is writing experimental fiction, the writer does not show us some purely accidental action and does not introduce characters at random that act without any apparent purpose. Instead, he creates his own characters, places them at specific points within his fictional world and causes them to act to some purpose. In other words, works of fiction are not accidents but works which have a purpose, a form and a meaning, all of which have been deliberately created by the author. In thus giving his work purpose, form and meaning, he was, however, forced to make certain decisions, which can often be located in the text. If we can find out just why he made these decisions, the overall meaning of the work should become much clearer.

The first decision he has to take concerns his **central purpose,** the **central idea** his story is meant to embody — he has to choose his **theme.** (For all practical purposes we can treat these three terms as synonymous). Every good short story is shaped by a controlling idea or theme, and in a good novel we can normally locate a **dominant theme** among a number of **secondary themes.** It is sometimes not easy to define such a dominant theme in a long and loosely-structured novel, and we may need a whole sentence to formulate it, but we can nevertheless be sure that a dominant theme is there, because the writer has of course selected and arranged everything that eventually went into his work, such as the action, the characters, the conflict and its resolution, according to some plan, some central purpose — his dominant theme. If we can find an idea, a concept, which gives coherence and meaning to all the elements in a fictional work, then we have in fact discovered its theme. And it is always worthwhile to look for such a theme because it will help us to understand the story much better, and it may also make the reading more enjoyable (especially a second or third reading).

The author's central purpose may be practically anything within the compass of human experience. Thus some works of fiction depict and analyse human emotions, such as love or sorrow, or they deal with actions and moral choices, or the theme may be a study in character, or simply the presentation of an aspect of life. But whatever the theme may be, it always provides a focus for all the elements in a story and thus gives them unity and infuses the story as a whole with a specific meaning.

Theme or central idea

<table>
<tr><td rowspan="2">This novel
This short story</td><td>deals with
is concerned with</td><td>the theme of...</td></tr>
<tr><td colspan="2">is a study of...</td></tr>
</table>

<table>
<tr><td>The problem of...</td><td>forms the central theme.
is the dominant theme.
provides the main theme.
is a secondary theme.</td></tr>
</table>

<table>
<tr><td colspan="2">The author's central purpose is</td><td rowspan="2">the presentation of</td><td rowspan="2">the extraordinary.
a moral problem.
character.
a human experience in depth.
an aspect of life.</td></tr>
<tr><td>The writer is</td><td>mainly concerned with
predominantly interested in</td></tr>
</table>

Typical questions

What is the story/novel about?
What does the story/novel present?
What is the author's central purpose?
What is the writer's theme?
How is the theme developed in the story/novel?

7.1.2 Action, plot, hero, and conflict

A second decision the writer has to take in composing his text is to decide on a **structure of action** to dramatize his theme. In other words, whatever the author wishes to communicate, he will have to make it concrete in terms of action. This interplay of characters which makes up the structure of action is called the **plot.** It is the backbone of a story and enables the writer to achieve his purpose. His main interest may be in character and motive, or he may want to explore a moral problem or portray some condition of society or expose some evil, or he may simply set out to make us laugh and generally entertain us. In all these cases he needs some action to express what he intends the reader to see — character for instance is revealed in action, and a moral issue becomes much more concrete and tangible if it is attached to certain characters in certain situations; action makes the problem explicit. If a writer wishes to achieve his purpose through fiction, his narrative must have a plot structure.

The plot always revolves around the main character of the story who commands the reader's chief interest; he or she is thus the **hero** or **heroine** of the story. This central character is also known as the **protagonist;** the opponent he or she is pitted against is the **antagonist** and the relation between the two is one of **conflict.** In this case — one character in opposition to another character — we speak of an **external conflict,** as also when the conflict is between the hero and fate itself, or when it is between a character and his environment, e.g. between the goal he has set for himself and certain circumstances that stand between him and this goal. We speak of **internal conflict** when the conflict can be located in the character himself, in opposing desires or conflicting values in the character's own soul. All these particular conflicts are themselves subordinate to the **central conflict,** which is always between fundamental and contrasting *qualities* or *forces,* such as honesty and hypocrisy, innocence and experience, individuality and the pressure to conform. This conflict is the core of the story's structure, the generating center out of which the plot grows. A story may contain more than one conflict of forces, but only the central conflict fully accounts for the events of the plot. Obviously, the central conflict of a story is intimately related to its theme: the two may even be identical[1].

Action, plot, hero, and conflict

<table>
<tr><td rowspan="2">The author</td><td colspan="2">creates his own characters.
causes his characters to act to his purpose.</td></tr>
<tr><td>presents</td><td>his theme concretely through characters in action.
his characters in action.</td></tr>
<tr><td rowspan="2">The action</td><td colspan="2">has the function of dramatizing the theme for the reader.</td></tr>
<tr><td>is</td><td>external.
internal.
both external and internal.</td></tr>
</table>

p. t. o.

Action, plot, hero, and conflict (continued)

<table>
<tr><td rowspan="6">The plot
The structure
of the action</td><td rowspan="2">dramatizes</td><td colspan="2">the theme.</td></tr>
<tr><td>the author's</td><td>purpose.
intention.</td></tr>
<tr><td colspan="3">enables the writer to achieve his purpose.</td></tr>
<tr><td colspan="3">is the backbone of a story.
propels the narrative forward.
is the dynamic whole to which the other parts relate.
is based on the interplay of characters.</td></tr>
<tr><td rowspan="2">revolves around the</td><td>main
central</td><td>character.</td></tr>
<tr><td colspan="2">hero.
protagonist.</td></tr>
<tr><td rowspan="3">The hero
The protagonist</td><td colspan="3">is pitted against the antagonist.</td></tr>
<tr><td>is locked in conflict with</td><td colspan="2">an opponent.
the antagonist.
another character.</td></tr>
<tr><td colspan="3">is the central character around whom everything revolves.</td></tr>
<tr><td rowspan="5">The conflict is</td><td colspan="3">external.
internal.</td></tr>
<tr><td colspan="3">intense.</td></tr>
<tr><td colspan="3">solved.</td></tr>
<tr><td rowspan="2">between</td><td colspan="2">one character and another character.
protagonist and antagonist.
the hero and fate itself.
a character and his environment.</td></tr>
<tr><td>opposing desires
conflicting values</td><td>within the character himself.</td></tr>
</table>

p. t. o.

Action, plot, hero, and conflict (continued)	
The **central conflict**	is between fundamental and contrasting qualities or forces. is the core of the story's structure. fully accounts for the events of the plot.
All the individual conflicts are subordinate to the central conflict.	

Typical questions and tasks

1) Describe the structure of the action in the story.
2) What is the writer's plot?
3) Describe the chain of causes and effects that makes up the writer's plot.
4) Draw a diagram illustrating the plot structure of the narrative.
5) Give a commentary on the structure of this story.
6) Who is the protagonist? (What makes you think so?)
7) Outline the (central) conflict in the story.
8) What kind of action is described?
9) Is the action mainly external or internal?
10) Show how external action and internal action are interrelated.

7.1.3 The component elements of plot; various forms of plot

Some narratives, especially those in the picaresque tradition, have an **episodic plot structure:** they present a number of episodes which are strung together into a single narrative about the same central character. Other narratives employ an **integrated plot structure:** they aim at a **unity of action** and a **unity of effect,** i. e., they try to achieve an artistic whole in which the component parts, or **incidents,** are all directed towards the intended effect and in which none of them is unnecessary. In the case of such a **unified plot,** the writer attempts to establish a clear sequence of beginning, middle, and end — he sets out to present a story which moves from the opening situation in the **introduction,** through the stages of **complication, conflict,** and **climax,** to a **resolution.** This type of plot with its definite resolution of conflict is called the **closed plot;** it is typical of fiction in the eighteenth and nineteenth centuries but is often used in twentieth century fiction as well, notably in popular detective fiction, where a closed plot is indeed essential and inevitable, for the mystery must be solved.

Generally speaking, however, the convention of the closed plot has largely been abandoned in serious fiction as it is felt that resolutions cannot be found for many of our basic conflicts. An **open plot** is thus often preferred because it favours the dramatic, simple narrative, has little or no resolution and rejects the convention of the **happy ending** in favour of the **open ending** where nothing is really decided and a finished interpretation of what we experience as a very complicated world is avoided.

A number of modern writers are prepared to go even further and to reject the concept of plot altogether. They would readily concede that it may be artistically much more satisfactory to construct a narrative artefact as well-balanced and economical as a geometrical shape than simply to present the totally unordered movement of real life. They believe, however, that the task of the writer of fiction is to present an imitation of the very formlessness of real life rather than a well-structured story which imposes what is felt to be an artificial order on things. It is of course true that in real life there are no clear-cut 'beginnings' and 'endings' and very few simple motives for action, but to try to mirror this situation in fiction is to destroy its very foundations. For this reason, and because such anti-fictional texts are very boring to read, this experimental movement of writing texts without any plot-structure whatsoever does not seem to have much of a future.
As regards the introduction, it seems useful to distinguish between the short story and the novel. The short story very often sets off *in medias res,* beginning at the point of the climax itself, whereas in longer narratives the writer may, if he so wishes, devote a whole chapter or two to the so-called **exposition** — the explanation of the whole set-up, the mentioning of important antecedent matters, the introduction of the theme and the main characters, and so on. The complication, sometimes called the **rising action,** begins when we see a conflict developing. This conflict will eventually reach a **climax**, which arrives when the conflict is at its most intense and when its resolution becomes inevitable. The direction in which the resolution of the conflict is going to move may be made obvious in a passage which indicates a **turning-point** or a **crisis;** from then on, we can speak of a **falling action,** with the fortune of one of the two antagonistic forces dropping lower and lower and the other correspondingly more and more controlling the course of events. In the resolution, or **denouement** (Fr. dénouement, literally "un-knotting", pronounced [deɪ'nu:mɑ̃]), the outcome of the conflict is finally decided, and the action ends in success or failure for the protagonist.
Of course, we should not expect to find all these elements in all narratives. In fact most of the technical terms for the various structural elements mentioned above were first used in a critical study of the structure of drama, especially tragedy, but they have been found extremely useful for the discussion of narrative fiction as well. The distinction between the **main plot** and one or more **subplots** was also first made in the critical analysis of drama, but it is equally an important feature of plot structure in many narratives. A subplot is a second story, complete in itself and interesting in its own right, which is introduced into the narrative in order to broaden our perspective on the main plot and to underline its meaning by similarity or contrast.
A common form of subplot is the so-called **frame story,** which, as the name suggests, provides a frame for the main story. That is to say, the central narrative is surrounded by the presentation of a situation in which a story like the main narrative might be told, such as a circle of people who have met for some purpose or other

and who act as the listeners. To strengthen the illusion of the frame story, they may interpose a question occasionally and make some closing comments at the end. The function of such a frame narrative is either to provide the central narrative with a greater authority and thus to increase its credibility, or to introduce a certain point of view through which the events of the main story can be interpreted.
Slightly different from the distinction between main plot and subplot are the concepts of **simple plot** and **complex plot.** In the first case we have a single story treating of one character's experiences, whereas in a complex plot the writer presents several sequences of events and the experiences of several characters, all of which have to be skilfully interwoven in a logically consistent manner, and with regard for probability, so that the unity of the whole is not endangered. But whereas in a story with a main plot the subplot or subplots are clearly of less importance, the various sequences of events in a complex plot are of about equal status.
In any case, even the most complex plots are extremely simple compared with the complexities — the chaos — of real life. Every writer who intends to give his fictional creations at least a semblance of coherence will have to impose an order of some sort on his material. A totally unordered listing of events, scraps of dialogue, etc., would simply be chaotic and meaningless, and the writer's purpose would be defeated at every turn, unless of course his purpose is just such a demonstration of the aimlessness and chaos of life.
In being selective, the writer's plot can make the links of cause and effect much clearer than we experience them in real life. Things of importance are granted a much more important status in fiction than in life itself, and irrelevant routines one takes for granted are simply ignored, unless the writer is especially interested in showing or implying the pressure of irrelevancies on a character's state of mind.

The component elements of plot; various forms of plot

This narrative This text This story This novel	has an	episodic integrated	plot structure.
	has a unified plot.		
	aims at a	unity of action. unity of effect.	
	employs makes use of uses	a closed plot. an open plot.	
	disposes of the concept of plot altogether.		

p. t. o.

The component elements of plot; various forms of plot (continued)

<table>
<tr><td rowspan="2">The **closed plot**</td><td colspan="7">is based on a clear sequence of beginning, middle, and end.</td></tr>
<tr><td>moves from the</td><td>introduction
opening situation
exposition</td><td>through the stages of</td><td>complication, or rising action, or a developing conflict, climax, turning-point, or crisis, and falling action</td><td>to the</td><td colspan="2">conclusion.
denouement.
resolution of the conflict.</td></tr>
<tr><td rowspan="3">The **open plot**</td><td>prefers
favours</td><td colspan="6">the dramatic, simple narrative.</td></tr>
<tr><td colspan="7">has little or no resolution.
avoids an over-simplistic resolution.</td></tr>
<tr><td colspan="7">rejects the convention of the happy ending in favour of the open ending.
rejects, on philosophical grounds, a finished interpretation of a complicated world.</td></tr>
<tr><td rowspan="2">This author
This writer</td><td colspan="2">has set out to present</td><td colspan="5">an imitation of the very formlessness of life.
the totally unordered movement of real life.
an anti-fictional text.</td></tr>
<tr><td colspan="2">rejects the</td><td colspan="5">concept of plot altogether.
convention of beginnings and endings.</td></tr>
<tr><td>The introduction
The **exposition**</td><td colspan="7">describes the general atmosphere.
explains the whole set-up.
introduces the main characters.
states the theme.
mentions important antecedent matters.
tries to awaken the reader's interest so that he wants to learn more.</td></tr>
<tr><td>The **complication**
The **rising action**</td><td colspan="7">sets in when a conflict begins to develop.
leads to the climax.
brings a development towards a crisis.
increases the reader's suspense.</td></tr>
</table>

p. t. o.

The component elements of plot; various forms of plot (continued)

<table>
<tr><td rowspan="3">The climax</td><td>arrives when</td><td colspan="2">the conflict is at its most intense.
the resolution of the conflict becomes inevitable.</td></tr>
<tr><td>brings</td><td>a new state of awareness
deeper self-knowledge</td><td>on the part of the protagonist.</td></tr>
<tr><td colspan="3">is identical with the turning-point in this text.</td></tr>
<tr><td rowspan="2">The turning-point
The crisis</td><td colspan="3">indicates the direction in which the resolution of the conflict is going to move.
is the beginning of the falling action.
is reached when...
reveals his fundamental error to the protagonist.</td></tr>
<tr><td colspan="3">occurs at the same moment as the climax in this story.</td></tr>
<tr><td colspan="4">A vital moment occurs when...</td></tr>
<tr><td rowspan="7">The conclusion
The denouement
The outcome
The resolution</td><td colspan="3">ends the conflict.
unties the knots of the conflict.
resolves the opposition of forces.</td></tr>
<tr><td rowspan="2">brings
ends in</td><td>success
failure</td><td>for the protagonist.</td></tr>
<tr><td colspan="2">the sudden disillusionment of the hero.</td></tr>
<tr><td>leaves the hero</td><td colspan="2">in a state of...
with a feeling of...</td></tr>
<tr><td colspan="3">shows the consequences of the hero's decision.</td></tr>
<tr><td colspan="3">comes rather abruptly.
comes when...</td></tr>
<tr><td colspan="3">is open-ended.</td></tr>
</table>

p. t. o.

The component elements of plot; various forms of plot (continued)

The conclusion The **denouement** The outcome The **resolution**	is	unexpected. surprising. plausible. well motivated. satisfying. appropriate.
The **plot structure** of this narrative	is	simple. complex. elaborate.
	is made up of a main plot and a subplot. contains the main story within a frame story.	
	is characterized by	the skilful interplay between main plot and subplot. a great amount of order and symmetry.
The **subplot**	is complete in itself. is interesting in its own right.	
	broadens the reader's perspective on underlines the meaning of	the main plot.
	reinforces the theme increases the general significance enhances the overall artistic effect	of the main narrative.
	takes the form of a frame story.	

Comprehension and revision

1) What is
   an 'episodic plot structure'?
   an 'integrated plot structure'?
   Explain the difference.
2) What is
   a 'closed plot'?
   an 'open plot'?
   Explain the difference.
3) What is the function of the exposition?

4) Explain the relationship between main plot and subplot.
5) Explain form and function of a frame story.
6) What is the precise difference between a simple plot and a complex plot?
7) Why must the writer of fiction be selective in the arrangement and presentation of his material?

Typical tasks and questions

1) Analyse the introduction. What are its functions?
2) Explain the character of the conflict and show where the climax is.
3) Comment on the handling of turning-point and denouement.
4) Try to suggest an alternative ending and explain your choice.
5) Analyse the mutual interdependence of main plot and subplot.

7.1.4 The movement of the plot

The **movement of the plot** raises questions in the reader's mind and appeals to his curiosity — he wants to know what happens next — and to his hopes and fears for the characters whose fate arouses his interest and sympathy. This anxious uncertainty about the future course of events is known as **suspense.** People enjoy suspense and excitement in their reading. But real suspense is based on **verisimilitude,** i.e. on an imitation of life-like situations, and on **causality.** If we cannot know what may happen next, because literally anything may occur in the world the writer has created, we feel lost and may well refuse to go on reading a story in which there are no probabilities and in which the principle of causality is neglected. A good plot carries the reader forward by keeping him in suspense and by enabling him to follow the workings of causality; "we may go forwards and see what leads to what, or backwards and find out why."[2]

Of course, there may occasionally be a development we have not foreseen because we have been led to expect something else. In this case we speak of a **surprise.**

> The interplay of suspense and surprise is a prime source of the magnetic power and vitality of an on-going plot. The most effective surprise is one which turns out, in retrospect, to have been well grounded in what has gone before though we have hitherto made the wrong inference from the given facts of circumstance and character. As E. M. Forster put it, the shock of the unexpected, "followed by the feeling, 'oh, that's all right', is a sign that all is well with the plot"[3].

When the outcome of a story is unexpected, we call it a **surprise ending.** The term has however acquired rather a negative meaning through its frequent association with plot resolutions which rely heavily on coincidence or are not really grounded in characterization or the course of events up to then. A surprise ending in this pejorative sense is like some practical joke played on the reader, but of course the joke is ruined after the first reading. When, however, the resolution is unexpected

but appropriate and plausible — because it has been adequately prepared even though the reader may have drawn the wrong inferences from what has come before — we can enjoy the unexpected denouement as often as we reread the story.
In this context, a word must be said about the convention of the **happy ending** — that at the end of a narrative the good achieve their wishes and the machinations of the wicked are thwarted. This conventional happy ending is rarely employed in serious literature today and its use is practically confined to more or less escapist fiction. In serious fiction, endings tend to be much more provisional — the protagonist has not been able to solve all the problems, but he has managed to sort out a few things and is now moving in a promising direction.

The movement of the plot can last of all guide the reader towards the meaning of the experiences which are presented in a narrative. We have understood the plot in the full artistic sense only when we have analysed the interplay of our desires and expectations as they are formed as the result of the movement of the plot — a well-constructed plot has the power to affect our opinions and emotions. At the very least, we want to know what is going to happen and how the problems the characters are confronted with will be solved. But, as we read, we also form expectations about what is coming and "we cannot help becoming, in a greater or less degree, emotionally involved; for some of the characters we wish good, for others ill, and, depending on our inferences as to the events, we feel hope or fear, pity or satisfaction, or some modification of these or similar emotions"[4]. The writer must of course have ordered his material in such a way that the elements of action, character, and thought combine to produce a complete and ordered whole and thus establish a connected series of expectations with which he can guide our responses and direct and control our attention. When we complain that a story is dull and boring because "nothing ever happens", it may well be that we have misinterpreted the questions the author meant us to ask of the story and, as a consequence, our attention is misdirected. Perhaps the writer is not mainly interested in showing us what is going on on the level of physical reality, the so-called **external action,** because his objective is to follow the wanderings of a character's thoughts, so that the emphasis in the story is almost entirely on **internal action.** Sometimes the action takes place on two levels, in the character's imagination and on the level of outward reality, and the external action simply provides the framework for the story and sets in motion the character's train of thought, which may wander freely in time and space.

The movement of the plot

The movement of the plot	carries the reader forward.	
	arouses	the reader's interest and sympathy. expectations in the reader about what is going to happen. responses of concern and excitement in the reader.
	raises questions in the reader's mind. affects the reader's opinions and emotions. makes the reader emotionally involved. directs and controls the reader's attention. guides the reader towards the meaning of the experiences which are presented.	
	creates	an anxious uncertainty about the future course of events. suspense.
	is based on the principles of verisimilitude and causality.	
	occasionally introduces a surprise.	
	may lead to	a surprise ending. an unexpected ending. a happy ending. a provisional ending. an open ending.
	may emphasize	external action. internal action.

Comprehension and revision

1) Explain what is meant when we speak of the 'movement of the plot'.
2) How is suspense created?
3) Why are the principles of verisimilitude and causality so important?
4) What is a 'surprise ending'?
5) Why has the convention of the 'happy ending' largely been abandoned in serious fiction?
6) How does the reader of a narrative become emotionally involved?

Typical tasks and questions

1) How has the writer managed to arouse the reader's curiosity?
2) Show how the author has created suspense.
3) How is the scene for the main action prepared?
4) What is the relationship between external action and internal action?
5) Why is the outcome so surprising?
6) Show that the ending is appropriate and artistically satisfactory.
7) Would you change the ending of the story? Give reasons.

To recapitulate, a plot is rather more than a selection of events arranged in time; it includes causality, motives, consequences, and relationships; one thing leads to another and some kind of pattern is established. We may say that the plot is as important to a work of fiction as the skeleton is to a human body — it holds the fictional organism together and gives it its structure[5].

7.2 The narrative process

There are many ways of telling a story, and the author has to decide which of them best suits his overall purposes. He has to choose the most suitable **narrator** from whose **point of view** the story is to be told. He has further to decide what **channels of information** he, or his narrator, is to use to convey the story to the reader — letters written by the characters, the protagonist's recollections, a minor character's report of what he saw and heard, and so on. He has to settle the question of what **mode of presentation** he ought to employ — whether to **tell** us about the events and their significance or whether to **show** only the words and actions of his characters without any commentary and leave the reader to draw his own conclusions. And he has last of all to decide just how much he wants to involve the reader in the action that is presented — at what **distance** he ought to place the reader from the story.

7.2.1 Point of view

Where there is a story, there is a storyteller. In many stories, this storyteller, or **narrator,** stands in a godlike position behind the scenes, managing his characters like puppets on strings and knowing precisely what each of them thinks and feels. In such a case we speak of an **omniscient narrator** because he seems to know everything about the characters, not only their present thoughts, perceptions and feelings, but also their characters as people and their past and future lives. We should, however, be careful with this concept of omniscience. What we normally find in omniscient narration is that only the *public* faces of the characters are shown, much as they might be noticed by a sensitive and detached observer. Only rarely do we penetrate to the innermost motives and feelings of the characters, although information is often given that could not possibly have been obtained by any participant in the events described.

An omniscient narrator who told the reader everything would indeed be a tiresome and boring guide through a story. If he revealed as much as he really knows of the characters, they would be so transparent as to be totally uninteresting. Most of the so-called 'omniscient narrators' are thus in effect hardly more than keen observers — the writer limits himself to throwing in this or that bit of commentary as he sees fit.

Many stories are explicitly presented as passing through the consciousness of a narrator, but where there is no such obvious **centre of consciousness** we must not forget that stories are always created — they do not write themselves, after all. There may be an explicit or **dramatised narrator** who is a character in the story and is involved in the action, but even where there is no dramatised narrator a story is never written by the author as he is in real life. An author is always in a godlike position with respect to his plot and characters, which no one in real life can ever be over his fellow men. For every story the author therefore necessarily assumes a second identity and becomes a 'second self', known as the **implied author,** who is always a superior version of the author as he exists in real life — usually more highly refined, wiser, more sensitive and perceptive than anybody in real life could be. The picture of the author's "second self" that emerges from a certain narrative is not normally identical with the one that is created before the reader's eye as he reads another story by the same author. The implied author in Hemingway's famous short story "The Killers", for instance, is rather different from the picture of the author that is built up in the reader's mind from a reading of Hemingway's *The Old Man and the Sea.* In any case, we must not make the mistake of identifying a narrator who has been given no personal characteristics whatever, i.e. an **undramatised narrator,** with the author himself. In many modern narratives we find fully dramatised narrators whose **point of view** completely dominates the tale they are presenting. This is to say that the method of narration the writer has chosen is to hand over the job of telling the story to one of his characters, as if he himself had nothing to do with the story. What this character knows, experiences, and feels controls everything. The objective in doing this is to establish some authority outside the author himself and with the help of this device to strengthen the illusion of reality the writer wants to achieve. And these are the two basic ways of telling a story — the writer can communicate his story from the outside, as a more or less omniscient narrator, or he can narrate it from the inside, with the help of one of the characters acting as the narrator.

In the case of what is called **editorial omniscience** the author includes in his text generalizations about life, manners and morals, which may have hardly any bearing on the story at hand, or he may comment here and there in the midst of the action as he likes. So he will not only report what happens or what goes on in the minds of the characters, but he will also criticize their actions and their plans and generally comment on the folly of mankind.

The situation is only slightly different if the author opts for **neutral omniscience.** He then abstains from directly interpolating his own ideas or intruding his comments, but his presence can still be felt if, for instance, he uses one of the characters as his mouthpiece, or when he intervenes between the story and the reader by describing the setting and everything concerning the characters in his own voice — as *he* sees it and not as his characters themselves might experience the situation they find themselves in.

In all these cases the narrator is outside the story and so refers to all the characters in it by name, or he calls them "he", "she", or "they". This so-called **third-person point of view** is often based on omniscience, but the author can also employ the device of **impersonal narration,** in which the narrator "gives up even the privilege of access to inner feelings and motives" and "describes, reports, or 'shows' the action in dramatic scenes, without introducing his own comments or judgments"[6]; or he can make use of a **limited point of view,** in which the story is told in the third person, but the narrator confines himself to the point of view of only a few, perhaps even only one, of the characters. This is to say that he limits his narration to what is experienced, thought, and felt by the character who is in the centre of attention at a given time in the action and thus provides a "focus", or "mirror", or "centre of consciousness". The story may be told sequentially, from the **shifting points of view** of many characters, or the writer may restrict the point of view almost exclusively to only one of his characters, showing only the action he takes part in and as it appears to him and giving only his thoughts. In this way the author can achieve a unity of focus and a strong identification of the reader with the viewpoint of the character who acts as the narrator. By closely following this character through his adventures or by following several of them in succession, the narrator can create a strong illusion of being present at the scene of the action. This illusion is even stronger when he impersonates one of his characters, or several in succession, and then uses **first-person narration,** writing as "I".

This "I" may be a minor character in the story who is more or less involved in the action and whose point of view is that of an observer or a witness. As a witness he has no more than ordinary access to the thoughts and feelings of others and, as a consequence of his limited point of view, can tell the reader only what he as a mere observer may legitimately know and discover and what he sees and hears others doing or saying. But it is of course always possible for a skilful writer to have recourse to all sorts of devices which increase the narrator's knowledge — he can use conversations his **observer-narrator** has with other characters, or this character may gain access to letters, diaries, and other writings which offer insights into the mental states of others, or he may of course make his narrator draw inferences as to the feelings and thoughts of others.

The "I" of first-person narration is often neither a simple witness of the events he relates, nor a minor or peripheral participant in the story, but the central character of the story himself. Because of his central role in the story itself, the **protagonist-**

narrator is much more limited in his mobility and in the range and variety of his sources than a witness-narrator who is not centrally involved in the action. The perspective of a protagonist-narrator therefore tends to be that of a fixed centre, over against what has been called the "wandering periphery" of an observer-narrator. In their attempts towards a complete objectivisation of the story material some writers have not only eliminated the author, who practically disappears in stories where characters are made to tell the story as they experience everything concerning it, but they have dispensed with a narrator altogether — the story is made to tell itself.

This can be done by a wholly **scenic presentation,** which provides information only as to what the characters do and say; what they think and how they feel is never openly stated, but may sometimes be inferred from the action shown and the dialogue given. A second method is the transmission of all the story materials — the action and words of the characters, their appearance and the setting — through the minds of the characters, i. e. the story is told as it is reflected in the mind of one of the characters. (For details see the following section 7.2.2).

Sometimes the narrator is aware of himself as a writer. Such a **self-conscious narrator** often discusses — seriously or for comic purposes — the various problems involved in the task he has set himself. Most narrators, however, do not mention the fact that they are composing a work of narrative art and seem to be totally unaware that they write or "reflect" a literary work.

A special problem for the reader is **fallible** or **unreliable narrators.** A story has a **reliable** narrator if he presents himself as fully understanding the plot, and if the reader is never in any doubt as to the narrator's role, but is able and expected to take everything the narrator says at its face value. If any of these elements are missing we speak of an **unreliable** narrator. This may be the case if he displays excessive innocence or oversophistication, or if he is blind to the moral problems involved in certain situations. All this "makes him a flawed and distorting 'center of consciousness' in the work; the result is an elaborate structure of ironies which, in some instances, frustrates the reader because he lacks sufficient clues to determine what the author intended as the true facts of the case, and the standards by which these facts are to be judged"[7].

In some instances a narrator presents himself as reliable whereas in fact he is not; he may be deliberately deceptive, as in some modern works of fiction, or the narrator may simply be mistaken, or he may pretend to qualities which he does not in fact possess. In the famous case of Mark Twain's *Huckleberry Finn* (1884), the titular hero and main character who is made to tell his own story in the first person "claims to be naturally wicked while the author silently praises his virtues, as it were, behind his back."[8]

Quite clearly, all of these forms of unreliability in the narrator — and there are a great many more — make great demands on the reader's power of inference, especially so if explicit corroborative or conflicting evidence is not supplied from within the action itself. Sometimes it is practically impossible to say whether a particular narrator is trustworthy or unreliable, because the clues provided by the story are inadequate, so that the interpretation and evaluation of the narrated events intended by the author remain uncertain and problematic.

There are advantages and disadvantages in employing this or that point of view. If the author decides to impersonate a character and to present everything as this character experiences it — irrespective of whether he uses first-person or third-person narration — he can achieve great vitality and conviction, but is then restricted to the experiences of one person only. An important advantage of omniscient narration, on the other hand, is that the writer "may follow any number of characters for short or long sections of the book, tell what he thinks is most interesting and comment if he wishes"[9]. He can give a large share of his attention to one character, but can turn aside at any time and follow another; or he can show a certain sympathy with this or that character or stand back from all the characters and confine himself to detached observing and reporting. The method of omniscient narration thus affords the author great freedom, but it involves one inescapable disadvantage — in varying degrees the writer always stands between the reader and the story, and the story-illusion may suffer.

Of course, it is well-nigh impossible to hit on a perfect point of view. Even first-rate writers of fiction must in each new work come to terms with the problem of just how much authorial guidance is needed for the story to have its proper effect. The author's crucial choice of the point of view best suited to his story material and the effects he wants to achieve usually leads him to adopting a mixture of points of view, for each new story requires the establishment of a particular kind of an illusion to sustain it.

> In dealing with point-of-view the novelist must always deal with the individual work: which particular character shall tell this particular story, or part of a story, with what precise degree of reliability, privilege, freedom to comment, and so on. Shall he be given dramatic vividness? Even if the novelist has decided on a narrator who will fit one of the critic's classifications — "omniscient," "first-person," "limited omniscient," "objective," "roving," "effaced," and so on — his troubles have just begun. He simply cannot find answers to his immediate, precise, practical problems by referring to statements that the "omniscient is the most flexible method," or "the objective the most rapid or vivid," or whatever. . . . the novelist discovers his narrative technique as he tries to achieve for his readers the potentialities of his developing idea. The majority of choices are consequently choices of degree, not kind. To decide that your narrator shall not be omniscient decides practically nothing... To decide that you will use first-person narration decides again almost nothing. What kind of first person? How fully characterised? How much aware of himself as a narrator? How reliable? How much confined to realistic inference, how far privileged to go beyond realism? At what points shall he speak truth and at what points utter no judgment or even utter falsehood?[10]

All these questions cannot of course be solved by generalisations: the writer of fiction has to work out the answers to them in his page-to-page progress through his story.

Point of view

<table>
<tr><td>Point of view</td><td colspan="2">is the position from which the reader perceives the events of a story.
refers to the perspective or perspectives established by an author through which the reader is presented with a story.</td></tr>
<tr><td rowspan="8">The author</td><td colspan="2">is not identical with the narrator.
is different from the implied author.</td></tr>
<tr><td colspan="2">must come to terms with the problem of how much authorial guidance is needed for the story to have its proper effect.
decides what channels of information he is to use to convey the story to the reader.
has to settle the question of what mode of presentation he ought to employ.
decides at what distance he wants to place the reader from the story.</td></tr>
<tr><td>creates a narrator</td><td>to establish an authority outside himself.
who tells the story (objectively).
whose point of view controls the entire story.</td></tr>
<tr><td colspan="2">chooses the most suitable narrator from whose point of view the story is to be told.</td></tr>
<tr><td>opts for</td><td>editorial omniscience.
neutral omniscience.
selective omniscience.
a limited point of view.</td></tr>
<tr><td colspan="2">impersonates a character and writes as "I".
closely follows a character through his adventures and refers to him as "he".</td></tr>
<tr><td>employs</td><td>an observer-narrator.
a protagonist-narrator.</td></tr>
</table>

p. t. o.

Point of view (continued)

<table>
<tr><td rowspan="6">The author</td><td rowspan="3">makes use of</td><td>an</td><td>outsider's
insider's</td><td rowspan="3">point of view.</td></tr>
<tr><td>a first-person</td><td>peripheral
central</td></tr>
<tr><td>a third-person</td><td>omniscient
limited</td></tr>
<tr><td colspan="4">adopts a mixture of several points of view.
uses multiple points of view.
moves from character to character.
employs a shifting point of view.
shifts the angle of vision from time to time.
employs drastic shifts in the point of view.</td></tr>
<tr><td colspan="4">uses an impersonal approach.
adopts an impersonal point of view.
pretends not to be there at all.
dispenses with a narrator altogether.
lets the story tell itself.
effaces himself completely.</td></tr>
<tr><td>tries to achieve</td><td colspan="3">a unity of focus.
a strong illusion of giving an inside view.
a strong identification of the reader with the viewpoint of the narrator.</td></tr>
<tr><td>The implied author
The author's "second self"</td><td colspan="4">is always a superior version of the author as he exists in real life.
may be different from story to story.</td></tr>
<tr><td>The subjective author</td><td colspan="4">directly judges or interprets the characters and the significance of the events.
makes use of "authorial intrusions".
comments on whatever he likes.</td></tr>
<tr><td>The objective author</td><td colspan="4">avoids describing even the characters' ideas and emotions.
lets the reader infer everything from the facts alone.</td></tr>
</table>

p. t. o.

Point of view (continued)

<table>
<tr><td rowspan="3">The narrator</td><td colspan="3">may be dramatised or undramatised.
completely dominates the tale he is presenting.</td></tr>
<tr><td>may be</td><td colspan="2">omniscient.
limited in his knowledge.
self-conscious.
reliable, trustworthy.
fallible, unreliable.
intrusive.
unintrusive.</td></tr>
<tr><td>may tell the story</td><td colspan="2">in the first person.
in the third person.</td></tr>
<tr><td rowspan="4">The omniscient narrator</td><td colspan="3">has a godlike sweep of vision.
seems to know the meaning of the events.
tells the story from a remote standpoint.
knows everything that needs to be known about the characters and the events.</td></tr>
<tr><td rowspan="2">is entirely free</td><td colspan="2">to move as he will in time and place.
to shift from character to character.</td></tr>
<tr><td>to report
to conceal</td><td>what he chooses of the characters' speech and actions.</td></tr>
<tr><td colspan="3">has access to the characters' thoughts, feelings, and motives.</td></tr>
<tr><td>The narrator who is limited in his knowledge</td><td colspan="3">confines himself to what is experienced, thought and felt by a single character.
uses a character as a focus, mirror, or centre of consciousness.
may present all the events and actions as they unfold before the particular consciousness of one of the characters.
seems to come by his knowledge through natural means.
seems to be roving around since he can be anywhere at any time except within the minds of the characters.</td></tr>
</table>

p. t. o.

Point of view (continued)

	is himself a character in the story.	
A first-person narrator	may be	a fortuitous witness of the matters he relates. a minor participant in the action. a noncentral character. the central character in the story.
	is limited in his point of view to what he himself knows, experiences, infers, or finds out by talking to other characters. knows and understands only what his temperament and talent permit. can describe with unchallenged authority his own sensations and ideas. can invest the story with (uncommon) credibility.	
A third-person narrator	stands outside the story. may tell the story from an omniscient position. may content himself with watching and observing. may restrict himself to the point of view of one character. may use a character as the viewpoint character and make the reader see everything through his eyes. may use the "seeing eye" of a single character. may add his own guesses and conclusions from what he observes.	
The self-conscious narrator	is aware that he is composing a work of art. takes the reader into his confidence about the various problems involved in the telling of his story.	
The fallible, unreliable narrator	may be	excessively innocent. oversophisticated. blind to the moral problems involved in certain situations. deliberately deceptive.
	gives a distorted view of the events. may pretend to qualities he does not possess. does not interpret and evaluate the matters he relates in accordance with the norms of the work. is used by the author for the purpose of irony.	

p. t. o.

Point of view (continued)	
The intrusive narrator	not only reports but freely comments on the characters. evaluates the characters' actions and motives. expresses his views about human life in general. makes authoritative judgments.
The unintrusive, impersonal narrator	describes or "shows" the action in dramatic scenes. does not intrude his own comments and judgments. gives up the privilege of access to inner feelings and emotions and presents only the external action.

Comprehension and revision

1) Explain the difference between the author and the narrator of a work of prose fiction.
2) Why is the story told by a narrator and not by the author himself?
3) Is it true to say that an undramatized narrator is identical with the implied author?
4) Try to explain the meaning of the following technical terms:
   — point of view;
   — implied author;
   — editorial omniscience;
   — neutral omniscience;
   — limited point of view;
   — impersonal narration;
   — shifting point of view;
   — self-conscious narrator;
   — unreliable narrator.
5) What are the advantages and disadvantages of
   — an omniscient point of view?
   — a limited point of view?
   — impersonal narration?

Typical tasks and questions

1) Try to characterize the narrator.
2) From what position does the narrator tell the story?
3) Explain the point of view from which this story is told.
4) What channels of information does the narrator use to present the story to the reader?
5) At what point in the story does a shift in the point of view take place? What is its function?
6) Is the narrator reliable? Try to find some evidence in the text for your answer.

7.2.2. Mode of presentation

The narrator's point of view directs the reader's attention to whatever the author wants him to hear, feel and see. This kind of involvement in the story can be achieved by conveying it primarily as **summary** (also known as **telling** or **panorama),** or as **scene** (also known as **showing** or, more rarely, as **picture)**, or — most commonly — as a combination of the two. These two **modes of presentation** are quite distinct and are used by writers of fiction for different purposes — summary provides a comprehensive and extensive view, whereas scene offers an intensive view, like a close-up photograph. Summary narrative is especially useful when the writer intends to give "a generalized account or report of a series of events covering some extended period and a variety of locales"[11] or when he wants to cover large tracts of the world of his narrative which are necessary to his tale, but are not worth narrating in detail. Other frequent uses of summary are the description of the setting and the sketching of some background to the main characters' specific activities or a rapid conveying of their past history.
If the narrator uses the method of telling, his own attitude towards the events he recounts is clearly dominant, whereas if he employs the method of showing, the event itself is in the centre of attention and is allowed to speak for itself. The scene method is thus used especially for intense moments and whenever an important action takes place. No amount of telling can replace the effect of immediacy that is achieved by showing setting, action and character in scenic presentation. With its concrete details of time, place, action, and character and its stress on 'living' dialogue, scenic presentation closely resembles the dramatist's method. Whenever this **dramatic mode** is used, the characters therefore present and interpret themselves in their words and actions, and the details of time and setting and the characters' appearance may be given by the author as in stage directions. This is to say that the reader is asked to infer the meaning of what is being shown without any help from the comments of the narrator.
Either method — telling or showing — would of course be a mere *tour de force* if used exclusively. The art of narrative is based on the proper use and the skilful blending of panorama and scene, as in the following extract from Charlotte Brontë's *Jane Eyre* (1847), which can serve as a typical example:

Panorama: The moon was set, and it was very dark;
Scene: Bessie carried a lantern, whose light glanced on wet steps and gravel road...
Panorama: Raw and chill was the winter morning;
Scene: My teeth chattered as I hastened down the drive...
The distant roll of the wheels announced the coming coach; I went to the door and watched its lamps approach rapidly through the gloom....
The coach drew up... my trunk was hoisted up; I was taken from Bessie's neck, to which I clung with kisses. "Be sure and

take good care of her!" cried she to the guard. "Ay, ay!" was the answer; the door was slapped to, and on we drove.

Panorama: We appeared to travel over hundreds of miles. . . .
We passed through several towns,

Scene: and in one, a very large one, the coach stopped; the horses were taken out, and the passengers alighted to dine. I was carried into an inn. . . .[12]

A special case is the presentation of what goes on in characters' minds. This dramatization in language of the workings of a character's consciousness tries to reflect the interior processes of perception, thought and speech by following his **stream of consciousness.** As a method of narration the so-called stream-of-consciousness technique is concerned with the presentation of the impressions made upon a character's conscious and unconscious mind by the experiences of life. In using this narrative method, the author never leaves the area of one person's immediate experience and restricts himself completely to this character's point of view.

He may introduce the reader directly into the interior life of a character by giving a direct quotation of the processes of this character's mind in all their disregard of formal logic or conventional concepts of time. This is to say that the reader is given access to the easy and effortless intermingling of past and present events as they come into the character's mind by random association. This disorganization of events out of time is typical of the whole process. The reader follows a character's thoughts as they move uninterruptedly from one thing to another and on through the whole of his "accumulated experience, stored in [his] memory and available for immediate recall as soon as the right word or image appears to trigger it off. . . . Things happen by random association rather than by any scheme of causation."[13]

When a writer does not try to record the whole consciousness of a character with the almost totally unpredictable workings of his mind, including the nonverbal elements, but limits himself to that area of his consciousness in which the mind formulates its feelings and thoughts as language, we speak of the technique of **interior monologue.** This translation into language of the character's thoughts and feelings is also known as **reported thought** or **substitutionary narration,** especially when a third-person point of view and the past tense group are used. If the author attempts to transmit the character's consciousness by intervening between the character's mind and the reader and giving a summary of the character's thought — and often an interpretation of what the character thinks and feels as well — we speak of **internal analysis,** "since it is the author's *analysis* of what is taking place inside the character. Internal analysis and the stream of consciousness technique are fundamentally different: the one *summarizes,* the other *dramatizes;* the one is *abstract,* the other is *concrete. . . .* If . . . the author intervenes in any way between the reader and the character's consciousness in order to analyze, comment, or interpret, then he is employing not the stream of consciousness technique but a fundamentally different method which may correctly be designated *internal analysis.* The latter is an indirect statement in the words of the author; the former is a direct quotation of the character's consciousness."[14]

There is, however, still considerable disagreement and confusion as to the precise meaning of these terms; many simply refer to all the three methods of narration we have mentioned by the comprehensive term of "the stream-of-consciousness technique". Whichever terms individual critics may prefer, there can be no doubt that the narrative methods which have enabled writers of fiction to move inside the minds of their characters have provided literature with a new convention for the presentation of the processes of the mind which will be used by authors for a long time to come.

Mode of presentation

<table>
<tr><td rowspan="3">The narrator</td><td>uses the method of</td><td>telling.
showing.</td></tr>
<tr><td>relies mainly on the presentation of</td><td>panorama.
scene.</td></tr>
<tr><td colspan="2">employs the dramatic method.
gives a panoramic view.
(skilfully) blends panorama and scene.
shifts the focus from panorama to scene.
makes use of several narrative methods.
effaces himself completely.
employs the stream-of-consciousness technique.</td></tr>
<tr><td>A story can be presented</td><td colspan="2">as summary or as scene or as a combination of the two.
as a direct quotation of the processes of thought in a character's consciousness.</td></tr>
<tr><td>Summary
Panorama
Telling</td><td colspan="2">provides a comprehensive and extensive view.
offers a panoramic view.
provides a comprehensive focus.
may help to establish setting, atmosphere and tone.
establishes the authority of the narrator.
is useful for the presentation of material which is necessary to the story but not worth narrating in detail.</td></tr>
</table>

p. t. o.

Mode of presentation (continued)		
Scene Showing The dramatic method	offers an intensive view. provides the focus of a close-up. lets the characters present and interpret themselves.	
	is used	for intense moments. when an important action takes place.
When the dramatic method is used, the reader		is brought close to the story's action. feels, hears and sees the action.
The stream-of-consciousness technique	attempts a presentation of what goes on in a character's mind. dramatizes in language the workings of a character's consciousness. tries to reflect the interior processes of perception, thought and speech. is concerned with the presentation of the impressions made upon a character's conscious and unconscious mind by the experiences of life. gives a direct quotation of the processes of a character's mind. gives the reader access to the chain of free association in a character's mind. allows the reader to follow a character's thoughts. tries to record the whole of a character's consciousness.	
Interior monologue	is limited to that area of a character's consciousness in which the mind formulates its feelings and thoughts as language. reports a character's consciousness insofar as it is translated into language.	
Internal analysis	gives a summary of a character's thought in the author's words. lets the author or narrator intervene between the reader and the character's consciousness in order to analyse, comment, or interpret.	

Comprehension and revision

1) Explain the difference between telling and showing.
2) What are summary and scene used for by writers of fiction?
3) Explain what a writer does when he makes use of
   — the stream-of-consciousness technique;
   — interior monologue;
   — internal analysis.

Typical tasks and questions

1) Analyse the mode of presentation used in this narrative.
2) What effect is achieved when the narrator
   — shifts the focus from panorama to scene at this point in the story?
   — effaces himself completely and gives a direct quotation of the workings of this character's mind?

For study

Study the following four extracts and then say whether they present the technique of stream of consciousness, interior monologue, internal analysis, or substitutionary narration (reported thought).

extract one:

Yes because he never did a thing like that before as ask to get his breakfast in bed with a couple of eggs since the *City Arms* hotel when he used to be pretending to be laid up with a sick voice doing his highness to make himself interesting to that old faggot Mrs Riordan that he thought he had a great leg of and she never left us a farthing all for masses for herself and her soul greatest miser ever was actually afraid to lay out 4d for her methylated spirit telling me all her ailments she had too much chat in her about politics and earthquakes and the end of the world let us have a bit of fun first God help the world if all the women were her sort down on bathingsuits and lownecks . . .[15]

extract two:

"The vagaries of the Fair, dear girl," he said presently, in a soft, blurred tone. That's one of his phrases, thought Miriam — that's old-fashioned politeness; courtliness. Behind it he's got some sort of mannish thought . . . "the unaccountability of women" . . . who can understand a woman — she doesn't even understand herself — thought he'd given up trying to make out. He's gone through life and got his own impression; all utterly wrong . . . talking about them with an air of wisdom to young men like Gerald . . . my dear boy, a woman never knows her own mind. How utterly detestable mannishness is; so mighty and strong and comforting when you have mewed up with women all your life, and then suddenly, in a second, far away, utterly imbecile and aggravating with a superior self-satisfied smile because a woman says one thing one minute and another the next. Men ought to be horsewhipped, all the grown men, all, all, horsewhipped until they apologize on their knees.[16]

extract three:

> The hushed happiness that had begun in the dining room half an hour ago seized her again suddenly, sending her forward almost on tiptoe. It was securely there; the vista it opened growing in beauty as she walked... bearing within her in secret unfathomable abundance the gift of old-English rose and white gracious adorable womanhood...[17]

extract four:

> In his normal condition, nothing could have exceeded Charles's terror and shame in such a situation. He had been the cause of a disturbance! He had broken the sacred law of self-effacing, mute compliance — he had made, the phrase ran, an *exhibition of himself!* Normally, he would not have waited, except to stammer out his apologies...[18]

7.2.3 Distance

Distance (also known as **aesthetic distance** or, more rarely, as **psychic distance)** is a factor in fiction "which helps to control the intensity and kind of attention the reader is asked to give to the story, especially to its dramatic scenes (close-ups). It helps to determine how near the author should bring the reader to the scene."[19] In most good stories the reader is meant to participate in the events of the plot, "but not to the extent of losing himself in his emotional reaction. The reader must be able to contemplate and feel the action almost simultaneously. If the distance between him and the action is too great, he cannot participate in the feeling; if the distance is too little, he cannot contemplate the intellectual content of the action."[20] In other words, distance refers to the degree to which the reader is asked to forget the artificiality of the story he is reading and to participate in the fortunes of the characters it shows him. Whatever device makes him aware that he has to do with a work of fictional art and not with real life increases the distance between him and the work.

The concept of distance does not, however, refer only to the reader's involvement or detachment with the work as a whole, but is also applied to the relation between the author and his narrator, the narrator and the other characters, and the reader's relation to any of these. The degree of a reader's involvement in a work of fiction is thus normally made up of many reactions to author, narrator or narrators, and to other characters.

There are some devices by which the reader's distance from the action that is presented to him may to a certain extent be controlled or manipulated. If, for example, the author wants to involve the reader directly in the story, he can use scenic presentation and make imagery and dialogue work before his eyes, as if no gap in time separated him from the action of the story. If the narrator shifts the focus back to panorama, the reader's involvement in the events becomes consequently more detached. Another point is that first-person narration tends, on the whole, to

be more intimate and involving than third-person narration, because readers tend to identify more easily with the narrator's experiences if he offers his own personal testimony.
In most narratives the reader is held in a flexible relationship with its events, and his experience of distance varies in the course of the story — sometimes involved, sometimes detached, as best serves the author's artistic purpose.

Distance

Distance Aesthetic distance	determines how near the author wants to bring the reader to the scene. helps to control the intensity and kind of attention the reader is asked to give to the events of the story. refers to the degree to which the reader is asked to forget the artificiality of the story he is reading. may also refer to the relation between the author and his narrator and between the narrator and other characters. may range from identification to complete opposition. may vary in the course of the story. may to a certain extent be controlled or manipulated.

Comprehension and revision

1) What ideas does the concept of 'distance' refer to?
2) What are some of the devices an author can use to control distance and what are their effects?

Typical tasks and questions

1) Analyse the degree of the reader's involvement in this section of the story.
2) How has the author managed to control distance?

7.3 Characters and characterisation

The **characters** in a narrative work are fictional representations. They are motivated to act as they do, just as are people in real life. They may remain essentially stable, i.e. unchanged in their outlook and dispositions, throughout the course of the narrative, or they may undergo various degrees of change, either slowly and gradually or as the result of a crisis of some sort. Irrespective of whether a character remains stable or undergoes some change, he is not credible as a character unless he shows **consistency** in his behaviour. This is not to say that he cannot occasionally surprise us, but the surprise must still be grounded in his temperament and general make-up as we have come to know it from his previous conduct.[21]

If we now go on to consider the roles characters have to play within a work, we can distinguish between **central characters, background characters,** and a wide variety of **intermediate figures.**
The **central characters** (also known as **protagonists** or **heroes** and **heroines)** are

> those characters whose motivation and history are most fully established, who conflict and change as the story progresses, who engage our responses more fully and steadily, in a way more complex though not necessarily more vivid than other characters. They are the vehicles by which all the most interesting questions are raised; they evoke our beliefs, sympathies, revulsions; they incarnate the moral vision of the world inherent in the total novel. In a sense they are endproducts; they are what the novel exists for; it exists to reveal them. . . . At the other end of the scale are those many different kinds of creation we lump together as **background characters.** These may . . . be allowed a moment of intensity and depth, but equally they may be almost entirely anonymous, voices rather than individualized characters. Singly they may be merely useful cogs in the mechanism of the plot, collectively they may establish themselves as a chorus to the main action . . . or may exist simply to establish the density of society in which the protagonists must move if they are to have any depth of realization.[22]

Between the central characters and the background characters we find a wide variety of **intermediate characters** who exist mainly to serve some particular function. We will thus come across characters who act as spokesmen and representatives — they may have been created to express the viewpoint of a social group; or they have to represent some idea or concept; or they may be used as mouthpieces for the views the author wants to repudiate and of course also for the views he wants to put across to his readers; or they may be meant to have about them something of a symbolic or mythical quality.
Another useful distinction is that made between **flat** and **round characters.**[23] A **flat character** is one that can be summed up in a single sentence because he is constructed round a single idea or quality and thus presented only in outline and without much individualizing detail. A **round character,** on the other hand, is hard to describe adequately because he is characterised by good and bad features, typically a mixture of weaknesses and strengths. Because of his very complexity, both in temperament and motivation, and also because of his ability to surprise us occasionally, he cannot be described in a single phrase. Flat characters tend to be background figures, mere **types,** perhaps even **caricatures,** who are easily recognized when they appear and are easily remembered by the reader afterwards, whereas round characters cannot be placed so easily because their creator has made them so many-faceted. This is the reason why round characters are often referred to as **three-dimensional** — as opposed to the **two-dimensional** nature of flat characters — but it is important to realize that even though the creation of round characters may signify a bigger literary achievement than the invention of flat ones,

two-dimensional characters may be entirely adequate for the author's purpose. "The degree to which a character needs to be three-dimensional depends on his function in the plot, and in many types of plot, such as in the detective novel or adventure novel or farce comedy, even the protagonist usually possesses only two dimensions."[24]

Characters

<table>
<tr><td rowspan="2">Characters in fiction</td><td colspan="2">are created to serve some function.
have a role to play in the story.
remain stable or undergo a change.
must show consistency in their behaviour to be credible.
may occasionally surprise us.</td></tr>
<tr><td>may be</td><td>flat or round.
two-dimensional or three-dimensional.</td></tr>
<tr><td rowspan="2">The central characters
The protagonists
The main characters</td><td colspan="2">evoke our beliefs, sympathies, and revulsions.</td></tr>
<tr><td>are those characters</td><td>whose motivation and history are most fully established.
who are at the centre of attention.</td></tr>
<tr><td rowspan="2">Background characters</td><td>may be</td><td>almost entirely anonymous.
mere cardboard figures.
mere types or even caricatures.</td></tr>
<tr><td colspan="2">are two-dimensional and flat.</td></tr>
<tr><td>Intermediate characters</td><td colspan="2">may be major or minor characters.
exist mainly to serve some particular purpose.
act as spokesmen and representatives.
may express the viewpoint of a social group.
may represent some idea or concept.
are often used as mouthpieces.
may have about them something of a symbolic or mythical quality.</td></tr>
<tr><td rowspan="2">Flat characters</td><td colspan="2">can be summed up in a single sentence.
are constructed round a single idea or quality.</td></tr>
<tr><td>are presented</td><td>only in outline.
without much individualizing detail.</td></tr>
</table>

p. t. o.

Characters (continued)			
Flat characters	tend to be background figures, mere types. are two-dimensional.		
Round characters	are hard to describe adequately. are complex and three-dimensional. may surprise us occasionally. are many-faceted.		
This character X	is sharply delineated. is drawn 'larger than life'. is (not) fully characterised. shows (no) complexity of emotion.		
	is	described presented portrayed depicted characterised	as a mere type. as a fully-rounded character.
			with psychological subtlety.

Character in a work of fiction is not nearly as complex and puzzling as character in real life — not even the best writers of fiction can give a total portrait of a complete person. Even if an author intends to present a character in depth in a work of fictional art, he must be selective in the organization of his material and thus cannot achieve a perfect picture. "Yet we do learn about character [in fiction] rather as we do in real life: from people's actions, from what they say about themselves, from what others say about them. We may be told just what to think, or be left with some of the ambiguities and perplexities we feel in real life."[25] In other words, the writer of fiction may handle characterisation in a number of ways.

He can first of all invent a name that fits the character and thus helps to describe him, as in the case of the villainous Murdstone, a character from Dickens's novel *David Copperfield* (1849—50); or he may give an explicit description of the character's moral nature and also provide telling comments on his actions **(direct characterisation).** Another type of evidence comes from the other characters in a narrative; they may function as foils to this character and by their differences from him and also by the various ways in which they resemble him, or even embody and personify certain traits in his character, help to establish his true nature; they may also discuss his person or comment on his behaviour and in this manner provide additional clues. The most important evidence, however, usually comes from the character himself. He may make direct statements about himself or show the significant traits of his character in what he says and does; or the author may prefer to employ the stream of consciousness technique and try to give a representation of what is going on in his mind at a crucial moment. Not infrequently a writer uses several of these methods in combination to achieve the particular effects he is aiming at, although we can normally say that his main mode of establishing character is one of **telling** or of **showing** (cf. 7.2.2 above), i.e. we may be given the most significant information about a character in the narrator's descriptions and comments, or we may have to infer what the character is like by closely following his own dialogue and behaviour, and perhaps also that of the other characters, which the author simply shows us and leaves it at that **(indirect characterisation).**

Characterisation

<table>
<tr><td rowspan="2">Characterisation in fiction</td><td rowspan="2">may be</td><td>attempted
handled</td><td>in a number of ways.</td></tr>
<tr><td colspan="2">achieved by telling or showing or by telling and showing in combination.</td></tr>
<tr><td rowspan="5">Character in fiction may be established</td><td>by giving</td><td colspan="2">the character a name that fits him.
an explicit description of the character's moral nature.</td></tr>
<tr><td colspan="3">by providing authorial comments on the character's actions.
by the other characters' comments.</td></tr>
<tr><td colspan="3">by surrounding the character with a number of other characters who
— exemplify certain traits in his character.
— dramatize the moral choices he has.
— act as foils to him.</td></tr>
<tr><td>by the character's</td><td colspan="2">own dialogue and actions.
stream of consciousness.</td></tr>
<tr><td colspan="3">by the language the character uses.</td></tr>
<tr><td colspan="4">Character is exposed when...</td></tr>
<tr><td colspan="4">The basic traits of X's character are...
One of X's striking characteristics is...
X is characterised by one outstanding quality, namely...
X has one besetting emotion, namely...
X stands in clear contrast to Y.
X is only described from the outside.</td></tr>
</table>

Comprehension and revision

1) What makes a character in a work of fiction credible?
2) Try to explain the difference between
   — central characters, background characters, and intermediate characters;
   — flat and round characters.

For study

Can you think of any work or works in which even the protagonist is only two-dimensional? Does this fact have any effect on the quality of this work or these works?

Typical tasks and questions

1) How are the characters presented in this story?
2) Try to explain the devices the author has used
   — to characterise X;
   — to make X's character emerge;
   — to bring out the contrasts between X and Y.
3) Trace the different stages of X's development.
4) Show that X and Y are two different types of character.
5) Try to summarize the information the reader gets about X.
6) What is X's position within the total structure of the story? Is he a major or a minor character? Give reasons for your opinion.

7.4 Language and style

The medium the literary artist must use to convey his work is, of course, **language,** but there are an infinite number of ways in which language can be used for literary purposes. In what follows we will try to indicate what seem to be the most frequent uses of language in fiction and to show how writers may achieve certain effects by using different **styles.**

Language is employed first of all to **communicate the facts of the story.** It serves the writer as a means of informing the reader about what generally takes place within the fictional world, and it can also transmit attitudes, experiences, emotions, and even ideas and values. In most mainstream fiction, i.e. fiction which is not experimental in character but is based on conventional techniques of storytelling, all this information can be conveyed through a mixture of ordinary narrative with passages of dialogue or conversation.

It is in these conversational passages that a second important use of language is to be found — it helps to **reveal character.** A skilful writer will find an appropriate diction for all his characters which will establish them as individual people. That is to say, he will differentiate them by making them use a particular style that suits their sex, age, education, class, occupation, social life, nationality, religion, and so on. They may also have speech defects, mannerisms, favourite phrases; some will be shy and inarticulate; some fluent and cogent, some merely loquacious; some witty, some dull; some may be prone to use vehement, emphatic language, or coarse and brutal language; some will be reticent or prim; some will like quotations, or slang, or proverbs; the talk of some will be muddled and inconsequential; some will have tact and some will not.[26]

The writer may also indicate how strong emotional stress in its many forms may modify speech, making it broken and confused, or more eloquent and poetic, or even obscene and grotesque; and he may underline developments in character by causing these characters to change their speech habits. Briefly, character emerges only partly through what a person does, the way he is made to talk is often of equal significance.

A third important use of language is to **bring out irony.** Irony basically refers to the difference between what is asserted and what is actually the case.[27] When the author's ironic purposes are accomplished through his use of language, we speak of **verbal irony** (for other forms of irony see 7.7 below). A writer may achieve an effect of irony through his choice of an inappropriate title, as with Hemingway's "The Undefeated", where the implications of the title are not borne out by the contents of the story; or, more often, the writer's ironic attitude towards his material may be brought out by the words he uses to describe his characters and their actions within the text itself. A special effect of verbal irony can be achieved when the first-person narrator is made to use language that — unnoticed by himself — reveals his self-contradictions, his self-deceptions, his prejudices, and his failure of insight in general. All this clearly establishes him as a fallible narrator (cf. under 7.2.1 above) who of course does not notice the effect of irony that his words bring about. It is in fact up to the reader to use his intelligence to discover the irony.

A fourth function of language in fiction is perhaps even less obvious than the ironic effects it may create. When language is used to **establish meaning** the writer tries to make use of words in a figurative manner and to set off conscious or unconscious resonances in the reader, who will then not only absorb the information that the literal meaning of certain words and phrases implies but also become aware to a certain extent of what these words and phrases suggest on a deeper level of meaning. The effect of employing this figurative dimension of language is often twofold — a certain image may trigger off in the reader's mind its own particular associations and it may also evoke in him a sense of the deeper significance of the events in the story.

Figurative language in this sense is used by many writers to **achieve an undercurrent of meaning** which helps to bring about the desired artistic effect and to attune the reader to the interpretation which the author is aiming at. For this he sometimes employs strongly **emotive language;** this is language which touches off reverberations in the reader's own mind and produces in him an emotional response to the many allusions and references in the text to aspects of the human condition and especially to mankind's eternal struggle on earth. William Faulkner (1897—1962), for instance, is a master of such a style, employing a language that carries many **overtones** and is fraught with dark meanings. This extra dimension of allusion in a work of fiction of this sort may in the end become as integral to our understanding of it as its overt subject matter. Our attitude may become so suffused with these references to the deeper meaning behind the story's events that we experience everything that occurs with all those allusions colouring our vision. In this way we are led to regard the story as a work of art which does not only present individual events but also expresses something of the larger significance of these events and thus **embodies a universal truth.**[28] Language can thus **function as a vehicle of interpretation,** especially when certain words and phrases are used again and again throughout a text and obviously operate as **motifs** or **symbols** or both.

Any recurring element in a piece of fiction may be called a motif. Its value lies in the fact that the frequent repetition of a certain phrase in the same work provides an important clue to the meaning of the whole. This is because such motifs have not been put there by the author by accident but in a conscious attempt to establish meaning. Motifs may also help to weld the work together.

A symbol, on the other hand, is something that stands for itself and yet also represents or suggests or means something else as well. In some cases symbols operate as motifs, too, and are thus reinforced and extended. Examples of this use of symbols as motifs can be found in a well-known modern novel, J. D. Salinger's *The Catcher in the Rye* (1951), in which recurring motifs, such as the ducks in the park or Holden's hunting cap that he likes to put on from time to time, all stand for something else besides actual ducks and caps and so act as symbols as well.

The difficulty with motifs and even more so with symbols is not only that they are more or less hidden in the text and have first of all to be recognized as such but that, once they have been recognized, their meaning has to be established. There are some conventional symbols whose meaning has long been fixed so that they do not present any problems, such as a red rose as a symbol of love. Most literary symbols, however, are 'private' or 'personal symbols' and as such may have meanings for which conventional symbols do not exist. We may recognize a detail in the story as symbolic if it is conspicuous for some reason other than its importance in the plot. In trying to find out just *what* it symbolizes familiar **connotations** may be relevant. "But this approach can be misleading. Connotations often conflict: fire suggests both danger and the friendly hearth." So a better approach seems to be to study the context in which we find the symbol. "Does it in any way repeat, resemble, or suggest an element of the scene in which it appears? Are any of its connotations specifically relevant to the scene?" When a symbol turns up in a number of situations, "we should ask not only how it is related to each context, but also how these contexts are related to one another. If the contexts form a pattern or progression of their own . . . or if they possess certain qualities in common, we have a further clue to the symbol's meaning."[29] All these methods of interpreting symbols may be found useful. The point is, of course, that if we can manage to properly understand a writer's symbols, we will have gone a long way in understanding the meaning of what he is trying to communicate.

Language

<table>
<tr><td>Language</td><td colspan="3">is the medium of fiction.
may be used in an infinite number of ways.</td></tr>
<tr><td rowspan="4">Language is used in fiction</td><td colspan="3">to communicate the facts of the story.
to inform the reader what generally takes place in the fictional world.</td></tr>
<tr><td colspan="3">to reveal character.</td></tr>
<tr><td colspan="3">to bring out irony.
to achieve an effect of irony.</td></tr>
<tr><td colspan="3">to establish meaning.
to achieve an undercurrent of meaning.
to function as a vehicle of interpretation.</td></tr>
<tr><td rowspan="4">The author</td><td>employs</td><td>informal
formal
figurative
emotive</td><td>language.</td></tr>
<tr><td>uses language</td><td colspan="2">functionally.
figuratively.
symbolically.</td></tr>
<tr><td colspan="3">employs verbal irony.</td></tr>
<tr><td colspan="3">tries to communicate meaning through language.</td></tr>
</table>

Even though no agreement has yet been reached as to a method of evaluating **style** objectively and in such a way that it shows its artistic force at the same time, we may say that a writer's use of a certain style may be among the most important elements in his success in accomplishing his artistic aims.[30]

The pragmatic insights that have been reached so far enable us to say that **general diction,** i. e. the use of ordinary language, is suitable when the aim is to summarize, to abstract and to abridge. **Specific and concrete diction,** on the other hand, tends to heighten the immediacy of the scene that is being described by its appeal to the senses.

A writer can often achieve humorous and ironic effects when he employs **informal language** full of colloquialisms and slang. Some famous examples of such usage are Twain's Huck Finn and Salinger's Holden Caulfield. On the other hand, **formal language,** which has a number of subcategories: **technical, foreign, allusive, learned,** tends on the whole to have a distancing effect (for 'distance' cp. 7.2.3 above). **Figurative language,** which makes use of imagery, symbols, metaphors, and analogy, may suggest emotional colouring and generally intensifies the implications of the material; a highly metaphorical style lends itself especially well to the purposes of **allegory.**

A whole range of effects may be obtained through **sentence structure.** Short sentences often carry overtones of urgency and seem to rush the action forward, whereas long sentences frequently "attain a momentum and rhythm appropriate to sustained action."[31] Highly coherent sentence structure can often refine the effect of what is being told, and a calmly balanced structure is appropriate for the discussion of philosophical concepts and ideas in general.

There are many more ways in which language may be used by the writer of fiction, especially with regard to the subversion of conventional syntax, the creation of stylistic effects from an exploitation of sound patterns and the rhythmic repetition of structure.

At a final level, style is thus not only a writer's characteristic use of language or merely "an index either of the narrator's personality or of individual characters whose speech and thought the novelist may stylize to reveal distinctive qualities of temperament", but "it is *a way of organizing and creating reality; it reflects and extends the basic vision of life contained by the [work]"*[32] and thus helps to create an artistic whole which can embody meaning.

Style

Style	is an author's characteristic use of language. intensifies the implications of the fictional material. is a way of organizing and creating reality. reflects and extends the basic vision of life expressed in a work. helps to create an artistic whole which can embody meaning. contributes to the story's success.

p. t. o.

Style (continued)			
The author	uses a characteristic style.		
	uses	general specific and concrete	diction.
	aims at creating certain stylistic effects.		

Comprehension and revision

1) How is language employed in fiction? Try to characterise its various uses.
2) Try to find definitions of the following terms:
   — motif;
   — symbol;
   — irony;
   — figurative language;
   — emotive language;
   — diction;
   — style.
3) How can the meaning of symbols be established?
4) Explain some of the effects that a skilful use of style can achieve.

For study and discussion

Can you think of any conventional symbols and the meanings they have? What private symbols, i. e. unconventional symbols used by writers in particular works, have you found in your own reading? Can you explain their meaning?

Typical tasks and questions

1) Examine the use of language in this work and comment on its function.
2) What sort of language does X characteristically use? What can his use of language tell us about his general background and his character?
3) Where does the writer use emotive language? Try to explain the effect he apparently wants to achieve.
4) ... is clearly used symbolically. Try to establish its meaning.
5) Can you find examples of irony in the text? Explain what makes them ironic.

7.5 The treatment of time

One of the distinguishing features of the modern consciousness seems to be an increased awareness of everything that happens as being part of the ever-changing process of history. This sense of the passing of time as something important is without doubt a most significant factor in our conception of the nature of reality as essentially dynamic, i.e. constantly moving and changing, as against the notion of an essentially static cosmos, i.e. one which remains basically stable and unchanging, which was accepted in the Middle Ages. These different conceptions of reality and thus of the nature of time have of course found expression in the work of the literary artists of every period.

The heroes and heroines of the medieval romances exist in a timeless world, and this is one of the reasons why they seem so remote from us. Robinson Crusoe, on the other hand, immediately goes and devises a calendar once he finds himself alone on his island. This action of the central character in what is perhaps the first novel in English (cp. under 6.1 above) epitomizes right at the beginning of the historical rise of the novel as a distinct genre its quintessential difference from the timeless world of the old romances — **modern fiction is concerned with a presentation of events as they happen in time.** That is not to say that everything must necessarily be told in a strictly chronological order — we will come back to this problem in a moment — but **modern fiction definitely implies the existence of some kind of time scheme,** with the inevitable consequence that the temporal setting of an individual narrative recedes further and further into the past as the years go by and that the narrative itself may thus lose much of its original appeal. It is certainly one of the characteristics of a great writer that his work can bridge the ever-widening gap between the date of composition and the date of reading by successive generations of readers. He can achieve this by creating a strong illusion of immediacy and directness in the reader's mind of the events that are presented, even though they are described in the past tense. This story illusion may in fact be so vivid that an impression of actual participation in the action is conveyed.

> In other words, the reader if he is engrossed in his reading translates all that happens from this moment of time onwards into an imaginative present of his own and yields to the illusion that he is himself participating in the action or situation, or at least is witnessing it as happening, not merely as having happened. Everything that antedates that point, as for instance exposition, is felt as a fictive past, while all that succeeds it, as for instance those premonitions and anticipatory hints that novelists find so useful for directing the attention forward to the climax or evoking a feeling of suspense, are felt as future. Verbally, all may be equally past; psychologically, once the point of reference has been established, each event presented in its time-order constitutes a point in the past series considered as a now, and whatever is out of sequence in relation to that series of points is considered as relatively past or future....
> To put it more concretely, someone may today be reading a novel written in the past tense about events that took place on a certain day in the year 1789, and feel as though they were happening now at his moment of reading, in his presence and presentness.[33]

When the **chronological past** of the story's action is thus translated into the **fictive present** felt by the reader, the story illusion is complete — the reader is made to forget his own present and sink himself into the fictive present of the story. Of course, all the elements of a work of fiction have to contribute towards achieving this effect, but the writer's handling of the time scheme of the story plays an important part in it.

For E. M. Forster, in his *Aspects of the Novel,* there was **a clock ticking away in every work of fiction;** some writers tried to follow this clock closely, others speeded it up or slowed it down; some set the hands back or forward, but none was able to abolish the clock altogether. If we apply this remark, which is generally accepted as valid in literary criticism, to the choices a writer is faced with in selecting the time scheme of a narrative, we may say that he can choose between three basic alternatives.

He can aim for a close correspondence of **acting time** and **reading time,** which is to say that the events described are transacted in approximately the same time as it takes to read about them. When acting time and reading time correspond in this way it is not normally possible to deal with more than a single day in the lives of the characters, whereas many years may be allowed to elapse between the beginning and the ending of a story if the writer has decided on **concentration** and **compression,** contracting and summarizing time. A third alternative is **expansion** of chronological time. Here the writer tries to catch the full impact of a 'moment of importance' in which the whole of life at its most intense is enclosed; he attempts to hold this moment of vision and to render in words all that he feels is expressed in it. This may be done by employing the stream-of-consciousness technique and giving a direct quotation of everything that passes through a character's consciousness at such a moment. James Joyce called such a sudden spiritual manifestation an **epiphany,** a sudden perception, in the space of a moment, of the total meaning and character of a scene, of a person, of a phrase.

Not many works of fiction are written throughout in one of these three basic approaches to the treatment of time. The writers of mainstream fiction usually vary the proportion of time allocated to particular incidents and in this way **achieve a flexibility in the narrative tempo** which is an important element in their creation of the illusion of immediacy in the mind of the reader; this flexibility of tempo is also helpful in the control of distance. We can lose ourselves in the events of a story much more easily when the writer indicates the relative value of each occurrence within the plot by his handling of pace — an important event may thus be described at greater length than it took to happen, whereas long periods of time may be dealt with in a single paragraph. Narrative speed is largely determined by the amount of detail allowed, but syntactical structure also has an important part to play. A string of short sentences, bound together with connectives like 'and' or 'then', tends to convey an impression of greater speed than elaborate construction with a number of subordinate clauses.[34] (For the influence of style in fiction see 7.4 above).

The temporal structure of a work of fiction is determined not only by the length of reading time allocated to the individual events it describes but also by the order in which they are told. Even "the simplest narrative is likely to *blend the processes of perception, memory and speculation.* Consider this sentence:

> As he sat in the taxi, the memory of his failure last week was strong in him: today's interview could be at least no worse than that.

One of the functions of the storyteller is to be everywhere at the same time, mindful of past history, conscious of the present and aware of the possibilities of the future. In his narrative all known or expected time can be brought to focus on the immediate event, and in the process the 'novelist's clock' is made to tell different times simultaneously."[35] There are many ways in which a writer can handle the difficult problems connected with the setting up of a time scheme that is adequate for the purposes of a particular story — at what point in time within the relative chronology that obtains in the story he ought to set the action in motion, how much of what went on before he should fill in later and at what point or points, and so on. The simplest method is obviously to present the action in strictly **chronological narration,** i. e. to tell about the events in the order in which they happen in time, one after another. We encounter this method mainly in action-centred stories. Where the artistic aim is to get the reader interested in the character's psychological make-up rather than in the action as such, as in fiction in the psychological mode (for details see 8.3 below), writers frequently try to "get in the character first with a strong impression, and then work backwards and forwards over his past."[36]

This method is known as **reverted narration;** some parts of the story are narrated in the obvious time-sequence, but others are presented in **flashbacks,** filling in what went on before the point at which the work opened. This may be done, for example, by shifting the point of view to another character and letting him reveal portions of the past. Or the time continuum may be broken down to such an extent that only a number of fragmentary impressions are given through which the total picture can be perceived in the end. This treatment of time is typical of the impressionist style. (for details see 6.2.2 above). Special effects may be created by the technique of **foreshadowing** (also known as **anticipation),** in which the narrator hints at what comes later and thus increases the suspense.

Generally speaking, the tendency in modern fiction is to give up the old theory which demanded that the narrative should begin somewhere in the middle or even towards the end of the action, then break off to tell about the events which happened before the story opened, "and finally continue with the main line of action from the point of interruption to the end." Instead, many modern writers "prefer to interweave the exposition with the main line of action in the form of short alternating or even intermingling retrospective and anticipatory flashes."[37] The novelty of this **time-shift technique** lies in the fact that what is conventionally called the exposition is now

> treated as part of the main action, not as a subordinate adjunct to it. The focus of presentness shifts continually; the relative pastness and presentness are deliberately dissolved; the tenses are confused or rather fused, so that the past is

> felt not as distinct from the present but included in it and permeating it. Every moment is conceived as the condensation of earlier history, and the past is not separate and completed but an ever-developing part of a changing present.[38]

In other words, some modern writers of fiction have discarded chronological narration because to them it suggests the immutable pastness of the past. As they see it, time is nothing but an eternal present in which the past is fused — there is no past as such, but only a **growing present.** This treatment of all chronological time as nothing but aspects of an eternal present is found mainly among impressionist writers using the stream-of-consciousness technique. They refuse to submit themselves to the conventional notion of the clock as the organizing principle of fiction and have established, at least for themselves, **the 'moment of importance' as the individually decisive time-unit in fiction.** The artistic aim is to present everything as a present experience — perceptions, feelings, memories, ideas, fantasies, and so on — as they pass through an individual's consciousness.

Comprehension and discussion

1) Explain the three basic alternatives a writer is faced with in selecting the time scheme of a narrative.
2) Why is flexibility of tempo so important in the creation of the story illusion?
3) How can the reader be made to forget about the chronological past of the story's action and to translate it into the fictive present?
4) Try to explain the difference between chronological narration and reverted narration.
5) What is meant by the term 'time-shift technique'?
6) Try to explain the idea of a 'growing present' in impressionist fiction.

Typical tasks and questions

1) In what sequence is the action presented in this story? Explain its temporal structure.
2) What is the relation between acting time and reading time?
3) Where has the writer used compression, where expansion? Try to explain what effects he may have wanted to achieve.

The treatment of time

<table>
<tr><td colspan="2">The medieval romances exist in a timeless world.</td></tr>
<tr><td>Modern fiction</td><td>is concerned with a presentation of events as they happen in time.
implies the existence of some kind of time scheme.</td></tr>
<tr><td colspan="2"></td></tr>
</table>

p. t. o.

<table>
<tr><th colspan="4">The treatment of time (continued)</th></tr>
<tr><td rowspan="5">The author</td><td>tries</td><td>to create a strong story illusion
to engross the reader in the story illusion</td><td>by varying the narrative tempo.</td></tr>
<tr><td colspan="3">sets up a time scheme that is adequate for the purposes of a particular story.</td></tr>
<tr><td colspan="3">opts for congruence between acting time and reading time.</td></tr>
<tr><td>makes use of
employs</td><td colspan="2">compression.
expansion.
chronological narration.
reverted narration.
flashbacks.
foreshadowing.
the time-shift technique.</td></tr>
<tr><td colspan="3">tries to present all the events in the story as forming part of a present experience.</td></tr>
<tr><td rowspan="2">The temporal structure
The time scheme
The chronology of a story</td><td>may be based on</td><td colspan="2">chronological narration.
reverted narration.
the idea of an ever-changing present.</td></tr>
<tr><td>may be marked by</td><td colspan="2">a striking disproportion between acting time and reading time.
a skilful handling of the narrative tempo.</td></tr>
</table>

7.6 Setting and atmosphere

By the **setting** of a narrative, we mean the environment of its action, the immediate world in which it takes place. Part of the setting is the physical background (the landscape and scenery), part of it is the whole environment in which the events occur (the climate, the customs of the country, the historical period, intellectual and cultural life, social levels, the general standard of living, and so on). Part of the setting may also be formed by people, such as the members of the social class in whose circles the protagonists move.

Setting is not of equal importance in all fiction, and different writers use setting in different ways. It may sometimes be the most important element, as in the case of fiction with a strong reformist purpose where the setting is used by the writer to expose the faults of society he wants to attack, or it may simply be one of the elements of the total structure of a work, the silent background before which the events are acted out. The setting may also have been invented as a negative example of what certain trends of an epoch might lead to; this is the case in utopian novels, such as Aldous Huxley's *Brave New World* and George Orwell's *1984.* Or it may be an integral part of the whole plot, as in works in which a deliberately exotic setting may help to underline the strange character of the events which are described, or where an alien background may put the alienation of the characters into sharper relief. And in fiction which deals with problems of human adjustment, a change in the setting may serve to bring out these problems more clearly. The details of the setting generally add to the sense of reality and three-dimensionality, but they may also exemplify the theme or have a symbolic function, as in Herman Melville's *Moby Dick,* where the isolated ship suggests Ahab's spiritual isolation. Sometimes we even find that the setting directly influences the characters[39] or that there is a visual interaction between character and physical location, as in E.A. Poe's rightly famous "The Fall of the House of Usher", where the sickly landscape seems to have taken charge of the characters "and they act out their story of a family's degeneration determined by the emotional tone of the visual setting. As people, they are entirely overshadowed by the physical presence of their surroundings: they have no moral qualities or choices; they are subject only to the inevitability of decay."[40]

When the setting evokes such a definite emotional tone or mood that surrounds the characters, we speak of **atmosphere** (also known as **tone).** It may be used to set up in the reader expectations as to the course of events, especially if the action is going to end tragically. It may also help to interpret the symbolic action as distinguished from the mere surface action of the plot. The atmosphere of almost unbearable drabness that permeates Orwell's *1984,* for instance, not only reflects the state of mind of the characters but also underscores Orwell's message — that an ideologically based system of totalitarianism will not lead to the happiness of mankind but only to a general atmosphere of spiritual and emotional frustration and thus to a loss of human dignity.

Comprehension and revision

1) Try to give definitions of 'setting' and 'atmosphere'.
2) What may setting be used for by a writer?
3) What are the functions of atmosphere?

For study and discussion

How may atmosphere be created?

Typical tasks and questions

1) Describe the setting in which the events occur.
2) Explain the function of the setting in this story.
3) Has the setting any symbolic significance?
4) What kind of atmosphere is evoked in the story?

Setting and atmosphere

<table>
<tr><td rowspan="3">Setting</td><td colspan="2">is the environment of a story's action.
is the immediate world in which the events of a story take place.</td></tr>
<tr><td>may be used</td><td>as the silent background before which the events of the story are acted out.
as a negative example of what certain trends of an epoch might lead to.
to underline the meaning of the events.
to add to the sense of reality and three-dimensionality.
to exemplify the theme.</td></tr>
<tr><td colspan="2">may have a symbolic meaning.
may directly influence character.</td></tr>
<tr><td rowspan="2">Atmosphere
Tone</td><td colspan="2">is the emotional mood that surrounds the characters.
is the mood that pervades a literary work.</td></tr>
<tr><td colspan="2">sets up expectations in the reader as to the course of events.
helps to interpret the symbolic action.</td></tr>
</table>

7.7 Author and reader

Any story is successful only to the extent that its author makes it credible; if he fails to make it credible, the story will fail. He must therefore try to make his fiction not merely possible, but probable, so that the reader willingly accepts the illusion of reality that is created for him and is prepared to exercise a "willing suspension of disbelief" (Coleridge). **If the reader is to lose himself in the story, the author must try to arouse his interest and involvement in the events which are going to be presented.** That is to say that he must manoeuvre his reader into a position where he wants to read on in order to find out more about the characters and the action.

This illusion of reality which every author must achieve if his fiction is to be credible is most easily conveyed if he presents a narrative with a strong story line, i. e. one of fast moving, emotionally charged events that keep the reader in suspense from beginning to end. Some readers may then in fact become so impatient in their desire to know what the eventual outcome of the action will be that they peek ahead to the last few pages.

The reader is allowed to share the experiences and emotions of the characters in a story, their awe, their terror, their joy, happiness and grief, and so comes to feel personally involved with one or more of the characters. He may even identify with the characters to such an extent that he readily yields to the illusion that he himself is participating in the action, at least as a witness, and in this manner translates the chronological past of the story's action into the fictive present felt by himself — as if the action were happening *now.* The more psychologically committed he is to the people in a narrative, the more likely he will be to think ahead to what might happen to them. The more his interest in character increases, the more he tries to anticipate the future turn of events, especially the likely outcome of the story. Consequently, **he begins to interact with the author,** setting up his desired or expected plot against the one he is following.[41]

These expectations about the characters' fate are derived partly from a knowledge of real life and an acquaintance with realistic characters, but they will also be dictated by the traditional plot or story formulas the reader is familiar with. This formulaic element may dominate a story so much that a discerning reader sometimes feels that the characters have no human life of their own and are nothing more than tools or pawns in an artificial plot, as in much popular escapist fiction. Writers of this type of fiction are usually quite happy to gratify the reader's hopes for the characters in whose fate his interest has been aroused by letting the action work out to a happy ending for the sympathetic characters and to a correspondingly bad ending for the despicable ones.

The serious literary artist, on the other hand, will use a story formula not as an end in itself, but only as a means of starting certain expectations in the reader. He will then induce him to revise these expectations as he makes him more and more aware by his structuring of his material that the formulaic approach that was suggested at the beginning of the story is totally inadequate for a fuller understanding of the meaning of the characters' experiences. **When the writer is skilful and interprets the reader's responses correctly, he can manoeuvre him into changing the nature of what he desired for the characters** at the beginning and steer him towards accepting a new range of values, the values that *the writer* thinks are more important.

In his *Great Expectations* (1860—61), for instance, Charles Dickens seemingly adopts the general plot of a classic fairy-tale sequence and thus leads the reader to

expect that Pip, the hero, will grow up to be rich and handsome, that he will earn the love of Estella, his beautiful childhood companion, and that they will live happily ever after. Gradually, however, Dickens makes us see that the "great expectations" Pip has of becoming a gentleman can only be realized at the cost of betraying his old friends. Pip discovers that "greatness" in life all too often implies "weaknesses and meannesses . . . committed for the sake of people whom we most despise", and so, "slowly but surely, the success we anticipated for Pip — becoming a gentleman of wealth and leisure — no longer looks as attractive as it once did. We are inclined to think, as we read on, that maybe Pip would be better off if he were poorer but happier, and more decent to his old friends." We grow disillusioned with the rewards that the fairy-tale beginning seemed to promise because we are made to see "not only that fairy tales do not come true, but that an attempt to live as if they did weakens one's will to act independently, for the dangerous allure of such fantasies is that good things magically happen to people without their making positive efforts in their own behalf." The "defeat of the expectations dictated by the fairy-tale formula" therefore "reinforces our conviction that humane qualities bring the most genuine satisfactions and that they require positive individual effort."[42]
When towards the close of the novel our expectations about the course of events in the book are finally reversed — Pip gives up his great expectations of wealth in order to save the man he earlier hoped would be returned to prison or even killed — we have been guided towards an appreciation of the meaning of Pip's experience. We can see now that in the final analysis the most important human values are compassion for other people, forgiveness, and sacrifice.

By being **manoeuvred by the writer into a position where we can appreciate a new set of values,** we are led to see the symbolic truth of what is presented to us — the universal significance of this particular story becomes clear.

If we can become more conscious of these shifts in our attitudes and what positions the writer is trying to steer us to, we will gain a sharper insight into his intentions and, consequently, into the meaning of the experiences that he invites us to share. This does not mean that we must necessarily accept the writer's values as our own. But we ought to try to understand and follow the movement towards these values, a movement which the writer has attempted to achieve by carefully playing upon our responses. By closely observing the modifications we are induced to make in our expectations and desires or anxieties, we will be able to analyse how they contribute to an elucidation of the meaning of the work as a whole and will thus have a basis for an intelligent critical evaluation of it.

It is not only through a skilful handling of plot that the good author can manoeuvre the reader into arriving at the interpretation of the events that the wants him to put on them.

In fiction in which plot does not play a major role he may have to establish the illusion of reality not so much by showing some characters in an exciting situation right at the outset of the story and inducing the reader to identify with them as by trying to create the illusion of presentness and immediacy, for instance through making the **viewpoint character,** i.e. the character from whose point of view the story is told, directly address the reader and thus take him into his confidence; or he may use seemingly 'objective' methods of narration, such as the **dramatic method,** the **lavish use of dialogue** and the **limited point of view.**

By employing one or more of these narrative devices (for details about the narrative process see 7.2 above) **the author in effect asks the reader to take an active part in the building up of the story illusion.** Instead of having everything that matters told by a reliable narrator, with suitable comments on the people's characters and the meaning of their behaviour, we may be required to create whole scenes in our imagination because we are given nothing but dialogue. We may not even be told who says what, i.e. who the speaker is in each case, and we may have to infer the meaning of the events we are shown ourselves because the author effaces himself completely and lets the story tell itself. Or we may have to build up the total picture largely by ourselves because everything is presented as seen by a single character who is perhaps not very intelligent or who may not even understand what he is experiencing or witnessing. **It is of the utmost importance to realize that in all these instances where the author *qua* author has practically disappeared from the story it is still he who controls everything — the action, the dialogue *and* the reader's reaction.**

He is thinking of the effect his story will have on the reader when he chooses his narrator and makes him omniscient or limited in his knowledge, a minor character in the action or the protagonist himself. He has the reader in mind when he selects from various modes of presentation the one that seems to transmit the action most adequately — most adequately for the author's purposes, that is. When he creates characters to dramatize his theme, when he decides on a closed plot or an open plot, and so on, all the author's choices are inextricably bound up with the problem of how he can best achieve his artistic aims and make the reader see the universal truth embodied in his fiction.

He may occasionally consider it necessary for his purposes to break up the story illusion at this or that point in a narrative by acting as an 'intrusive author' and interposing occasional comments which draw attention to the *fictionality* of the events and thus achieve a kind of **alienation effect** (cf. Brecht's use of this device in his dramas) which increases the distance between reader and work. Or he may employ irony and thereby invite or cause the reader to understand the situation differently from the literal meaning of the surface statements. In the case of Dickens's *Great Expectations,* for instance, **verbal irony** is used in the choice of this title — Pip's "great expectations" must be seen in a different light from what the term ostensibly asserts. Modern writers sometimes use **structural irony,** which "depends on a knowledge of the author's intention shared by the audience, but unknown to the speaker".[43] That is to say that the author makes the reader aware of the narrator's limited insight or lack of comprehension. When a writer thus establishes an ironic relationship of this kind between narrator and reader, he gives the reader the satisfaction of superior understanding and thus induces evaluation and criticism. Through the obvious need of setting up his own interpretation against the one the naive hero or the fallible narrator persist in putting on affairs, the reader is made to think more deeply about the distorting perspective of the narrator's prejudices and private interests than he would otherwise be prepared to do.

Whichever way we look, there is no getting away from the fact that it is the author who is in total command everywhere. We may even say that **he creates the reader as the story develops,** starting him on a particular way by letting him form expectations about the future course of events and then inducing him to revise these expectations and to turn in any direction he wants him to go. And so every work of fiction not only has its **implied author** but also its **implied reader.**

We can recognize the difference between, say, the implied author in Dickens's *Hard Times,* who seems to be a grim prosecutor full of dry indignation at an inhumanly utilitarian culture, and the implied author in others of Dickens's novels, who can assume geniality, high spirits and tenderness. In much the same way as the author can create different images of his 'second self' for different works, he is able to create different images of the implied reader. In this work the implied reader may, for example, take every word the narrator says as gospel truth, whereas in that work he may join hands with the author behind the narrator's back, as it were, because he has been caused to see the inadequacy of the narrator's evaluations and judgements and so takes up an ironic stance towards him. Or the writer may create an implied reader who loses himself in the story illusion to such an extent that he willingly accepts certain elements in the fictional world which he would never dream of wasting a thought on in real life, such as interventions in the course of events by ghosts and other supernatural phenomena, or as encounters with all sorts of fantastic extraterrestrial beings, as in many science fiction stories. Again, the author may shatter the story illusion occasionally in order to increase the distance between the reader and the events and thus make him stand back from them and view them with a much more critical eye than he would have done had the story illusion continued unbroken.

In short, **the author manipulates the reader's response to the story from beginning to end, and if he is skilful he can manoeuvre him into precisely the positions he wants him to take up.** The reader is thus like clay in the author's hands — he can model him as he wants him for the accomplishment of his artistic purposes.

Comprehension and revision

1) Why is it so important that the author builds up an 'illusion of reality' for his story?
2) How can the reader be led to identify with the characters?
3) Why is it so important for us to become conscious of shifts in our attitudes towards the characters and their situation?

4) Explain what devices the author can use to establish an illusion of reality if he cannot rely on the movement of the plot.
5) How can the use of irony help the author in guiding the reader towards the interpretation of the events which he wants him to put on them?
6) Explain the concept of the 'implied reader'.

For study and discussion

1) "The author always loads his dice, but he must never let the reader see that he has done so, and by the manipulation of his plot he can engage the reader's attention so that he does not perceive what violence has been done him."

   (from W. Somerset Maugham, *The Summing Up,* Harmondsworth, 1938, p. 147.)

   Discuss the implications of Maugham's statement.

2) "Enjoy the illusion, but remember that an author is presenting the story and that presenting it requires more than the mere reciting of facts. When you find evidences of his manipulation ... try to determine their effect, their relevance to the events, characters, and purpose of the story. And then read the story once more, with the increased and deepened pleasure that comes from knowing what the story really *is*."

   (from Robert Stanton, *An Introduction to Fiction,* New York, 1965, p. 36.)

   Think over the ideas put forward by Stanton and then try to say whether there is an ideal way of approaching a story.

Typical tasks and questions

1) Explain the devices the author has used in building up a convincing story illusion.
2) Try to explain into what attitudes the author manoeuvres the reader.
3) Explain how the author makes use of irony in this text and comment on its effect.
4) What kind of implied reader is created by the story?

Author and reader

<table>
<tr><td rowspan="2">The author</td><td colspan="2">makes the story credible by creating the illusion of reality.</td></tr>
<tr><td>creates the illusion of reality</td><td>through the movement of the plot.
through his choice of a reliable narrator.
by letting the narrator directly address the reader and take him into his confidence.</td></tr>
</table>

p. t. o.

<table>
<tr><td rowspan="6">The author</td><td>creates the illusion of reality</td><td colspan="2">by creating an atmosphere of objectivity through the use of 'objective' methods of narration.
by confronting the reader with characters who present themselves in their own characteristic language.
by properly motivating the action of the characters to make the plot probable.
by effacing himself completely and letting the story tell itself.
by asking the reader to take an active part in the building up of the story illusion.</td></tr>
<tr><td>tries to</td><td>achieve
create</td><td>an impression of immediacy.</td></tr>
<tr><td colspan="3">arouses the reader's interest in the characters.
engages the reader's attention through the movement of the plot.
directs the reader's interest through a skilful use of the shaping devices of fiction.
carries the reader along from page to page.
focuses the reader's attention on...</td></tr>
<tr><td>creates
maintains
increases</td><td colspan="2">(the) tension.
suspense.</td></tr>
<tr><td colspan="3">keeps tension at a high pitch.
keeps the reader in suspense.
creates a general atmosphere of nervous tension.</td></tr>
<tr><td colspan="3">arouses certain expectations in the reader.
deliberately leads the reader astray.
induces the reader to revise his expectations.
causes the reader to shift his attitudes.
induces in the reader the mood he desires.
steers the reader towards accepting the values that he thinks are important.
induces the reader to make modifications in his expectations and desires or anxieties.</td></tr>
</table>

p. t. o.

Author and reader (continued)

<table>
<tr><td rowspan="4">The author</td><td colspan="3">causes the reader to understand the situation differently from the narrator and thus achieves an effect of irony.</td></tr>
<tr><td colspan="3">guides the reader towards the meaning of the experiences in the story.
attempts to make the reader see the universal truth embodied in his fiction.
tries to make the reader arrive at a certain interpretation of the meaning of the action of the story.</td></tr>
<tr><td>leads the reader to see</td><td>the symbolic truth embodied
the universal significance of the events</td><td>in this particular story.</td></tr>
<tr><td colspan="3">manipulates the reader's response to the story from beginning to end.
manoeuvres the reader into precisely the positions he wants him to take up.
creates the implied reader.</td></tr>
<tr><td rowspan="3">The reader</td><td colspan="3">willingly suspends disbelief.
is prepared to accept the story's illusion of reality.
is encouraged to imagine that what is portrayed is real or probable.</td></tr>
<tr><td colspan="3">shares the characters' emotions.
identifies with the characters.
places himself imaginatively in the situation of the characters.
is psychologically committed to the characters.
is made to transfer the chronological past of the story's action to the fictive present felt by himself through his identification with the characters.</td></tr>
<tr><td colspan="3">forms expectations about what will happen.
is deeply involved in the story.
feels intense interest and excitement.
is kept in suspense.
is concerned over what is going to happen to the characters.
desires to know what will happen to the people in whom his interest has been aroused.</td></tr>
</table>

p. t. o.

Author and reader (continued)

The reader	tries to anticipate the future turn of events. gradually develops his own conception of what he would like to see happen to the characters.	
	wants to know	what is going to happen. how the problems faced by the characters are going to be solved.
	is kept at a certain distance.	
	is left to draw his own conclusions. has to build up the total picture largely by himself. is required to infer the meaning of the events he is shown. has to set up his own interpretation against that of the fallible narrator.	
	interacts with the author. is like clay in the author's hands.	

8. THE INTERPRETATION OF FICTION

8.1 Preliminary remarks

When we speak of 'interpreting' fiction, we have in mind the twofold task of analysing and appreciating a piece of narrative prose. The task of **analysis** consists in a critical study of its component parts, such as the narrative process, language and style, the treatment of time, and so forth. This detailed study and description of the various elements that make up a work of fiction must be supplemented by an assessment of their interrelation and their function within the text as a whole, within its total structure. This process of assessment is called the **appreciation.** Analysis and appreciation together form the **interpretation.**

There are many people who strongly object to the interpretation of fiction. They feel that readers who attempt a critical analysis of a work of fiction may all too easily read all sorts of things into it; they are also convinced that its author cannot possibly have meant all that the critics claim to discover. Some even go so far as to suggest that the motive of scholarly criticism lies in the critic's wish to draw attention to his own cleverness and ingenuity rather than in a genuine attempt at interpreting an interesting work of imaginative art.

All these accusations usually come from people who have never worked hard at understanding a literary text in its total meaning and in all its implications. Yet, if we try to refute their charges, we will find that only their claim that literary critics simply try to be clever can be dealt with fairly easily. This can be done by pointing out that nobody who only wants to give the impression of cleverness will be prepared to risk contradiction, in this case the scathing remarks of other critics. No serious critic can afford to lose his scholarly reputation by writing articles about a work of fiction which are mainly products of his fancy and self-conceit.

The situation is not quite so easy with the other two objections. We can readily admit that occasionally people do get carried away in their interpretations so that they do in fact read too much into the text, but this can quickly be put right by a critical examination of the text itself. If our tentative conclusions cannot be validated from the material of the story, then they will have to be modified or even dropped entirely.

At this point, an important feature of 'good' literature can be mentioned in passing — that an author has often deliberately left a character's behaviour or attitude ambiguous or that he makes this character undergo a change in the course of his experience in the story; in other words, our author has attempted to present people in their real complexity. To determine in such a case whether any inconsistencies between our interpretation and the evidence of the text mean faulty reading on our part or imply a deliberate ambiguity that was intended as such by the writer is not always easy to decide. We have to use our own judgement here, in much the same way as when we judge people's motives in real life.

The accusation about the writer not having intended all that an interpretation claims to see in a work is a bit tricky.

It cannot really be refuted because it is quite a well-known fact that numerous writers have admitted that they cannot really say in advance what their intentions are with the literary work they are writing until they have completed it, and perhaps not even then. Some writers have given accounts of how at various stages in the creation of a new work the characters simply took on a life of their own and seemed to come alive, thereby moving the work in quite a different direction from the one originally intended, and of how unanticipated insights came to the surface and unconscious inspiration directed the writing. (Another point we can mention incidentally is the rather curious fact that even world-famous writers have not infrequently erred in evaluating their own work and have regarded as their masterpieces works which since then have been shown to be far less valuable than some others by the same author, which, however, he himself did not consider particularly important.)

On the other hand, we must realize that the argument that the writer did not mean all that our interpretation claims to find in his text does not make that interpretation invalid. The question, "Did the author really mean all of that?" is in fact beside the point. The author's own insights and interpretations, where we know them, can of course be an immense help for our own efforts, but the fact remains that any work of fiction must be interpreted according to its own merits and nothing else. This is to say that our own interpretation need not be wrong even if the writer, in the process of creating his text, did not foresee or intend it. **It is part of the timelessness of great art that it speaks to different generations, even to individual people, in many different ways,** and often in ways that the author could not possibly have anticipated. Charles Dickens (1812—1870), the famous nineteenth century novelist, certainly

> never heard of the modern concept of alienation — a feeling that one does not belong to one's world or to any of the people or things in it — that many modern critics use in order to interpret his novels, but Dickens wrote about men and women who behaved as though they were alienated, and it is valid for us to talk about them in these, our own terms. For the same reasons, the contemporary theater companies that give Shakespeare's *Hamlet* a Freudian interpretation have a certain justification for it even though the psychological concepts of Shakespeare's time are radically different from those of Freud. There are constants in human nature that enable literature to speak to various ages. So long as we do not distort the work of art, we can engage in this kind of analysis ...[1]

A final objection to the critical analysis of fiction is based on the fear that the reading experience itself will be ruined if one reads with the intention of paying a studious attention to literary concerns. It is felt that one goes to fiction for enjoyment and not for intellectual challenge. But although it is true that many of the best writers of fiction wanted their works first of all to be good stories which kept the reader's interest, it is also true that it would increase our pleasure in fiction and enrich our appreciation of it if we could fully understand this or that fictional narrative in all its aspects or at least were able to put its message into clearer perspective. The point we are trying to make is that **the interpretation of fiction** (based on critical analysis of individual aspects and of the structure of the work as a whole) **will give us additional pleasure in reading** and will enlarge the potential area of our enjoyment.

> Even if we turn to fiction for escape — to lose ourselves awhile in fantasy when life becomes too dull or crass or heavy — we will discover that the trip into imagination is more intriguing when we have become unconsciously attuned to the manipulative devices a good writer uses to exploit our hidden anxieties, fears and desires. No matter how lightly we take our reading, then, a familiarity with the way fiction operates upon us will add other dimensions of interest, pleasure and even excitement. The writer needs our personal involvement before he can achieve his best dramatic and imaginative results, because literature functions, as no other study of human relationships does, in the realm of personal responses and interactions.[2]

It is important to understand that the interpretation of fiction is not a mechanical operation dealing only with an analysis of the writer's methods and his technical skill in presenting his material (for details see 8.5 Various critical approaches), but a creative activity concerned with the tracing of the pattern or patterns of a work of fiction. One's past reading and one's own imagination are essential here. We will find that **the study of fiction is cumulative;** this is to say that what we have learnt from one book can very often help us in understanding another, but only if we are prepared to make a real effort and read each new work of fiction as carefully as the one that went before. Whether we will in fact reach a high standard in our interpretations largely depends on our willingness to search for ideas and concepts in our own experience and knowledge which we can apply.
In what follows, we are going to present a range of ideas and concepts, starting with 'universal story types', which may be of help to you in your interpretative work. The suggestions made in the following sections are by no means exhaustive, but they have been found useful in starting students in the right direction and in making their attempts at interpreting fiction something less of the nature of a hit-or-miss operation.

For revision

1) What is the difference between an 'analysis' and an 'appreciation'?
2) What is an 'interpretation'?
3) What reasons do people give for their dislike of the interpretation of fiction?
4) How can each of these objections against the interpretation of fiction be refuted?

The interpretation of fiction

<table>
<tr><td>Fiction can be</td><td colspan="2">critically examined.
studied critically.
analysed.
appreciated.
assessed.
evaluated.
interpreted.</td></tr>
<tr><td rowspan="2">A literary text can be</td><td>understood</td><td>in its total meaning.
in all its implications.</td></tr>
<tr><td>misunderstood</td><td>through faulty reading.
through missing the ambiguities it contains.</td></tr>
<tr><td rowspan="2">Conclusions
Tentative conclusions</td><td colspan="2">must take the evidence of the text into account.</td></tr>
<tr><td>must be</td><td>validated.
modified.
revised.</td></tr>
</table>

8.2 Universal story types

> Many types of stories center on heroic action, and these are quite different from stories where the chief interest lies in how a girl meets a boy and love is born. Still another kind of story focuses on the unraveling of some mystery, and while it may well contain elements of both heroism and romance, these are clearly subordinate to the search for truth. Other types of stories derive their fascination from the imaginary encounter with some monster or situation of fantasy.[3]

The **four main formal archetypes** mentioned in these lines — **adventure, romance, mystery,** and **encounter with the supernatural or quasi-supernatural** — can be found in so many stories that we have probably long stopped noticing them as such. To be sure, these story types can be found particularly often in popular fiction, but even 'high' or 'serious' literature makes use of them occasionally. It will be useful to take a close look at them.[4]

Universal story types

A fictional narrative may	centre on concentrate on focus on	adventure. romance. mystery. the encounter with the supernatural or quasi-supernatural.
	be chiefly concerned with be chiefly interested in	
	deal with put the emphasis on stress	

In a story of **adventure,** the hero, an individual or a group of people, has to overcome obstacles and dangers in order to accomplish some important and moral mission. Sometimes, especially in stories of the popular type, the hero's problems and trials are caused by the machinations of a villain. This latter will be overthrown in the end, whereas the hero normally receives, as a kind of side benefit, the love of an attractive young lady.

> The interplay with the villain and the erotic interests served by attendant damsels are more in the nature of frosting on the cake. The true focus of interest in the adventure story is the character of the hero and the nature of the obstacles he has to overcome. This is the simplest and perhaps the oldest and widest in appeal of all story types. It can clearly be traced back to the myths and epics of earliest times and has been cultivated in some form or other by almost every human society. At least on the surface, the appeal of this form is obvious. It presents a character, with whom the audience identifies, passing through the most frightening perils to achieve some triumph.[5]

Adventure

The chief interest lies in The focus of interest is on		heroic action. the development of a love relationship. the investigation and discovery of some hidden secret. the encounter with the unknown or unknowable.
The dominant structural principle The dominant line of action	is	
The structure of action The organizing structural principle	is	

p. t. o.

<table>
<tr><th colspan="7">**Adventure** (continued)</th></tr>
<tr><td rowspan="4">The hero of a story of adventure</td><td colspan="2">has to</td><td colspan="4">overcome obstacles.
face dangers.
undergo trials.
escape the machinations of a villain.
pass through some frightening perils.
accomplish an important mission.</td></tr>
<tr><td colspan="6">achieves some triumph.</td></tr>
<tr><td>is</td><td colspan="3">victorious
triumphant</td><td colspan="2">in the end.</td></tr>
<tr><td colspan="3">receives
gets
gains</td><td>the love
the favours</td><td colspan="2">of one or more attractive young ladies.</td></tr>
</table>

Although there is probably no exclusive sexual property in these structural archetypes, the fact remains that most stories of adventure have a male protagonist, whereas in stories of **romance** the central character is usually female. The structure of action in this story type is the development of a love relationship, with everything else relegated to secondary importance. It is of course true that a certain element of adventure, and perhaps also of mystery, is contained in many romances, but quite clearly the dangers and the mysterious events function merely as a means of challenging and perhaps strengthening the love relationship. The dominant line of action, the organizing structural principle, is definitely the development of a love interest. A long-lasting happy marriage is the usual outcome, normally after some combination of social or psychological barriers has been overcome. More sophisticated types of romance occasionally "end in the lovers' death, but always in such a way as to suggest that the love relation has been of lasting and permanent impact."[6] It seems that it is the very intensity of the lovers' passion itself which brings about their ruin. The passion of their love simply cannot continue to exist, either for social or for psychological reasons, or both, and so necessarily results in the death of one or both of the lovers. We call this the *Liebestod*-motif.

Romance

<table>
<tr><td>A love relationship is</td><td colspan="3">established.
strengthened.
cemented.
challenged.
doomed.</td></tr>
<tr><td>A love interest is
Erotic interests are</td><td colspan="3">included in a story.</td></tr>
<tr><td>Love</td><td colspan="3">is triumphant and permanent.
overcomes all obstacles and difficulties.</td></tr>
<tr><td rowspan="4">The lovers</td><td colspan="3">are brought to a deeper and more secure love for each other.</td></tr>
<tr><td rowspan="2">have to overcome</td><td>social
psychological</td><td>barriers.</td></tr>
<tr><td colspan="2">temporary obstacles.</td></tr>
<tr><td colspan="3">are guided by an intense passion.
establish a perfect relationship which has a lasting and permanent impact.</td></tr>
<tr><td>The lovers' passion</td><td colspan="3">brings about their death.
results in their death.
redeems the lovers.
leads to a Liebestod.</td></tr>
</table>

The **mystery** is a story type in its own right, but mystery has always been far more important as a subsidiary issue in stories of adventure or romance than as the dominant structural principle, with the single exception of the socalled "classical detective story". The reason for this lies in the fact that the investigation and discovery of some hidden secret, which is basic to the structure of action in a mystery story, is mainly, and almost exclusivelly, an intellectual activity. The search for the key to the secret — in the case of a detective story the attempt to find the murderer or criminal from among a number of suspects — involves the isolation of clues and the process of making deductions from these clues, which in the end puts them in a complete scheme of cause and effect. In other words, the main emphasis is on the use of reason, of man's reasoning powers, on the process of thought, deduction and inference, and on rational solutions. The pure mystery has obvious limitations because of the basic intellectual demands it makes on its audience; most people quickly lose interest in a predominantly rational structure and prefer mystery as a means of intensifying and complicating heroic or romantic action by increasing suspense and uncertainty and so creating increased interest in the final outcome.

Mystery

<table>
<tr><td rowspan="8">The mystery story</td><td rowspan="4">is concerned with</td><td colspan="3">the investigation and discovery of some secret.</td></tr>
<tr><td>the search for</td><td>the key clues</td><td>to the secret.</td></tr>
<tr><td colspan="3">making deductions from clues.
rational solutions.</td></tr>
<tr><td>looking for</td><td colspan="2">a complete scheme of cause and effect.</td></tr>
<tr><td colspan="4">has a predominantly rational structure.
makes intellectual demands.</td></tr>
<tr><td colspan="2">is based on one's powers of</td><td colspan="2">reasoning.
making deductions.
drawing inferences.</td></tr>
<tr><td colspan="2">places the emphasis on</td><td colspan="2">intellectual activities.
the processes of thought.</td></tr>
<tr><td colspan="4">has obvious limitations.</td></tr>
<tr><td>Mystery can</td><td colspan="4">intensify heroic and romantic actions.
increase suspense and uncertainty.
create additional interest in the final solution.</td></tr>
</table>

The mystery is often assumed to be identical with the story type of **encounter with the supernatural or quasi-supernatural.** Stories of ghosts, demonic possession or madness, etc. are however fundamentally different from the mystery in that in them mystery surrounds something unexplained and perhaps inexplicable and is never cleared up in the sense of being rationally explained, but is only dealt with in some way. In Bram Stoker's *Dracula,* for instance, the vampire is controlled in the end by some more or less rationalistic-religious activity, but the mystery remains, and the way is prepared for Count Dracula to rise as a vampire again and again. "This sort of conclusion is the very antithesis of the mystery story where, once discovered and explained, a secret is no longer capable of disturbing or troubling us."[7]

In the real stories of terror, on the other hand, such as Henry James's "The Turn of the Screw" or Poe's "The Fall of the House of Usher", the incomprehensibility of the unknown and the limits of the knowable are vividly brought home to the audience — they know that something terrible is happening or about to happen, but they cannot find out, and never will, whether supernatural causes are at work or not. All they can be sure of is that the events which are presented are somehow frighteningly real.

The unknown or unknowable

<table>
<tr><td rowspan="3">Stories of</td><td colspan="2">ghosts
monsters</td><td>are not identical with
are different from</td><td>stories of
mystery.</td></tr>
<tr><td>imaginary</td><td>beings
creatures</td><td colspan="2" rowspan="2">are based on the incomprehensibility of the unknown or unknowable.
explore the limits of the knowable.
introduce supernatural or quasi-supernatural causes.
create horror and terror.</td></tr>
<tr><td colspan="2">demonic possession
madness
supernatural influence</td></tr>
<tr><td rowspan="3">The mystery of the unknown or unknowable</td><td colspan="4">remains.</td></tr>
<tr><td>is never</td><td colspan="3">cleared up.
rationally explained.
resolved.</td></tr>
<tr><td colspan="4">cannot be explained away.
is somehow dealt with.</td></tr>
</table>

For revision and further study

1) Describe the typical structure of action
   — in an adventure;
   — in a romance;
   — in a mystery;
   — in a story about an encounter with the supernatural or quasi-supernatural.
2) Explain the basic difference between a mystery story and one about an imaginary or quasi-real, perhaps even surpernatural, creature.
3) Try to find out about
   — Bram Stoker's *Dracula*;

— Henry James and his “The Turn of the Screw”;
— E. A. Poe’s “The Fall of the House of Usher”;
— “Gothic” romances and novels.

8.3 Modes of fiction

We can distinguish between different modes of fiction. The three most important categories are:

1) fiction in the **social mode;**
2) fiction in the **psychological mode;** and
3) fiction in the **mode of symbolic action.**

When speaking of **‘mode’** here, we refer to the way material is presented in fiction and do not have in mind structure and shape; this would be ‘form’. Of course, the categories are hardly ever pure. But we can say that most books clearly belong primarily to this or that mode. The point is that by identifying the mode of a text, we can make a good estimate of the sort of issues it is dealing with — the nature of a society, the pattern of a person’s thoughts and sensibilities, or a philosophical idea. Having this as a starting-point will help us immensely in our interpretation.

Fiction in the **social mode** generally presents lifelike characters in a well-defined social context. Whole societies with a great many characters whose actions are followed over a period of time may be depicted; or we may get a representative cross-section of a class of people, of a particular world. In any case, one acquires from such a piece of fiction a concrete sense of what it is like to live in this world. It is in fact one of the identifying characteristics of fiction in the social mode that the reader is given enough information to be able to project himself into the world that is being presented. Another such characteristic is the importance of social interaction — the main characters in this type of fiction tend to define their problems and seek to solve them through confrontations with other people, normally in a series of human encounters. Most of what takes places is thus not internalized within the individual character, but is acted out in the open, between the characters. Each of these encounters will then lead to a slight change in the interpersonal relationship; it may be strengthened and deepened, or it may be ruined in the course of time. We can say that a third characteristic of social fiction is this emphasis on the dynamics of change, both between individuals and within the larger context of the social milieu, of the class of society, etc. that is described. People are shown in their manifold social interactions and an attempt is made to capture the dynamics of cultural and economic change. This sense of time passing and things changing can be achieved in the reader by informing him well about what happens when and where and what comes before and after.

Since one of the objectives of social fiction is to present the texture of life within a certain society, our interpretation will first of all have to concentrate on elucidating the nature of this society — what shape it is, how it operates, what tensions exist within it, and what its guiding principles and values are. This can best be done by closely following all the hints the author gives us about places and times, about manners and ideas, and about characteristic activities. A second important aspect in the interpretation of fiction in the social mode lies in tracing the patterns of human behaviour as they emerge from the portrayal of the web of interrelationships that is presented as typical of the society in question. We will find that some scenes between characters are crucial for the shaping of such patterns and thus deserve our special attention. In looking at people's behaviour, we will also notice causes and effects, which will not normally be difficult to discover as social fiction tends to emphasize the outward manifestations of human behaviour and not the sometimes inexplicable internal sources of motive. A last area of interest in social fiction is a typical concern with the tensions which exist within a society and which lead to a number of ethical questions. They will be focused in a relatively objective form because causes and effects will normally not be hidden, but presented quite openly — in scenes in which confrontations between characters take place. Our task in interpreting this aspect of fiction in the social mode is to show how the answers to the ethical questions that have been raised can be found in the crises of the individual characters as they take shape and manifest themselves in a series of human encounters and how individual behaviour is affected by the surrounding social order.

Since social fiction intends to give us a vicarious experience of a social situation by drawing us into the world being described, we must realize that this is possible only because a close relationship exists between the fictional world and our own. This is to say that we can, and indeed must, respond to and evaluate the fictional in terms of the real world — we are invited to discover insights about human societies in general and more specifically about our own lives. In interpreting the fictional world, we are being asked to interpret our own by transferring meaning from the one to the other.

Social fiction

Social fiction	presents	a whole society. a class of society. a social milieu. a particular world.
		instances of social interaction. people's behaviour in chains of cause and effect.

p. t. o.

Social fiction (continued)

Social fiction		the web of interrelationships that is typical of the society in question.
	emphasizes	the dynamics of change. the outward manifestations of human behaviour.
	is concerned with	the tensions which exist within a society. ethical questions. moral problems.
	aims at presenting the texture of life within a certain society.	
The interpretation of fiction in the social mode	tries to elucidate the nature of the social order which is presented. traces the patterns of human behaviour as they emerge from the depiction of social situations. analyses causes and effects.	
	attempts	to show how individual behaviour is affected by the surrounding social order. to suggest the answers to the ethical questions which have been raised.

If we turn to fiction in the **psychological mode** now, we will first of all notice that its organisational principle, its structure of action, is the psychological experience of one or several characters. This does not mean that social interaction is excluded and that the characters move in a world that is not described at all. But the description of a society, of a particular world, is not in the centre of interest as in fiction in the social mode; the focus is rather on individual development — on the movement of thought, on experiences which are important for the development of personality and on the complex internal motives that animate a character's behaviour.

We can say that the focal areas of fiction in the psychological mode are the conflicts and developments that take place within one or several characters and that the depiction of the nature of a society clearly takes second place. In fiction in the social mode, on the other hand, the psychology of individual characters is not ignored, but the uniting principle is the presentation of social interaction; the stress is on external action and not so much on internal action, on the thoughts, feelings and perceptions of a character, whereas in psychological fiction it is just the other way round — the sphere of internal processes and mental activities takes clear precedence over the presentation of outward action. The reader does learn something about the nature of the social setting, but it is sharply subordinated to the unfolding of a character's mind and sensibility.

A first consequence of this approach is that frequently several moments in time are contracted and that generally the sense of time is dominated not by the objective chronology of events, but by a presentation of only those moments in the character's experience which are psychologically significant in the sense of being intensely meaningful to him. The clear sequence of events that is typical of fiction in the social mode is often missing here. Instead the unfolding of the story usually gives a distorted picture of the actual time sequence because the narration can move from present to past and back to present again and repeat this process. In fact, the use of repeated flashbacks is typical of psychological fiction; any emotional impulse may trigger off memories and remembrances and thus start entirely new trains of thought. "In any case, what is important are the formative moments in an individual's development or state of mind..."[8] We can say that fiction in the psychological mode stresses internally significant events and not externally significant ones. In this way the reader is invited to share a character's experiences and to see the world through his eyes, in his uniquely personal way. And this is what fiction in the psychological mode is aiming at — to project the reader into a person's consciousness and his highly individualistic and essentially inimitable experience and in this way to enlarge his own sensibilities.

In interpreting psychological fiction, we have to try to comprehend the formation of feeling and attitude in one or several characters. We can say that "our critical energies will be engaged not so much with understanding the nature and workings of society, or even how people interrelate, but how one individual experiences life" and that "we will be looking less for objective data and more for those patterns and nuances of self-revelation that make up a man."[9] Since we share so extensively the inner experience of other people, we can perhaps discover the complex patterns of association and rationalization which go together to form a person's character and his emotional situation. But we should not expect to be asked to pass moral judgement on the way this person thinks and feels; we have to try to understand a character and find out what motivates and animates him and what memories, aspirations and anxieties are at work in him, but we do not have to judge him.

In summary we can say that we find in fiction in the psychological mode a stress on personal experience at the cost of a grander overview of society and its values. In other words, we encounter a preoccupation with the primacy of individual experience, rather than with the objective importance of social and historical events. In fact, everything in psychological fiction may be distorted to fit the character's perspective and his mood.

Psychological fiction

<table>
<tr><td rowspan="2">Fiction in the psychological mode</td><td>is concerned with
deals with
concentrates on
focuses on
tries to describe
stresses
emphasizes</td><td>individual development.
internal action.
the psychological experience of one or several characters.
the complex internal motives which animate a character's behaviour.
the conflicts and developments that take place in a person.
the sphere of internal processes and mental activities.
the unfolding of a character's mind and sensibility.
the formative moments in an individual's development or state of mind.</td></tr>
<tr><td>aims at</td><td>enlarging the reader's sensibilities.
projecting the reader into the intensity of another individual's experiences.
letting the reader enter a person's consciousness and share his experiences.</td></tr>
<tr><td>The interpretation of fiction in the psychological mode</td><td>tries to understand
attempts to comprehend</td><td>how one individual experiences life.
a character's emotional situation.
the formation of feeling and attitude in a character.
what motivates and animates a character.</td></tr>
</table>

We can say that fiction in the **mode of symbolic action** is written mainly to dramatize a theme or a philosophical concern and that in interpreting such fiction we are asked to understand its theme in all its implications. If a text focuses on an idea of human nature, such as violence as an expression of something that is perhaps natural to the human condition, as in Anthony Burgess's well-known novel *A Clockwork Orange* (1962), the governing emotional situation will lead to a darkening of the world of the story. Such a world frequently seems to be deliberately unreal, even heavily distorted or bizarrely exaggerated. In this way it becomes possible for the writer to single out a certain aspect of society and isolate it from its usual contexts. He can thus achieve a sharp focus on his theme and a remarkable intensity of narration. This tendency to isolate a single idea or feeling at the cost of neglecting other aspects is in fact one of the identifying characteristics of the mode of symbolic action. Everything in the world of symbolic fiction is projected like imaginary shapes on a wall. This is to say that the world we are shown is in reality the world of the protagonist's state of mind; what happens in the story is thus a reflection of his emotional situation or a projection of the way he sees himself and everything around him. As a consequence, we must be careful in trying to understand the action in the story too literally. As the name suggests, action in fiction of this mode is often symbolic — a projection of the hero's emotional situation. As such, it is not intended as a literal rendering of reality, but as a dramatization of an idea, state of mind, or mood.

We must not expect too much from the characters in symbolic fiction either. Most of the time we are allowed only a limited knowledge of their full development. They appear to possess no complexity of emotions and to be unable to change or effect shifts of thought. They are presented as two-dimensional only, as being in the grip of a single emotion or even an all-governing obsession; and this is all the information we get about them.

What follows from this is that it would be an entirely wrong approach if we tried to criticize a story of the symbolic mode for not showing three-dimensional characters. For its objective is an almost exclusive concern with the dramatization of a state of being and of the ideas that are grouped around it. In the example mentioned above — Burgess's *A Clockwork Orange* — this state of being is the human potentiality for evil, and so the story focuses on the sad fact that it is possible for human beings to want and to carry out evil.

By projecting the reader into the dramatic context, mainly through a fascination with the protagonist and his actions and a compelling interest in the events described, the theme is presented in symbolic fiction with such forceful immediacy that the reader often finds himself reading on with fascination, even though some truly terrifying action may be described, as in *A Clockwork Orange*.

To recapitulate, we can say that fiction in the mode of symbolic action is concerned with an all-pervading idea which is given a sharp dramatic focus in a symbolic story. The action is usually full of suspense because the reader is almost inevitably drawn into the anxiety of the emotions felt by the characters and thus he participates in the symbolic activity. Symbolic fiction neglects in-depth characterization in its concentration on a single idea, emotion, state of mind, or even a cluster of ideas and feelings. It can thus reach a deep emotional intensity, a sharp focus and a high degree of artistic integrity, perhaps even more so than works written in either of the two other modes. All the experiences and all the images which are used often relate to or illustrate the governing state of mind or feeling which is being explored. The story itself may be unfolded into a kind of extended image and induce the reader to share as he is reading those special feelings and experiences which are typical of the state of mind or emotion under discussion.

Fiction in the mode of symbolic action

<table>
<tr><td rowspan="5">Fiction in the mode of symbolic action</td><td colspan="2">explores a state of being or a state of mind.
is concerned with an all-pervading idea.
focuses on a single idea, feeling, or mood.</td></tr>
<tr><td>dramatizes</td><td>a theme.
a philosophical concern.</td></tr>
<tr><td colspan="2">deals with the idea it presents in a complex and impressionistic way.
tries to single out a certain aspect of society.
sharply focuses on its theme.
does not intend a literal rendering of reality.</td></tr>
<tr><td>presents</td><td>a world which seems to be unreal, distorted and bizarrely exaggerated.
symbolic actions.
events which are reflections or projections of the hero's emotional situation.</td></tr>
<tr><td colspan="2">achieves a high degree of artistic integrity.
emotional intensity.</td></tr>
<tr><td>Characters in fiction of the symbolic mode</td><td colspan="2">are not fully developed.
are two-dimensional only.
are not presented in an extended in-depth portrait.
are in the grip of a single emotion or obsession.
possess no complexity of emotions.
act in a symbolic way.</td></tr>
<tr><td rowspan="2">The interpretation of fiction in the mode of symbolic action</td><td>tries to understand</td><td>action as symbolic.
the events as projections of the hero's situation.</td></tr>
<tr><td colspan="2">elucidates the governing emotional situation in all its aspects and implications.</td></tr>
</table>

Comprehension and revision

1) What is meant by speaking of a 'mode' of fiction?
2) What are the identifying characteristics of
3) What is the objective of
4) Where must the stress be put when trying to interpret

} a) fiction in the social mode?
b) fiction in the psychological mode?
c) fiction in the symbolic mode?

For further study

Try to find out more about *A Clockwork Orange* — about the story as such, the way the theme is presented and characterization is handled, and in what sense the action (or the individual events) can be called 'symbolic'.
There is also an interesting film version of the book.

8.4 'Good' and 'bad' literature

Mickey Spillane is an American author whose murder fiction books sell in larger quantities than those of any other paperback writer. Many of his stories — the most famous is *The Big Kill* — are about a tough and ruthless private detective called Mike Hammer. He is over six feet tall, he smokes and drinks heavily, and he is irresistible to women. Hammer does not bring guilty people to justice. In his view the police are tied down by rules and regulations and the law is far too slow and cannot be relied on. He therefore deals with the guilty himself, acting as detective, Judge, jury and executioner. Hammer is a superman fighting the forces of evil and licensed to do so with their own weapons of violence and death. He believes in an eye for an eye and a tooth for a tooth and in wicked people deserving to die brutally.

The stories are set against a big city background, but we do not learn much about the city because it is not fully described. The characters in the stories have few emotions other than fear, hatred, lust and greed, although Hammer is sentimental about children and has an old and loyal friend who is a policeman. But generally speaking such things as friendship, affection, good-nature and even politeness do not seem to exist. The same stock characters are used again and again in book after book and none of them have any true reality.

There are several other American writers of 'hard-boiled' crime fiction. For example, men like Dashiell Hammett and Raymond Chandler have written about racketeers and crooked cops in an economical style that catches the tone of a cool American toughness. Spillane's books offer us a shabby imitation of their work. His writing is often inconsistent, he misuses words, and there are often mistakes in grammar. The detectives created by Hammett and Chandler are tough, but they use intelligence and observation to meet crime. All that Mike

Hammer offers is a bestselling mixture of sex and sadism. It is significant that Spillane is an ex-comic strip writer, for most of his books are written at that level.[10] Confronted with this mixture of sex, sadism, violence, brutality and murder that is the accepted conduct in stories by Spillane and other crime fiction writers, many people would tend to say, 'This is not literature at all.' In the sense, however, in which we understand 'literature' here they would simply be wrong because they mix up a question of literary taste with the quite different problem of identifying a piece of writing as literature. **Literature must be defined independently of value judgements.** Thus we may want to say that Spillane is a bad writer and that his stories are of a poor quality, but this is not the same as asserting that he is not a writer and that what he produces are not stories. Quite clearly even a work of the poorest literary quality can still be literature in the sense of being essentially an imaginative creation if the central attribute of all literature, fictionality, is there, which it undoubtedly is in Spillane's books, even though, as the text quoted above states, stock characters are used and none of them is true to real life.

There is obviously a big difference between **a 'serious' author** who writes because he thinks he has something of lasting value or interest to communicate and **the 'popular' writer** who simply churns out book after book in an attempt to supply what he hopes is a bestselling mixture of elements which notoriously appeal to a wide readership. In other words, this type of author is not interested in communicating anything of permanent importance and literary merit; his only interest is in making a lot of money out of the low literary tastes of a large part of the reading public.

We must, however, not confuse the problem of literary merit with the question of financial reward. There is of course nothing wrong in a professional writer wanting to make money from his books. A famous historical example is Walter Scott (1771—1832), who was trying to work off his huge debts by producing book after book, and nobody has accused him of thereby showing a narrow-minded and vulgar spirit of commercialism. In fact, we are glad to have these books, as they undoubtedly possess remarkable literary qualities, even though they were written under great pressure of time and practically exclusively for the money they would make. An author's motive in writing a book cannot normally be a factor in deciding on its merit as literature. **It is the literary quality of the work alone that counts,** and again we must avoid the danger of equating all the books produced by the paperback industry with literary trash. We would be doing popular bestseller authors a grave injustice by suggesting that their products are literature of the lowest quality. From a strictly literary point of view most bestsellers are probably second-rate, but the mass reading public is not worried about questions of literary quality. Some people even think that it is possible for a clever author to find out what a large section of this public wants and then sit down and produce a bestseller. It has actually been suggested by serious critics that a writer like Harold Robbins does in fact do this, that he has a formula of sex + blood + money + power which puts novels like *Stiletto, The Betsy, The Inheritors* and *The Adventurers* in the bestseller lists every time.

> Whether they write to a formula or not, most authors of bestselling fiction set out to provide their readers with (a) sensation, (b) escape, (c) topical interest, (d) a strong story line, and (e) strong characterization. The use of this recipe means that there is a tendency for publishers to turn out the same kind of bestselling novel, and this produces masses of books that offer the same experience. They are all equally 'sensational', 'powerful', 'frank' or 'ruthless', and one can do the same job as well as another.[11]

An author cannot of course be held responsible for the way his publisher tries to advertise his book. But we can say that a 'serious' author will normally try to find a 'serious' publisher, whereas a 'popular' writer will turn to publishers who regard books exclusively as a market commodity and then use the language and methods of the detergent men and super-marketeers to sell them. In any case, the question whether a writer intended to produce a work of lasting quality and of permanent value, or whether he simply wanted to cash in on what occupied people's minds at the time, or even make a quick profit by pandering to the vulgar tastes of a certain section of the public, is normally fairly easy to decide. But the point is that **we must study the quality of the finished product** to be able to say, 'This is good literature and this bad.' It does occasionally happen that a book which was originally meant as 'popular' and not at all intended as 'serious' literature, in the sense of meant to last, suddenly or gradually turns out to be of high literary quality and to be of lasting interest to generation after generation. Daniel Defoe and his world-famous *Robinson Crusoe* (1719) come to mind here. It would have come as a complete surprise to him to be told that his *Robinson Crusoe* would be regarded as one of the great books of all time and that it would make his name and that of his hero immortal. There is no guarantee, on the other hand, that a writer with a very serious artistic purpose will in fact produce something of lasting value. Quite obviously, having artistic intentions is not enough.

What is in fact 'enough'? When can literature be said to be of permanent worth? The question is not an easy one to decide. Literature may be bad, indifferent, good or even great. Most of the literature produced in the world is of mediocre quality; some of it is bad, some is good, and only a very little is great. But on what basis can we make value judgements in literature? **What are the criteria by which we distinguish 'good' from 'bad' literature?**

We might think of the **quality of permanence** here. When a work of literary art has stood the test of time then it must be good. But this can be decided only in retrospect and so 'permanence' is not a helpful criterion in trying to evaluate the literary quality of a contemporary work. Quite obviously, there must be methods of evaluation which are independent of the judgements of literary history. All we can really say about the possible permanence of a large percentage of contemporary fiction is that we strongly suspect that this or that work will not last for very long and will be on the market only for a limited period of time. It may even be a success there, in the sense of selling a large number of copies, but will disappear again sooner or later and leave hardly any trace, especially so if it was devised and published as a paperback right from the start. Anybody who has ever tried to buy the popular fiction of yesterday or to obtain certain works from public lending libraries will have found this all but impossible. In fact, any surviving copies of the pre-war production of fiction of this type have become much-coveted collector's items. All this throws us back of course to the question of what the intrinsic positive criteria are by which we can evaluate the literary quality of a work of fiction.

Two important negative criteria have already been mentioned in connection with Mickey Spillane's fiction — that stock characters are used and that none of them is true to real life.

We can say that a writer who produces 'bad' literature makes little or no attempt at a life-like portrayal of character and uses only crudely-drawn stereotypes. A world of black and white is presented, a world in which right and wrong, truth and falsehood, are distinguishable with absolute certainty, a world of hero and villain. "The protagonists are flat types; the hero and heroine are pure as the driven snow and the villain is a monster of malignity"[12] (cp. the good guys and the bad guys of the run-of-the-mill westerns). In the end, the villain bites the dust and the good heart triumphs over all. The author's aim is quite obviously to flatter the readers' moral sense: the bad are punished and the good are rewarded.

The writer of 'good' fiction, on the other hand,

> paints a world in which there is, in the beginning, neither black nor white, neither right nor wrong which can be defined with absolute certainty. The certainty can only come in terms of the process, and must be *earned,* as it were, through the process... The artist realized that, if the opponent... is a straw man, the conflict will lack interest... It would have no psychological center for tension, either in terms of the main character or in terms of the audience.[13]

Very often the 'good' author uses irony to intensify the implications of the conflict that is presented and to raise the issue above the level of a simplistic wholesale condemnation of the hero's antagonists. Another function of irony is to "indicate an awareness" of the complexity of the issues involved and "of the multiplicity of options in conduct, idea, or attitude — an awareness of the full context."[14] This **'awareness of the full context'** is generally missing from what we can call 'bad' literature. The popular author's concern with the psychological basis of action is minimal; he concentrates almost exclusively on the presentation of a fast-moving narrative in which the psychological motivation of the characters' behaviour remains largely in the dark or is not even psychologically probable, whereas the writer of 'good' literature draws a psychologically very accurate picture. **He 'holds the mirror up to nature'** (Shakespeare, *Hamlet)* **and presents a 'criticism of life'** (Matthew Arnold) in the sense of passing on to his audience feelings and ideas which they immediately recognize as belonging to real life and not to a world of fantasy, which is peopled by heroes and villains, by supermen and by fiends in human form, as in so many stories of popular fiction. It is this closeness to life, this concern with thoughts and feelings which are recognized by the audience as part of their own experience, either actually or potentially, that is one of the distinguishing features of 'good' literature.

> . . . it follows that good writing can only come out of actual human experience. It is not, of course, the *quantity* of the writer's experience that counts; if this were so, young writers would necessarily be less good than old writers — a clear absurdity when we compare the best work of Shelley and Keats with that of older but less good writers. It is the *quality* of the experience, its strength and vitality, from which good writing comes.[15]

Conversely we can say that where we find a drastic reduction of **the complexity and range of human emotions** — in the case of Mickey Spillane's fiction people seem to be motivated only by fear, hatred, lust or greed — and where "credibility both of character and plot is sacrificed for violent effect and emotional opportunism"[16] we are dealing with literature of poor quality. A search for heightened and intensified narrative and cheap dramatic effects is characteristic of this type of literature. It is generally associated with violence, sensationalism and a heightening of feeling for its own sake (not as an integral element of structure).

In 'good' literature, on the other hand, an organic relation exists among the individual elements which make up the story. It is a typical feature of high literary achievement when all the elements in a work of fiction are arranged so that they are interrelated and that they highlight, each in its individual fashion, the general character of the whole, that they all contribute to an overall impression of **organic unity.** In this manner literary artists of the first rank accomplish a balance of interest between external action and character: "Hemingway's *The Short Happy Life of Francis Macomber* is as violent in its packed events as the most lurid tale of adventure, but every detail of the action is contrived to test and reveal, with a surprising set of reversals, the moral quality of all three protagonists."[17]

Another characteristic element of 'good' literature is **originality,** not in the sense of being original through and through — that is almost impossible because almost every imaginable human situation has been dealt with in one way or another — but in the sense that these situations are shown in some quite new and perhaps fascinating light.

> It must be remembered that the central themes of all literature — life, love and death — are in themselves unchanging; so are most of our ideas about these great subjects. Yet writers continue to discover new ways of looking at them, and will continue to do so as long as mankind exists. Originality, then, consists not of inventing new themes, but of seeing and expressing the old unalterable themes in a new way.[18]

In the type of fiction, on the other hand, which is meant to have a 'popular' appeal, originality is for all practical purposes regarded as an undesirable thing — writers of popular fiction naturally assume that the reading their stories provide has to help people to unwind after a day's work in the office or factory, and so anything too complicated and original would mean that the readers could not 'lose themselves' in the stories and thus escape from the reality of their everyday lives. As a consequence, one story is very much like another, the characters are stereotypes, only their names differ from book to book, and it is normally easy to guess how each story ends. It has even been suggested that it is possible for such stories to be written by a team of writers, with each of them contributing a certain share to the formula they use in the 'production' of stories, and that this is in fact the normal practice. All that one needs to qualify as a writer in this sense is some technical skill in the use of suitable words and phrases on the right language level and the ability to produce so and so many words per day.

The idea that the art of writing can be studied and learnt like some other trade cannot be accepted in the realm of 'good' literature. The 'serious' writer has of course to acquire technical skill or craftsmanship, too, if he wants to be absolute master of a style suitable to whatever subject matter he wants to take up. But even if he could reach a level of proficiency, after much practice and effort, he would still not necessarily be a good writer. It is true that without the art of the right word in the right place no good writing is possible. It is, however, equally true that "literature can only come alive through the **creative imagination"** and that good literature is never created by technique alone.[19]

Another, and very important, characteristic which is to be found in almost all good literature is a **concern with truth.** This is to say that the serious literary artist tries to give some true picture of life, in the sense of presenting a sincere, well observed, and enlightening picture of an aspect of human life, whereas the commercial writer of stories intended to have a 'popular' appeal is not so much concerned with truth, but rather with playing up to the readers' expectations, especially their sense of right and wrong and their sense of justice. Consequently, the good are rewarded in the end and the bad get punished. That life is not like this, that the good do not always win, that even the very concept of 'good' people and 'bad' people is highly doubtful because **an incongruous mixture of good and evil** may exist in the same person is conveniently overlooked in this type of fiction. In any case, even at the lowest level we find that literature cannot get along without the recognition that good and evil have a real meaning and that therefore even what we might call 'escape literature' is concerned in some way with truth. One of the main differences, however, between light reading of this type and great literature is that in great works of literary art a far deeper level of truth is reached.

> There is a quest for truth in the realms of psychology and morality; motives, emotional complexities, moral development, interplay of character and emotion; our self-deceptions and our slow evolutions towards an awareness of self and others; questions of purpose, of principle, of the deeper reaches of the conflict of good and evil; truth in portraying something of the tangled, inexhaustible

complexity of our emotional, moral, social and spiritual being and its relationship with others.
Great literature is not only harder to write, but harder to read. The hero of an adventure story is usually up against either a well defined villain whom it is plainly meritorious to thwart, or some task or hazard.[20]

The demands made on the characters in great literature are quite different; they have to come to grips with very **complex situations** and with many moral ambiguities. We can perhaps say that a large part of the moral truth in much of twentieth century literature is precisely an increasing awareness of such moral ambiguities. Of course, no literary work can offer any 'total truth', but 'good' literature leaves one with some moral and psychological insights which provide at least some sense of fragmentary **truthfulness.** The audience is confronted with "a very complex, very multiple impression of a portion of life and its problems, communicating many diverse insights, some explicitly, some by implication."[21]
This leads us to a final distinguishing feature of great literature — it possesses a **'multivalence', an aesthetic value that is so rich and comprehensive that it can give satisfaction to one admiring generation after another.** In a literary work of that stature, an imaginative integration of a great amount of diverse material has been achieved and such a large variety of human experience has been embodied that all its systems and strata and levels of structure cannot be realized all at once. This is what people mean when they say that they can discover in each successive reading something new and exciting in Shakespeare's *Hamlet,* in James Joyce's *Ulysses,* or in some other great literary work.

Comprehension questions

1) What type of story is Mickey Spillane known for?
2) Can his books be regarded as 'literature'?
3) What is the basic difference between a 'serious' author and a 'popular' writer?
4) What are the criteria by which we distinguish 'good' literature from 'bad'?

Points for discussion

1) What could be the reasons for Mickey Spillane's fantastic commercial success with his books?
2) What is the relationship between personal experience and literary expression? E.g. is it necessary for a writer to have personally experienced a situation he wants to write about to be able to present it in an artistically utterly convincing manner?

General language practice

1) Try to express the meaning of the following words and phrases in your own words:
   a) paperback writer;
   b) bestseller;

c) character stereotype;
d) stock character (can you think of any?);
e) straw man;
f) literary trash;
g) escape literature.

2) Try to explain what the difference between 'quantity' and 'quality' in a writer's experience is.
3) The elements of 'sensation', 'escape', 'topical interest', 'a strong story line', and 'strong characterization' are said to be essential for the success of a work of popular fiction. Explain in your own words what is meant in each case.

'Good' literature and 'bad' literature

<table>
<tr><td rowspan="3">Literature may be</td><td colspan="3">bad.
indifferent.
good.
great.</td></tr>
<tr><td>of a</td><td>high
mediocre
second-rate
third-rate
low
poor</td><td rowspan="2">quality.</td></tr>
<tr><td>of the</td><td>lowest
poorest</td></tr>
<tr><td rowspan="3">A work of fiction</td><td colspan="3">is (not) intended to last.</td></tr>
<tr><td>is (not) of</td><td colspan="2">lasting value.
permanent worth.</td></tr>
<tr><td colspan="3">has (not) stood the test of time.
possesses literary qualities (does not . . .).
is second-rate.
is trash.</td></tr>
<tr><td>A character is</td><td colspan="3">(not) portrayed as life-like.
(not) true to real life.
a stock character.
a stereotype.</td></tr>
</table>

p. t. o.

'Good' literature and 'bad' literature (continued)

<table>
<tr><td rowspan="5">The 'popular' writer</td><td colspan="2">uses a bestselling formula.
provides a mixture of elements which appeal to a wide readership.
has nothing of lasting value to communicate.
is only interested in making a lot of money.</td></tr>
<tr><td>presents a world of</td><td>fantasy.
black and white.
hero and villain.</td></tr>
<tr><td colspan="2">plays up to the readers' expectations and wishes.
tries to flatter the readers' moral sense.
avoids complex issues.
reduces the complexity and range of human emotions.</td></tr>
<tr><td>is not concerned with the psychological</td><td>basis of action.
motivation of the characters' behaviour.</td></tr>
<tr><td colspan="2">concentrates on the presentation of a fast-moving narrative.
searches for cheap dramatic effects.
sacrifices credibility both of character and plot for violent effect and emotional opportunism.</td></tr>
<tr><td>The serious literary artist
The 'good' writer</td><td colspan="2">has something of lasting value or interest to communicate.
'holds the mirror up to nature'.
passes on to his audience feelings and ideas which belong to real life.
achieves an organic relation among the individual elements which make up the story.
imposes an organic unity on his work.
accomplishes a balance of interest between external action and character.</td></tr>
</table>

p. t. o.

'Good' literature and 'bad' literature (continued)		
The **serious literary artist** The 'good' writer	is (fully) aware of	the complexity of the issues involved. the multiplicity of options. any moral ambiguities.
	is (absolute) master of the style suitable to his subject matter. is concerned with truth. gives a sincere and enlightening picture of an aspect of human life. provides some moral and psychological insights. shows a certain situation in a new and fascinating light.	

8.5 Various critical approaches

> The most widespread and flourishing methods of studying literature concern themselves with its setting, its environment, its external causes. ... Most students try to isolate a specific series of human actions and creations and to ascribe to that alone a determining influence on the work of literature...
>
> ...
>
> The natural and sensible starting-point for work in literary scholarship is the interpretation and analysis of the works of literature themselves. After all, only the works themselves justify all our interest in the life of an author, in his social environment and the whole process of literature...[22]

These two extracts from what must surely be the best-known book on literary theory introduce in a concise manner the two main critical approaches to the interpretation of literature. Wellek and Warren call the first of them 'extrinsic' criticism and the second 'intrinsic' criticism, but we prefer the terms **external criticism** and **internal criticism,** because they seem to express more clearly what is meant. (In what follows, we shall speak exclusively about criticism as it concerns fiction, although what is being said actually applies to literature in general).

External criticism relies heavily on information drawn from outside the literary work, but its exponents are by no means agreed as to where the stress is to be put, and various positions can be distinguished.
There are those who are convinced that fiction must be regarded mainly as the product of an individual author and that his work basically constitutes an act of communication between himself and his reader. In other words, they believe that he is moved by certain ideas which he wishes to communicate in his fiction and that

it is the reader's task to understand as well as he can the message that is being conveyed. When fiction is thus regarded primarily as the expression of a didactic or propagandistic aim, the attempt to get at the corresponding message is usually coupled with a close study of the **author's biography.** The idea is that his total experience, conscious and unconscious, during the time of writing necessarily found its way into the work and that by knowing his state of mind some light may be thrown on the message the work contains and on his intentions in general. But even though some works of fiction are doubtlessly designed with the intention of influencing the reader in a certain direction, this approach quite obviously creates a number of problems if an exclusive claim is made for its validity, as is frequently the case.

Although it can of course yield valuable results in quite a number of cases, one of its obvious weaknesses is its inability to give a fair and objective evaluation of fiction in which no clear moral, social, or political message can be detected. What message, for example, is there in Laurence Sterne's *Tristram Shandy* (1760—67), or in Graham Greene's *Our Man in Havana* (1958), or in Dashiell Hammett's *The Maltese Falcon* (1930)? Even where such a message can be found, it is often not central to the work but emerges more or less incidentally, for instance as the result of the presentation of the moral choices the characters are confronted with. Another area where this approach lays itself open to criticism is the importance it attaches to the author's intentions. Quite clearly, however, a piece of fiction must be evaluated not according to what it may, or may not, be *intended to be,* but by *what it actually is,* quite apart from the fact that, as has already been pointed out above (cf. 8.1 Preliminary remarks), not even the writer himself can always know what his exact intentions are in a certain work.

Another group of critics is convinced that fiction, and literature in general, is the product of the **writer's environment** — of the economic, social, and political conditions obtaining in his time, of the prevailing philosophical and theological or religious attitudes, and generally of the *Zeitgeist.*

There can be no doubt that this is also a valuable approach to the interpretation of fiction, because literature, and in fact all art, must somehow be related to the way of seeing the world which was dominant in the period which produced the work of literature; it must also in some way reflect the prevailing experience at the time of the conditions of human life in its socio-cultural context. Thus the dramatic rise of detective fiction in the second half of the nineteenth century is obviously a reflection of the rapid growth of the big cities with their unprecedented opportunities for crime and the simultaneous evolution of an efficient police force using sophisticated methods of investigating crime.

This attempt to regard fiction as a characteristic product of a certain period and a certain socio-political and philosophico-cultural background, of which the best-known variety is probably Marxist criticism with its insistence that literature, like everything else, is based on economic relationships, is not free from weaknesses either. Why, for instance, if the writer is only a kind of middleman between the climate of opinion, the *Zeitgeist,* or the social context, and the work of fiction he writes, is there such a vast qualitative difference between the various works produced in the same period? Or, why do conventions and indeed fashions in literature hardly ever reflect the rhythms of certain shifts in society, the dominant economic situation, the political climate, etc.? Imaginative literature often seems to be related not so much to prevailing cultural attitudes but to live rather within the domain of the counter-culture, or else it may be ahead of its time. Another question which this approach cannot answer is why fiction of the eighteenth and nineteenth centuries can still give so much aesthetic pleasure to twentieth-century readers.

Internal criticism is not so much interested in interpreting a work of literature in the light of what message it is intended to convey or of the conditions under which it was produced, but instead attempts **a description, analysis, and evaluation of the work itself.** This is to say that the exponents of this approach try to understand the work as an entity in itself, perhaps even as a self-sufficient object, as some critics do, which must be studied and evaluated by 'internal' criteria such as conflict, characterization, mode of presentation, and other structural elements, and their interrelation. They are convinced that internal criticism must precede external criticism, or as some of them maintain, replace it altogether, because the literary work must first be rightly assessed in and for itself before it can be used for gaining insight into 'external' affairs — the author's state of mind and his message, the psychological situation of his readers, the nature of the society that produced the work, and so on.

There can be no doubt that this approach is a healthy reaction to the almost exclusive preoccupation with the external setting of a work of literature which characterized the history of literary criticism for a long time, but the point that internal criticism is making is not without its weaknesses either, valuable though it is. The problem is that the idea that a work of fiction ought to be discussed mainly in terms of its structural elements can lead to an excessive concern with aspects of the technical presentation of fiction and so ignore the human context, without which literature is only a lifeless accumulation of words.

Summing up we can say that none of these approaches to the interpretation of fiction is without its problems. As the advocates of the individual approaches often act as if their own view-point were the only one possible, it is not surprising that these approaches are often regarded as being mutually exclusive. Most critics nowadays try however to make the best of all of them by combining them freely as the situation seems to demand. **Although the purists are not happy about this, it appears to be a sensible procedure to approach each work in a way which promises to**

do justice to it — first of all as a work of art, but also as the product of a certain period and as the expression of what the author wants to communicate. But this is precisely where the centre of the difficulty in all interpretation of fiction lies — even if we can isolate, compare and evaluate the individual factors which seem to determine the work of art, we still have to face the question of where we are going to put the stress in our interpretation. In other words, the question is which of all these factors can be expected to be the most important and thus the decisive factor. No general answer is of course possible, because literary art is never uniform and each work is a highly individual creation, even though it has many elements in common with other works.

Comprehension and revision

1) Explain the basic difference between external criticism and internal criticism as applied to fiction.
2) What are the problems that can arise when fiction is regarded as being primarily the expression of the message the author wants to communicate?
3) What are the weaknesses of the approach to fiction as the product of the author's environment?
4) What danger is inherent in internal criticism?
5) Why is it a sensible idea to combine various critical approaches in one's own interpretation of fiction?

For discussion

1) What are the strengths of each of the various critical approaches to fiction?
2) Which of them seems to be the most promising in your opinion?
   Try to give reasons.

Critical approaches to the interpretation of fiction

<table>
<tr><td>A critical study of fiction</td><td>may be concerned with</td><td>its setting.
its environment.
its external causes.
the analysis of the structure of the work itself.</td></tr>
<tr><td rowspan="2">External criticism</td><td colspan="2">relies heavily on information drawn from outside the fictional work.</td></tr>
<tr><td colspan="2">sees the author only as a kind of middleman between the contemporary climate of opinion and his fictional work.</td></tr>
</table>

p. t. o.

<table>
<tr><td colspan="6">Critical approaches to the interpretation of fiction (continued)</td></tr>
<tr><td rowspan="8">External criticism</td><td colspan="2" rowspan="3">regards fiction as</td><td colspan="3">the product of an individual author.
an act of communication between author and reader.
the expression of a didactic or propagandistic aim.</td></tr>
<tr><td colspan="2">the product of</td><td>the writer's environment.
a certain period.</td></tr>
<tr><td colspan="3">the presentation of the dominant experience of human life in its socio-cultural context.
the demonstration in fictional form of the dominant way of seeing the world at the time the author wrote his work.</td></tr>
<tr><td colspan="5">in a Marxist sense insists that fiction, like everything else, is based on economic relationships.</td></tr>
<tr><td rowspan="3">is unable to</td><td colspan="4">give a fair account of fiction without an obvious message.</td></tr>
<tr><td colspan="2" rowspan="2">explain</td><td colspan="2">the qualitative difference between the various works produced in the same period.</td></tr>
<tr><td colspan="2">why fiction of an earlier period can still provide aesthetic pleasure.</td></tr>
<tr><td colspan="5">ignores the fact that fiction is often not in harmony with prevailing cultural attitudes.</td></tr>
<tr><td>Internal criticism</td><td colspan="5">attempts a description, analysis and evaluation of the work itself.
studies the various structural elements and their interrelation.</td></tr>
</table>

p. t. o.

<table>
<tr><th colspan="4">Critical approaches to the interpretation of fiction (continued)</th></tr>
<tr><td rowspan="4">Internal criticism</td><td rowspan="2">tries to</td><td>understand the work as</td><td>an entity in itself.
a self-sufficient object.</td></tr>
<tr><td colspan="2">do justice to the work as a work of art.
assess the work in itself.</td></tr>
<tr><td colspan="3">may be excessively concerned with aspects of the technical presentation of fiction.</td></tr>
<tr><td colspan="3">cannot do justice to fiction with obviously didactic intentions.</td></tr>
<tr><td colspan="2" rowspan="3">Practical criticism ought to</td><td colspan="2">avoid the dangers of attributing to any of these approaches an exclusive validity.</td></tr>
<tr><td colspan="2">combine the insights of external and internal criticism for a more comprehensive interpretation.</td></tr>
<tr><td colspan="2">put the stress in the interpretation where the character of the work seems to demand it.</td></tr>
</table>

8.6 Study guide to the interpretation of narrative prose fiction

In **practical criticism** it is generally a good idea to go through the work of fiction under discussion, or through an extract of it, and ask the following questions:

1) **What does the author want to communicate to the reader?**
- What seems to be his primary preoccupation?
- Is he interested in giving an authentic picture of the social setting and of the psychological state of mind of his characters?
- What information and what impressions are being conveyed?
- Is anything withheld from the reader? What is stressed or played down, and why?
- How do the author and his narrator manipulate the reader's response?
- etc.

2) **What are the social conditions which produced the text, or at least strongly influenced its production?**

— What conclusions about the social setting can be drawn from the constellation of characters and from the nature of their activities?
— Does the author approve or disapprove of certain elements of the social background and what is his attitude towards certain characters? What does this tell us about his own social origins?
— Can the way in which the author describes certain events and selects for description only certain details tell us anything about his own personal background?
— What can the emphasis the author puts on such and such details tell us about the readership he envisages for his fiction?
— What do the ethical problems and the social and cultural issues touched upon reveal about the situation that produced this work?
— etc.

3) **How has the author managed to solve the artistic problems concerned with the technical presentation of his material?**

— What devices have been used to dramatize the theme? What form of plot has the writer opted for? How has he handled the conflict and its resolution?
— What kind of narrator has been employed? Is he detached? Is he reliable? Through whose point of view is the reader made to see the events? Are we given an inside view? What mode of presentation has the author selected — telling or showing — and in what combination?
— Has the author created round or flat characters? Do they change in the course of the story? How has he managed to show the psychological complexity of his characters? By what manners of speech has he characterized them?
— Has the author used a matter-of-fact tone or is the tone humorous and ironical? How has he achieved an effect of irony?
— How has he handled the time scheme of his story and how has he managed to evoke a certain atmosphere?
— By what means has the writer created suspense and engaged the reader's interest and concern? How has he controlled distance?
— etc.

By answering these or similar questions for yourself you will get a much clearer idea of what the decisive features of the text are and what therefore your interpretation of it ought to concentrate on.

SUGGESTED READING

In this section we are going to list a number of publications which will be found useful by students who want to follow up this or that line of study. For this purpose, we have considered it more helpful to offer these suggestions for further reading than to give an extensive bibliography of specialist literature. That is to say that we have tried to select works which can be recommended to the student because they provide information of a more introductory character on the subject or subjects they deal with; scholarly treatises and footnote-laden articles in specialist magazines have therefore been ignored here. Anybody who wants to explore further will easily find more than enough material in the bibliographies appended to most of the publications given below.
We have also thought it helpful to draw attention to a number of anthologies which provide the most important original texts; most of these are available in paperback form.

General works

Abrams, M.H., *A Glossary of Literary Terms* (New York, 3rd ed. 1971);
a standard reference work.

Beckson, Karl, and Ganz, Arthur, *A Reader's Guide to Literary Terms* (London, 1961);
a standard reference work.

Boulton, Marjorie, *The Anatomy of Literary Studies. An introduction to the study of English Literature* (London, 1980);
gives much sensible advice.

Cuddon, J.A., *A Dictionary of Literary Terms* (London, 1977);
by far the best reference work of this type — includes many items not easy to find elsewhere; recommended for libraries because rather expensive.

Cunliffe, Marcus, *The Literature of the United States* (Harmondsworth, 1954; many impr., some with revisions);
for reference purposes.

Gillie, Christopher, *Longman Companion to English Literature* (London, 1973);
for reference purposes.

Hart, J.P. (ed.), *Oxford Companion to American Literature* (London, 4th ed. 1965);
a standard reference work.

Harvey, Paul (ed.), *Oxford Companion to English Literature* (London, 4th. ed. 1967);
a standard reference work.

Herzberg, Max J. (ed.), *The Reader's Encyclopedia of American Literature* (New York, 1962);
for reference purposes.

Hoffmann, Daniel (ed.), *Harvard Guide to Contemporary American Writing* (Cambridge/Mass., 1979);
contains, among other things, useful essays on "Southern Fiction", "Jewish Writers", "Experimental Fiction", "Black Literature", and "Women's Literature".

Sampson, George, *The Concise Cambridge History of English Literature* (London, 1941);
for reference purposes.

Wellek, René, and Warren, Austin, *Theory of Literature* (New York, 1949; Penguin Book, 1963; many impr.);
possibly the best-known book on literary theory.

Newspaper Literature and Journalism

Examples of good journalism are most likely to be found in newspapers and magazines with an international reputation, such as
The Observer, The Sunday Times, The Guardian, The Economist (all published in Britain) *and The New York Times, The International Herald Tribune, The Washington Post, Newsweek, Time* (all published in the U.S.).
Some of the most interesting articles are reprinted in *World and Press* (published fortnightly by Eilers & Schünemann in Bremen).
The following works can be consulted for general guidance and much inside information:

Diamond, Edwin, *Good news, bad news* (Cambridge/Mass., 1978).
Hohenberg, John, *The Professional Journalist* (New York, 1978).
Johnson, Michael L., *The new journalism. The underground press, the artists of nonfiction, and changes in the established media* (Lawrence, 1971).
Weisberger, Bernhard A., *The American Newspaperman* (Chicago, 1961).
Wolseley, Roland E., and Campbell, Lawrence R., *Exploring Journalism* New York, 1949).

The Essay

Hepburn, James G., and Greenberg, Robert A. (eds.), *Modern Essays. A Rhetorical Approach* (New York, 1962);
has an introduction, prints many complete essays by well-known British and American authors and provides questions after each essay.
Rhys, E. (ed.), *A Century of English Essays* (London, 1913; numerous impr.); prints 100 essays by British writers from Caxton to Hilaire Belloc.
Scholes, Robert, and Klaus, Carl H., *Elements of the Essay* (New York, 1969);
with a readable general introduction, four complete essays plus extensive commentaries, a section on the 'dramatic essay', with Swift's "A Modest Proposal" as an example, questions on Swift's essay, and hints on "Approaching an Essay"; can be recommended (only 89 pages).
Stewart, John L. (ed.), *The Essay. A Critical Anthology* (Englewood Cliffs/N.J., 1952);
distinguishes between various types of essay, gives general introductions plus comments on some of the essays that are printed, has questions on all the essays (essays by well-known British and American authors).
Williams, W. E. (ed.), *A Book of English Essays* (Harmondsworth, 1942; many impr.); a useful anthology of essays by British authors.

Short Narrative Forms

Lindner, Hermann, *Fabeln der Neuzeit. England, Frankreich, Deutschland. Ein Lese- und Arbeitsbuch* (München, 1978);
pp. 47—95 offer a number of fables (in the original English) by British and American writers; extensive notes (in German) and bibliography.
Raith, Josef, *English Anecdotes* (München, 1971);
a little booklet of miscellaneous anecdotes, mostly humorous.
Sutherland, James, *The Oxford Book of Literary Anecdotes* (Oxford, 1975);
a large collection of anecdotes connected with literary figures through the centuries.
Thurber, James, *Fables for Our Times* (New York, 1931), available as a Penguin Book; contains some of the best-known modern fables by one of America's foremost humorists.

The Short Story

Freese, Peter, Groene, Horst, and Hermes Liesel (eds.), *Die Short Story im Englischunterricht der Sekundarstufe II. Theorie und Praxis* (Paderborn, 1979);
provides a number of essays on various aspects of short story theory and offers excellent introductions to the presentation in class of science fiction stories, stories of initiation, stories of violence, detective stories, etc.; especially useful are the essays on methods of analysis and on short story theories and the extensive bibliographical material that is presented, ranging from a listing of anthologies of short stories (school editions only) and of volumes providing interpretations of individual stories;
warmly recommended for teachers and staff libraries.

Useful short story anthologies not listed in Freese et al. include

Dolley, Christopher (ed.), *The Penguin Book of English Short Stories* (Harmondsworth, 1967; many impr.).

id. (ed.), *The Second Penguin Book of English Short Stories* (Harmondsworth, 1972; many impr.).

Cochrane, James (ed.), *The Penguin Book of American Short Stories* (Harmondsworth, 1969; many impr.).

American Short Stories of the Nineteenth Century, introduction by John Cournos (London, 1930; numerous reprints); available as an Everyman paperback.

Hadfield, John (ed.), *Modern Short Stories* (London, 1939; many reprints); available as an Everyman paperback.

O'Mara, Michael (ed.), *Great Tales of Humour* (London, Everyman paperback ed., 1978); a fuller version of this anthology was first published in 1976 under the title *Classics of Humour.*

(There are a number of other Everyman anthologies of detective stories, ghost stories, tales of supernatural, etc.).

Adkins, Alex, and Shackleton, Mark (eds.), *Recollections. Ten stories on five themes* (London: Edward Arnold, 1980);
prints two stories each on the themes of "Innocence and Experience", "Discovery", "Conflict", "Barriers", and "Looking Back"; provides a glossary and questions.

Anthologies of subtly simplified versions of well-known British and American short stories are available from Cambridge University Press ("Cambridge Fiction Readers") and from Longman (titles from the "Longman Simplified English Series" and "The Bridge Series").

The Novel

Freese, Peter, and Hermes, Liesel (eds.), *Der Roman im Englischunterricht der Sekundarstufe II. Theorie und Praxis* (Paderborn, 1977);
gives very useful hints about the criteria which ought to govern the selection of suitable texts and about didactic objectives for reading novels in class, lists the available school editions of novels and makes valuable practical suggestions about teaching perspectives using eight American and two British novels (F. Scott Fitzgerald, *The Great Gatsby,* 1925; Ernest Hemingway, *A Farewell to Arms,* 1929; Richard Wright, *Native Son,* 1940; Carson McCullers, *The Member of the Wedding,* 1946; J. D. Salinger, *The Catcher in the Rye,* 1951; James Baldwin, *Go Tell It on the Mountain,* 1953; William Golding, *Lord of the Flies,* 1954; Alan Sillitoe, *Saturday Night and Sunday Morning,* 1958; Keith Waterhouse, *Billy Liar,* 1959; Kurt Vonnegut, Jr., *Slaugherhouse-Five,* 1969);
warmly recommended for teachers and staff libraries.

Pinnells, James R., *The Modern Novel in Britain and America. Contemporary Critical Theory and Practice* (Frankfurt, 1979);
warmly recommended as an excellent introduction to the theory of the novel based on a great number of extracts from a variety of modern novels; with valuable practical exercises; teacher's key available.
Booklets providing background information about individual novels and their authors and offering model interpretations and various other helpful material are available in the following series:
Coles Notes; Methuen Notes; Methuen Study-Aids; Monarch Notes; Notes on Chosen English Texts (James Brodie); Pan Study Aids; Studies in English Literature (Edward Arnold); York Notes (Longman).

The Craft of Fiction

Boulton, Marjorie, *The Anatomy of the Novel* (London, 1975);
deals systematically with the major elements of fiction, such as plot, character, point of view, etc., and gives numerous illustrations from many major novels.
Forster, E. M., *Aspects of the Novel* (London, 1927; numerous reprints);
a small classic; still a readable introduction to the writer's craft by a leading novelist.
Henkle, Roger B., *Reading the Novel. An introduction to the techniques of interpreting fiction* (New York, 1977);
a valuable introduction to a critical reading of fiction; very methodical in its approach to the elements of fictional technique.
Raban, Jonathan, *The Technique of Modern Fiction. Essays in Practical Criticism* (London, 1968);
makes many useful practical points and provides extracts from a number of modern novels and critical analyses.
Stanton, Robert, *An Introduction to Fiction* (New York, 1965);
provides a critical vocabulary and defines the basic elements of fiction, such as plot, character, theme, and setting.
Werlich, Egon, *Understanding short narratives from modern fiction* (Dortmund, 1979);
prints a number of interesting extracts highlighting various aspects of fictional technique and provides notes on the texts, vocabulary explanations, key terms, and suggestions for guided analysis and practice; teacher's key available.

NOTES

1. LITERATURE AND LITERARY STUDY

1. René Wellek and Austin Warren, *Theory of Literature,* 3rd. ed. 1963 (Harmondsworth: Penguin University Books, 1973), p. 21f.
2. Wellek and Warren, op.cit., p. 25.
3. Wellek and Warren, op.cit., p. 19. We are generally indebted to Wellek and Warren for the content of this section.
4. pronounced ['færənhaıt fɔ: faıv 'wʌn]
5. Cleanth Brooks Jr. and Robert Penn Warren, *Understanding Fiction* (New York, 1943), p. 8.
6. R.J. Rees, *English Literature. An Introduction for Foreign Readers* (London, 1973), p. 12.
7. Marjorie Boulton, *The Anatomy of the Novel* (London, 1975), p. 5f.

2. NEWSPAPER LITERATURE — FACT AND FICTION

1. *The New York Times,* November 23, 1963.
2. ibid.
3. *The New York Times,* May 5, 1960.
4. R.E. Wolsely and L.R. Campbell, *Exploring Journalism* (New York, 1949), p. 452.
5. *The New York Herald Tribune,* November 24, 1963. (The text is quoted from the *Herald Tribune,* but the text, a syndicated column, appeared in a number of other papers, too).
6. *The Washington Post,* April 19, 1981.
7. *The Washington Post,* September 28, 1980.

3. THE ESSAY

1. W.E. Williams (ed.), *A Book of English Essays* (Harmondsworth, 1942; new and enlarged ed. 1951, repr. 1952), p. 11.
2. Paul Harvey (ed.), *The Oxford Companion to English Literature* (London, 1932; 3rd ed. 1946, 8th impr.), p. 741.
3. Williams, op.cit., p. 239 and p. 238.
4. Robert Scholes and Carl H. Klaus, *Elements of the Essay* (London, 1969), p. 2.
5. cp. Williams, op.cit., p. 218.
6. cp. his essay "Religion and Literature", from his *Essays Ancient and Modern;* reprinted in K.L. Knickerbocker and H. Willard Reninger (eds.), *Interpreting Literature* (New York, 1955; rev.ed. 1960), pp. 728—35.
7. cp. his essay "Dreams and Facts", from his *Sceptical Essays;* reprinted in Knickerbocker, op.cit., pp. 736—40.
8. Bertrand Russell, "Dreams and Facts"; quoted from Knickerbocker, op.cit., p. 737.
9. Archibald MacLeish, "Trespass on a Monument", *The New York Times,* December 7, 1958; here reprinted from Knickerbocker, op.cit., pp. 782—85.
10. quoted from Williams, op.cit., p. 159.
11. quoted from Williams, op.cit., p. 92.
12. quoted from Williams, op.cit., p. 268.
13. quoted from Williams, op.cit., p. 230.

14. quoted from Williams, op. cit., p. 82f.
15. quoted from Williams, op. cit., p. 268 and p. 269.
16. quoted from Williams, op. cit., p. 155.
17. quoted from Williams, op. cit., p. 349.
18. quoted from Knickerbocker, op. cit., p. 776.
19. quoted from Williams, op. cit., p. 187.
20. quoted from Williams, op. cit., p. 215.
21. quoted from Williams, op. cit., p. 223f.
22. quoted from Williams, op. cit., p. 178.
23. quoted from Williams, op. cit., p. 295.
24. quoted from Williams, op. cit., p. 211.
25. quoted from Williams, op. cit., p. 122.
26. quoted from Williams, op. cit., pp. 201, 198 and 199.
27. quoted from Williams, op. cit., pp. 341—46.

4. SHORT NARRATIVE FORMS

1. quoted in Wellek and Warren, op. cit., p. 213.
2. R. Scholes and R. Kellogg, "The Problem of Reality", in Philip Stevick (ed.), *The Theory of the Novel* (New York, 1967), p. 371.

5. THE SHORT STORY

1. from George S. Hellmann (ed.), *Letters of Washington Irving to Henry Brevoort* (New York, 1918), pp. 398—401; here quoted from Alfred Weber and Walter F. Greiner (eds.), *Short-Story-Theorien 1573—1973* (Wiesbaden, 1977), p. 24f.
2. E. A. Poe in his "Review of N. Hawthorne's 'Twice-Told Tales'", originally published in *Graham's Magazine,* May 1842; here quoted from Hans Bungert (ed.), *Die Amerikanische Short Story* (Darmstadt, 1972), p. 2f.
3. originally published in *The Dial,* October 16, 1901; here reprinted from Eugene Current-Garcia and Walton R. Patrick, *What is the Short Story?* (Glenview, Illinois, 1961; rev. ed. 1974), p. 40f.
4. from *The Philosophy of the Short Story* (New York, 1901); here quoted from Bungert, op. cit., pp. 10ff.
5. from W. D. Howells, *Anomalies of the Short Story* (New York, 1901); here quoted from Bungert, op. cit., p. 47; our italics.
6. R. L. Stevenson in *Vailima Letters,* vol. 1 (London, 1895); here quoted from Weber, op. cit., p. 50f.
7. from H. E. Bates, *The Modern Short Story. A Critical Survey* (London, 1941); here quoted from Weber, op. cit., p. 142.
8. Victor S. Pritchett in *Harper's Bazaar,* LXXXVII, July 1953; here quoted from Weber, op. cit., p. 162f.
9. here quoted from Current-Garcia, op. cit., p. 68.
10. from Ring Lardner, *How to Write Short Stories* (New York, 1924); here quoted from Current-Garcia, op. cit., pp. 75—77.
11. from *A Story Teller's Story* (New York, 1924); here quoted from Weber, op. cit., p. 103; our italics.
12. from *The Atlantic Monthly,* July 1915; here quoted from Current-Garcia, op. cit., p. 59f.
13. Herschel Brickell, "What Happened to the Short Story?", *The Atlantic Monthly,* September 1951; here quoted from Current-Garcia, op. cit., p. 111.

14. from *The Triumph of the Egg: A Book of Impressions from American Life in Tales and Poems* (New York, 1921); here quoted from Weber, op. cit., p. 94f.
15. Bonaro Overstreet, "Little Story, what now?", *The Saturday Review of Literature*, November 22, 1941; here quoted from Current-Garcia, op. cit., pp. 88—90; our italics.
16. from Malcolm Cowley (ed.), *Writers at Work* (New York, 1958); here quoted from Current-Garcia, op. cit., p. 127; our italics.
17. from *The Modern Short Story. A Critical Survey* (London, 1941); here quoted from Weber, op. cit., p. 139f.; our italics.
18. in "The Short Story: Notes at Random, *Lovat Dickson's Magazine*, II, March, 1934, p. 281f.
19. quoted in Klaus Lubbers, *Typologie der Short story* (Darmstadt, 1977), p. 59.
20. here quoted from James Joyce, *A Portrait of the Artist as a Young Man*. Text, Criticism, and Notes, ed. by C. and G. Anderson, (New York, 6th impr. 1970), p. 287f.
21. originally published in *The Saturday Review of Literature*, January 5, 1935; here quoted from Current-Garcia, op. cit., 80f.
22. from *The Faber Book of Modern Short Stories* (London, 1936); here quoted from Weber, op. cit., p. 125.
23. ibid., p. 124.
24. from Falcon O. Baker, "Short Stories for the Millions", *The Saturday Review*, December 19, 1953; here quoted from Current-Garcia, op. cit., p. 120.
25. ibid., p. 121f; our italics.
26. from Angus Wilson, "The Short Story Changes", *The Spectator*, October 1, 1954; here quoted from Weber, op. cit., p. 165.
27. from Granville Hicks (ed.), *The Living Novel: A Symposium* (New York 1957); here quoted from Current-Garcia, op. cit., p. 132f.
28. Ronald Sukenik, *The Death of the Novel and Other Stories* (New York, 1969), p. 41.
29. Marcus Klein, "Quiet Voice in the Market Place", *The New Leader*, March 6, 1951; here quoted from Peter Freese (ed.), Die *Amerikanische Short Story der Gegenwart. Interpretationen* (Berlin, 1976), p. 16.
30. Jack Hicks, in the preface to *Cutting Edges: Young American Fiction for the 70's* (New York, 1973); here quoted from Freese, op. cit., p. 15.
31. Irvin S. Cobb, quoted in Freese, op. cit., p. 16.

6. THE NOVEL

1. quoted from the article on "novel" in *Collier's Encyclopedia*, vol. 9, p. 701.
2. quoted in Ian Watt, *The Rise of the Novel. Studies in Defoe, Richardson and Fielding*, Penguin ed. (Harmondsworth, 1963; 5th impr. 1979), p. 236.
3. from 'Author's Preface' to *Joseph Andrews*, 1742.
4. from the article on "novel" in *The New Encyclopaedia Britannica in 30 Volumes*, vol. 13, p. 238.
5. Marcus Cunliffe, *The Literature of the United States* (Harmondsworth, 3rd ed., 8th impr., 1980), p. 218.
6. quoted in M. H. Abrams, *A Glossary of Literary Terms* (New York, 3rd ed., 1971), p. 86.
7. ibid.
8. from the article on "novel" in *The New Encyclopaedia Britannica in 30 Volumes*, vol. 13, p. 281; we have made use of this article also for much else in this section.
9. ibid., p. 282; shortened and adapted.
10. Stevick, op. cit., "Introduction", p. 1.
11. Quoted in Boulton, op. cit., p. 4.

12. Wellek and Warren, op. cit., p. 212.
13. Stevick, op. cit., "Introduction", p. 1.
14. ibid., p. 8.
15. *The Oxford Companion to English Literature,* ed. by Paul Harvey, 3rd ed. (London, 1946; 9th impr., 1964), p. 92.
16. Abrams, op. cit., p. 114.
17. The idea for this exercise comes from James R. Pinnells' excellent little volume *The Modern Novel in Britain and America. Contemporary Critical Theory and Practice* (Frankfurt, 1979), pp. 19—21.
18. The sources:
    1) Harper Lee, *To Kill a Mockingbird* (1960), a novel;
    2) G. B. Harrison, *Introducing Shakespeare* (1939), a popular outline of Shakespeare's life and work;
    3) Truman Capote, *Breakfast at Tiffany's* (1958), a novel, or novelette;
    4) Charles Dickens, *Great Expectations* (1861), a novel;
    5) G. M. Trevelyan, *A Shortened History of England* (1942), a history book;
    6) Laurie Lee, *Cider with Rosie* (1959), a novel;
    7) Pierre Berton, *The Comfortable Pew* (1965), a personal account of how the Church looks to the outsider;
    8) J. B. Phillips, *Your God is Too Small* (1952), a theological account of the images of God many people have;
    9) Ernest Hemingway, *For Whom the Bell Tolls* (1942), a novel;
    10) Jane Austen, *Emma* (1816), a novel.
19. For some of what follows we are indebted to Maurice Z. Shroder, "The Novel as a Genre", in Stevick, op. cit., pp. 13—29.
20. cp. Abrams, op. cit., p. 110.
21. ibid., p. 112.
22. Roger B. Henkle, *Reading the Novel. An introduction to the techniques of interpreting fiction* (New York, 1977), p. 44.
23. cp. Arnold Kettle, *An Introduction to the English Novel. Volume I. To George Eliot* (London, 1951; 2nd ed., 1967, 6th impr., 1977), p. 31 f.

7. THE CRAFT OF FICTION

1. Robert Stanton, *An Introduction to Fiction* (New York, 1965), p. 16; his italics.
2. Boulton, op. cit., p. 48.
3. Abrams, op. cit., p. 128 f.
4. R. S. Crane, "The Concept of Plot", in Stevick, op. cit., p. 143.
5. cf. Boulton, op. cit., p. 45.
6. Abrams, op. cit., p. 135.
7. ibid., p. 136.
8. Wayne C. Booth, "Distance and Point of View", in Shiv K. Kumar and Keith McKean (eds.), *Critical Approaches to Fiction* (New York, 1968), p. 326.
9. Boulton, op. cit., p. 37.
10. Booth, loc. cit., p. 331 f.
11. Norman Friedman, "Point of View in Fiction", in Stevick, op. cit., p. 119.
12. This extract is given as an example in Phyllis Bentley, "Art of Narrative", in Stevick, op. cit., p. 55, and is quoted from there (slightly adapted).
13. Jonathan Raban, *The Technique of Modern Fiction. Essays in Practical Criticism* (London, 1968), p. 47.

14. L.E. Bowling, "What is Stream of Consciousness?", in Kumar and McKean, op. cit., pp. 363—65.
15. from James Joyce, *Ulysses;* quoted from Raban, op.cit., p. 47; (stream of consciousness).
16. from Dorothy Richardson, *Honeycomb;* quoted from Bowling, "What is Stream of Consciousness?", loc.cit., p. 360f.; (interior monologue).
17. from Dorothy Richardson, *Interim;* quoted from Bowling, "What is Stream of Consciousness?", loc.cit., p. 364.; (internal analysis).
18. from John Wain, *Hurry on down* (Harmondsworth, 1960), p. 27; quoted from Egon Werlich, *Understanding short narratives from modern fiction — Lehrerausgabe* (Dortmund, 1979), p. 25; (reported thought or substitutionary narration).
19. Knickerbocker, op.cit., p. 94.
20. ibid.
21. cp. Abrams, op.cit., p. 21.
22. from W.J. Harvey, *Character and the Novel* (1965); quoted from Stevick, op.cit., p. 235f.; slightly adapted.
23. For what follows cp. E.M. Forster, "Flat and Round Characters", in Stevick, op.cit., pp. 223—231. The article was originally published in 1927 as part of Forster's *Aspects of the Novel.*
24. Abrams, op.cit., p. 21.
25. Boulton, op.cit., p. 89.
26. ibid., p. 109f.
27. cp. Abrams, op.cit., p. 80.
28. cp. Henkle, op.cit., p. 124f.
29. Stanton, op.cit., p. 32f.
30. For what follows we are indebted to Richard M. Eastman, "Style", in Kumar and McKean, op.cit., pp. 147—161.
31. Eastman, "Style", loc.cit., p. 152.
32. ibid., p. 159; our italics.
33. from A.A. Mendilow, *Time and the Novel* (1952); quoted from Stevick, op.cit., p. 265.
34. cp. Raban, op.cit., p. 57f.
35. ibid., p. 56f.; our italics.
36. from Ford Madox Ford, *Joseph Conrad: A Personal Remembrance* (1924); quoted from Stevick, op.cit., p. 270.
37. from Mendilow, *Time and the Novel;* quoted from Stevick, op.cit., p. 269f.
38. ibid., p. 270.; we are indebted to Mendilow's work also for what follows.
39. cp. Stanton, op.cit., p. 18f.
40. Raban, op.cit., p. 113.
41. cp. Henkle, op.cit., p. 50.
42. ibid., p. 53f.; we are generally indebted to Henkle for this short analysis of Dickens's manipulation of reader expectation in *Great Expectation.*
43. Abrams, op.cit., p. 81.

8. THE INTERPRETATION OF FICTION

1. Henkle, op.cit., p. 18f.
2. ibid., p. 3f.; shortened and adapted.
3. John G. Cawelti, *Adventure, Mystery, and Romance: Formula Stories as Art and Popular Culture* (Chicago, 1976), p. 37.
4. In what follows, we are much indebted to Cawelti's excellent study of story archetypes (cf.

n. 3 above). We do not, however, follow him in regarding 'melodrama' as a story type in its own right.

5. Cawelti, op. cit., p. 40.
6. ibid., p. 42.
7. ibid., p. 44.
8. Henkle, op. cit., p. 31; for much in this section we are indebted to Henkle's book, esp. ch. 2.
9. ibid., p. 32f.
10. R.B. Heath, *The Popular Press* (London, 1975), p. 89f.
11. ibid., p. 88f.
12. Abrams, op. cit., p. 91.
13. Cleanth Brooks, Jr., and Robert Penn Warren, *Understanding Fiction* (New York, 1943), p. xvii.
14. ibid., p. xviii.
15. Rees, op. cit., p. 6.
16. Abrams, op. cit., p. 91.
17. ibid., p. 158.
18. Rees, op. cit., p. 7.
19. ibid., p. 8.
20. Boulton, op. cit., p. 23.
21. ibid., p. 28.
22. Wellek and Warren, op. cit., pp. 73 and 139.

INDEX

Authors

Subjects

Acknowledgements

List of quoted copyright material and copyright holders:

The New York Times: article 'Kennedy is Killed by Sniper' by Tom Wicker; article 'The Right to Bear Arms; essay 'Trespass on a Monument' by Archibald MacLeish; *The New York Herald Tribune:* article 'Desperate Battle to Save the President's Life' by Jimmy Breslin; *The Washington Post:* article 'Janet's World. The Story of a Child Who Never Existed' by Bill Green; article 'Jimmy's World. 8-Year-Old Heroin Addict Lives for a Fix' by Janet Cooke; Penguin Books, Inc.: essay 'On Doing Nothing' by J. B. Priestley; Little, Brown and Company: 'The Oxford Method' from *Unforgotten Years* by Logan Pearsall Smith; Harper Brothers, New York: 'The Very Proper Gander' by James Thurber.